Key Concepts in Politics and International Relations

Palgrave Key Concepts

Palgrave Key Concepts provide an accessible and comprehensive range of subject glossaries at undergraduate level. They are the ideal companion to a standard textbook, making them invaluable reading for students throughout their course of study, and especially useful as a revision aid.

Accounting and Finance
Business and Management Research Methods
Business Practice
Criminology and Criminal Justice
Cultural Studies
Drama and Performance (2nd edn)
e-Commerce
Human Resource Management
Information and Communication Technology
Innovation
International Business
Law (2nd edn)

Leisure
Management
Marketing
Operations Management
Philosophy
Politics and International Relations (2nd edn)
Psychology
Public Relations
Social Research Methods
Sociology
Strategic Management
Tourism

Palgrave Key Concepts: Literature

General Editor: Martin Coyle

Contemporary Literature
Creative Writing
Crime Fiction
Literary Terms and Criticism (3rd edn)
Medieval Literature
Modernist Literature
Postcolonial Literature
Renaissance Literature
Romantic Literature
Victorian Literature

Palgrave Key Concepts: Language and Linguistics

Bilingualism
Language and Linguistics (2nd edn)
Phonetics and Phonology
Second Language Acquisition

Further titles are in preparation

www.palgravekeyconcepts.com

Palgrave Key Concepts
Series Standing Order ISBN 978–1–4039–3210–5
(outside North America only)

You can receive future titles in this series as they are published by placing a standing order. Please contact your bookseller or, in the case of difficulty, write to us at the address below with your name and address, the title of the series and the ISBN quoted above: Customer Services Department, Macmillan Distribution Ltd, Houndmills, Basingstoke, Hampshire, RG21 6XS, UK.

KEY CONCEPTS IN POLITICS AND INTERNATIONAL RELATIONS

Second Edition

Andrew Heywood

macmillan education   palgrave

First edition (*Key Concepts in Politics*) 2000
Second edition 2015

Published by PALGRAVE

Palgrave in the UK is an imprint of Macmillan Publishers Limited,
registered in England, company number 785998, of 4 Crinan Street,
London, N1 9XW.

Palgrave Macmillan in the US is a division of St Martin's Press LLC,
175 Fifth Avenue, New York, NY 10010.

Palgrave is a global imprint of the above companies and is represented throughout the world.

Palgrave® and Macmillan® are registered trademarks in the United States,
the United Kingdom, Europe and other countries.

ISBN 978-1-137-48961-6

This book is printed on paper suitable for recycling and made from fully
managed and sustained forest sources. Logging, pulping and manufacturing
processes are expected to conform to the environmental regulations of the
country of origin.

A catalogue record for this book is available from the British Library.

A catalog record for this book is available from the Library of Congress.

Printed in China

For Jean

CONTENTS

USES AND ABUSES OF POLITICAL CONCEPTS

Concepts have a particular importance for students of politics and international relations. It is no exaggeration to suggest that political argument often boils down to a struggle over the legitimate meaning of terms. Enemies may argue, fight and even go to war, each claiming to be 'defending freedom', 'upholding democracy' or 'supporting justice'. The problem is that words such as 'freedom', 'democracy' and 'justice' have different meanings to different people, so that the concepts themselves come to seem problematic.

At least three reasons can be suggested to explain the unusual importance of concepts in political analysis, whether domestic or international. The first is that political analysis typically deals in generalizations. The significance of this can be highlighted by considering differences between politics and history in this respect. Whereas a historian is likely to want to make sense of a particular event (say, the French Revolution, the Russian Revolution or the Eastern European Revolutions of 1989–91), a political analyst is more likely to study such events with a view to making sense of a larger or more general phenomenon, in this case the phenomenon of revolution. For historians, a special study of the concept of 'revolution' is of marginal value, because their primary interest is in what is different, even unique, about a particular set of events. For political analysts, on the other hand, a study of the concept of 'revolution' is not only necessary, it is the very process through which political enquiry proceeds.

The second reason is that the language used by students of politics is largely the same as that used by practitioners of politics, and particularly by professional politicians. As the latter are interested primarily in political advocacy rather than political understanding, they have a strong incentive to use language to manipulate and sometimes to confuse. This, in turn, forces students of politics to be especially careful in their use of language. They must define terms clearly and refine concepts with precision to safeguard them from the misrepresentations often current in everyday political debate.

The final reason is that political concepts are frequently entwined with ideological beliefs. Since the emergence of modern political ideologies in the late eighteenth and early nineteenth centuries, not only has a new language of political discourse emerged, but the terms and concepts of political debate have also been imbued with complex, and often conflicting, meanings. Political concepts are therefore particularly challenging creatures: they are often ambiguous and not infrequently the subject of rivalry and debate; and they may come 'loaded' with value judgements and ideological implications of which their users may be unaware.

WHAT IS A CONCEPT?

A concept is a general idea about something, usually expressed in a single word or a short phrase. A concept is more than a proper noun or the name of a thing. There is, for example, a difference between talking about a cat (a particular and unique cat) and having a concept of a 'cat' (the idea of a cat). The concept of a cat is not a 'thing' but an 'idea', an idea composed of the various attributes that give a cat its distinctive character: 'a furry mammal', 'small', 'domesticated', 'catches rats and mice' and so on. In the same way the concept of 'presidency' refers not to any specific president, but rather to a set of ideas about the organization of executive power. Concepts are therefore 'general' in the sense that they can refer to a number of objects, indeed to any object that complies with the general idea itself.

What, then, is the value of concepts? Concept formation is an essential step in the process of reasoning. Concepts are the 'tools' with which we think, criticize, argue, explain and analyse. Merely perceiving the external world does not in itself give us knowledge about it. To make sense of the world we must, in a sense, impose meaning on it, and we do this through the construction of concepts. Quite simply, to treat a cat as a cat, we must first have a concept of what it is. Precisely the same applies to the process of political reasoning: we build up our knowledge of the political world not simply by looking at it, but through developing and refining concepts that will help us make sense of it. Concepts, in that sense, are the building blocks of human knowledge. Nevertheless, concepts can also be slippery customers, and this is particularly the case in relation to political concepts. Among the problems posed by political concepts are that they are often value-laden, that their meanings may be subject to argument and debate, and that they are sometimes invested with greater substance and significance than they actually possess.

NORMATIVE AND DESCRIPTIVE CONCEPTS

Normative concepts are often described as 'values', and they refer to moral principles or ideals which *should*, *ought* or *must* be brought about. A wide range of political concepts are value-laden in this sense – 'liberty', 'rights', 'justice', 'equality', 'toleration', and so on. Values or normative concepts therefore advance or prescribe certain forms of conduct rather than describe events or facts. Consequently, it is sometimes difficult to disentangle political values from the moral, philosophical and ideological beliefs of those who advance them. In contrast, descriptive or positive concepts refer to 'facts' that supposedly have an objective and demonstrable existence: they refer to what *is*. Concepts such as 'power', 'authority', 'order' and law' are in this sense descriptive rather than normative. It is possible to ask whether they exist or not.

The distinction between facts and values is often regarded as a necessary precondition for clear thinking. Whereas values may be regarded as a matter of opinion, facts can be proved as either true or false. As a result, descriptive concepts are thought to be 'neutral' or value-free: they stand up to the rigour of scientific examination. Indeed, under the influence of positivism, the pressure to develop a science of politics meant that in the middle decades of the twentieth century normative concepts were often discarded as being 'metaphysical' and therefore nonsense. However, the problem with political concepts is that facts and values are invariably interlinked, even apparently descriptive concepts being 'loaded' with a set of moral and ideological implications. This can be seen, for example, in the case of 'authority'. If authority is defined as 'the right to influence the behaviour of others', it is certainly possible to use the concept descriptively to say who possesses authority and who does not, and to examine the basis on which it is exercised. However, it is impossible to divorce the concept completely from value judgements about when, how and why authority *should* be exercised. In short, no one is neutral about authority. For example, whereas conservatives, who emphasize the need for order to be imposed from above, tend to regard authority as rightful and healthy, anarchists, who believe government and law to be evil, invariably see authority as being nakedly oppressive. All political concepts, descriptive as well as normative, therefore need to be understood in the light of the ideological perspectives of those who use them.

One response to the value-laden character of political concepts that has been particularly influential since the late twentieth century has been the movement to insist on 'political correctness' in the use of language. Political correctness, sometimes simply known as PC, has been advocated by feminists, civil rights activists and representatives of minority groups generally, who wish to purge language of racist, sexist and other derogatory or disparaging implications. It is based on the belief that language invariably reflects the power structure in society at large, and so discriminates in favour of dominant groups and against subordinate ones. Obvious examples include the use of 'Man' or 'mankind' to refer to the human race, references to ethnic minorities as 'negroes' or 'coloureds', and the description of developing world countries as 'third world' or 'underdeveloped' (though 'developing world' is also attacked for implying that the Western model of development is applicable throughout the world). The goal of political correctness is to develop bias-free terminology that enables political argument to be conducted in non-discriminatory language. The difficulty with this position, however, is that the hope of an unbiased and objective language of political discourse is illusory. At best, 'negative' terms can be replaced by 'positive' ones; for example, people who are 'disabled' can be referred to as 'differently abled', and 'negroes' can be described as 'black'. Critics of political correctness argue, however, that it imposes an ideological straitjacket on language that both impoverishes its descriptive power and denies expression to 'incorrect' views.

CONTESTED CONCEPTS

A further problem is that political concepts often become the subject of intellectual and ideological controversy. It is not uncommon, as pointed out above, for political argument to take place between people who claim to uphold the same principle or ideal. Conceptual disagreement is therefore one of the battlegrounds of politics itself. This is reflected in attempts to establish a particular conception of a concept as being objectively correct, as in the case of 'true' democracy, 'true' freedom, 'true' justice and so on. A way out of this dilemma was suggested by W. B. Gallie (1955–6), who suggested that in the case of concepts such as 'power', 'justice' and 'freedom', controversy runs so deep that no neutral or settled definition can ever be developed. These concepts should be recognized, he argued, as 'essentially contested concepts'. In effect, each term encompasses a number of rival concepts, none of which can be accepted as its 'true' meaning. To acknowledge that a concept is 'essentially contested' is not, however, to abandon the attempt to understand it, but rather to recognize that competing versions of the concept may be equally valid.

The notion that most, if not all, concepts are many-faced or 'essentially contested' has nevertheless been subject to criticism, particularly by Terence Ball (1988). Two lines of argument have been advanced. The first notes that many theorists who attempt to apply Gallie's insights (as, for example, Lukes (2004) in relation to 'power') continue to defend their preferred interpretation of a concept against its rivals. This refusal to accept that all versions of the concept are equally valid produces ongoing debate and argument which could, at some stage in the future, lead to the emergence of a single, agreed concept. In other words, no concept is 'essentially' contested in the sense that rivalry and disagreement are fundamental to its nature. The second line of argument points out that Gallie's analysis is ahistorical. Certain concepts are now contested which were once the subject of widespread agreement. It is notable, for example, that the wide-ranging and deep disagreement that currently surrounds 'democracy' only emerged from the late eighteenth century onwards alongside new forms of ideological thinking. As a result, it is perhaps better to treat contested concepts as 'currently' contested (Birch, 2007) or as 'contingently' contested (Ball, 1997).

WORDS AND THINGS

A final problem with concepts is what may be called the fetishism of concepts. This occurs when concepts are treated as though they have a concrete existence separate from and, in some senses, holding sway over, the human beings who use them. In short, words are treated as things, rather than as devices for understanding things. Max Weber (1864–1920) attempted to deal with this problem by classifying particular concepts as 'ideal types'. An ideal type is a mental construct in which an attempt is made to draw out meaning from an otherwise almost infinitely complex reality through the presentation of a logical extreme. Ideal types are thus explanatory tools, not approximations of reality; they neither 'exhaust reality' nor offer an ethical ideal. Concepts such as 'democracy', 'human rights' and capitalism' are thus more rounded and coherent than the shapeless realities they seek to describe. Weber himself treated 'authority' and 'bureaucracy' as ideal types. The importance of recognizing particular concepts as ideal types is that it underlines that concepts are only analytical tools. For this reason it is better to think of concepts or ideal types not as being 'true' or 'false', but merely as being more or less 'useful'.

Further attempts to emphasize the contingent nature of political concepts have been undertaken by so-called postmodern theorists. They have attacked the 'traditional' search for universal values acceptable to everyone on the grounds that this assumes there is a moral and rational high point from which all values and claims to knowledge can be judged. The fact that fundamental disagreement persists about the location of this high point suggests that there is a plurality of legitimate ethical and political positions, and that our language and political concepts are valid only in terms of the context in which they are generated and employed. However, perhaps the most radical critique of concepts is developed in the philosophy of Mahayana Buddhism. This distinguishes between 'conventional' truth, which constitutes nothing more than a literary convention in that it is based on a willingness among people to use concepts in a particular way, and 'absolute' truth, which involves the penetration of reality through direct experience and so transcends conceptualization. In this view, thinking of all kinds amounts to a projection imposed on reality, and therefore constitutes a form of delusion. If we mistake words for things we are in danger, as the Zen saying puts it, of mistaking the finger pointing at the moon for the moon itself.

KEY CONCEPTS: THEIR MEANING AND SIGNIFICANCE

ABSOLUTISM

Absolutism is the theory or practice of absolute government. Government is 'absolute' in the sense that it possesses unfettered power: government cannot be constrained by a body external to itself. The most prominent manifestation of absolute government is the absolute monarchy. However, there is no necessary connection between monarchy and absolute government. Unfettered power can be placed in the hands of the monarch, but it can also be vested in a collective body such as the supreme legislature. Absolutism nevertheless differs from modern versions of dictatorship, notably totalitarianism. Whereas absolutist regimes aspire to a monopoly of political power, usually achieved by excluding the masses from politics, totalitarianism involves the establishment of 'total power' through the politicization of every aspect of social and personal existence. Absolutism thus differs significantly from, for example, fascism.

Significance

Absolutism was the dominant political form in Europe in the seventeenth and eighteenth centuries. It was usually linked to the claim that sovereignty, representing unchallengeable and indivisible legal authority, resided in the monarchy. Absolutist rule was justified by both rationalist and theological theories. Rationalist theories of absolutism, such as those of Jean Bodin (1530–96) and Thomas Hobbes (1588–1679), advanced the belief that only absolute government can guarantee order and social stability. Divided sovereignty or challengeable power is therefore a recipe for chaos and disorder. Theological theories of absolutism were based on the doctrine of divine right, according to which the absolute control a monarch exercises over his or her subjects derives from, and is analogous to, the power of God over His creation.

However, absolutist theories are now widely regarded as politically redundant and ideologically objectionable. They are politically redundant because the advance of constitutionalism and representation has fragmented power and resulted in a strengthening of checks and balances, and because, where dictatorship has survived, it has assumed a quite different political character. It is ideologically objectionable because absolutism serves as a cloak for tyranny and arbitrary government, and is, by definition, irreconcilable with ideas such as individual rights and democratic accountability. Nevertheless, a form of constitutional absolutism can be seen to survive in political systems based on respect for the principle of parliamentary sovereignty.

1

ACCOUNTABILITY

Accountability means answerability; it implies a duty to explain one's conduct and be open to criticism by another. Accountability requires that the duties, powers and functions of government bodies are defined in such a way that the performance of subordinate ones can be monitored and evaluated by 'higher' bodies. In this sense, accountability can operate only in a context of constitutionalism; being accountable does not mean being subject to arbitrary authority or capricious punishment. However, accountability may also amount to a weak form of responsibility, since it establishes a duty to answer and explain one's conduct, but not necessarily to bear guilt and accept punishment.

Significance

Accountability is an important feature of limited government, effective policy-making and democracy. It limits government power by establishing mechanisms of political control through which one institution oversees the working and performance of another. It can promote the quality of public policy by ensuring that policy proposals are carefully scrutinized and political performance is rigorously monitored. When this is achieved through regular and competitive elections, it amounts to a system of public control, public accountability being the practical face of democratic rule. However, accountability is effective only under certain circumstances. These include that the mechanisms for monitoring performance are rigorous; that 'higher' institutions or bodies have sufficient access to information to make critical and informed judgements; and that appropriate sanctions can be applied in the event of blunders or under-performance. The main drawback of accountability is that it may constrain independent judgement and action. For example, the accountability of civil servants to ministers can lead to politicization and allow bureaucratic power to be harnessed to the needs of the government of the day.

ANARCHISM

Anarchism is an ideology that is defined by the central belief that political authority in all its forms, and especially in the form of the state, is both evil and unnecessary (anarchy literally means 'without rule'). Anarchists believe that the state is evil because, as a repository of sovereign, compulsory and coercive authority, it is an offence against the principles of freedom and equality, the core value of anarchism being unrestricted personal autonomy. The state and the accompanying institutions government and law are therefore rejected as corrupt and corrupting. However, the belief that the state is unnecessary is no less important to anarchism. Anarchists reject 'political' order but have considerable faith in 'natural' order and spontaneous social harmony, ultimately underpinned by optimistic assumptions about human nature. Government, in other words, is not the solution to the problem of order, but its cause.

Nevertheless, the anarchist preference for a stateless society in which free individuals manage their own affairs through voluntary agreement and cooperation has been developed on the basis of two rival traditions: socialist communitarianism and liberal individualism. Anarchism can thus be thought of as a point of intersection between socialism and liberalism, the point at which each ideology generates anti-statist conclusions. Anarchism has therefore been thought of as a combination of 'ultra-socialism' and 'ultra-liberalism', taking the form, respectively, of collectivist anarchism and individualist anarchism. *Collectivist anarchism* (sometimes called 'classical' anarchism or 'social' anarchism) is rooted in the idea of social solidarity, or what Pyotr Kropotkin (1842–1921) called 'mutual aid', the belief that the natural and proper relationship among people is one of sympathy, affection and harmony. Collectivist anarchists have typically stressed the importance of social equality and common ownership, supporting Pierre-Joseph Proudhon's (1809–65) famous assertion that 'Property is theft', most radically expressed in the form of anarcho-communism. *Individualist anarchism* is based on the idea of the sovereign individual, the belief that individual conscience and the pursuit of self-interest should not be constrained by any collective body or public authority. Individualist anarchism overlaps with libertarianism and is usually linked to a strong belief in the market as a self-regulating mechanism, most obviously manifest in the form of anarcho-capitalism.

Significance

Anarchism is unusual among political ideologies in that it has never succeeded in winning power, at least at a national level. As no society or nation has been re-modelled according to anarchist principles, it is tempting to regard anarchism as an ideology of lesser significance. As a political movement, anarchism has suffered from three major drawbacks. First, its goal, the overthrow of the state and all forms of political authority, is often considered to be simply unrealistic. The most common criticism of anarchism is that it is an example of utopianism in its negative sense, in that it places excessive faith in 'human goodness' or in the capacity of social institutions, such as the market or social ownership, to maintain order and stability. Second, in viewing government as corrupt and corrupting, anarchists have rejected the conventional means of political activism, such as forming political parties, standing for election and seeking public office, and have relied instead on the willingness and capacity of the masses to engage in spontaneous rebellion. Third, anarchism does not constitute a single, coherent set of political ideas: apart from anti-statism, anarchists disagree profoundly about the nature of an anarchic society and particularly about property rights and economic organisation.

However, the significance of anarchism is perhaps less that it has provided an ideological basis for acquiring and retaining political power, and more that it has challenged. and thereby fertilized, other political creeds. Anarchists have high-lighted the coercive and destructive nature of political power, and in so doing have countered statist tendencies within other ideologies, notably liberalism, socialism and conservatism. In this sense, anarchism has had growing influence on modern political thought. Both the New Left and New Right, for instance, have exhibited libertarian tendencies, which bear the imprint of anarchist thinking. Indeed, the continuing importance of anarchism is perhaps merely concealed by its increasingly diverse character. In addition to, and in some ways in place of, established political and class struggles, anarchists address issues that range from ecology, transport and urban development to sexual relations, and they have been in the forefront in the campaign against neoliberal or 'corporate' globalization. To argue that anarchism is irrelevant because it has long since lost the potential to become a mass movement perhaps misses the point. As the world becomes increasingly complex and fragmented, it may be that it is mass politics itself that is dead.

ANARCHY

Anarchy literally means 'without rule', the absence of a supreme or sovereign power. In domestic politics, anarchy suggests there is no authority higher than the individual (or, possibly, the group). In international politics, anarchy suggests there is no authority higher than the nation-state. The term nevertheless generally carries heavily pejorative connotations, implying chaos, disorder and, not uncommonly, violence. In sharp contrast, within anarchism, anarchy is not only viewed as compatible with order, but it is taken to be the very foundation of stable and peaceful existence.

Significance

The concept of anarchy has played an important role in both mainstream political theory and international relations theory. In the former, it has been used to establish the legitimacy of the state and provide a basis for political obligation. Social-contract theorists, dating back to Thomas Hobbes (1588–1679) and John Locke (1632–1704), have argued that citizens should behave as though the state had arisen out of a voluntary agreement, or social contract, made by individuals who recognized that only the establishment of a sovereign power could safeguard them from the insecurity, disorder and brutality of the 'state of nature' (a stateless or anarchic society). Without a state, individuals abuse, exploit and enslave one another; but with a state, order and civilized existence are guaranteed and liberty is protected. The obligation to obey and respect the state thus arises, ultimately, from self-interest and the awareness that anarchy would degenerate into a 'civil war of each against all' (Hobbes).

In a tradition that can be traced back to Thucydides (c. 460–406 BCE), such thinking about the link between anarchy and disorder has been applied to relations between societies and not merely within societies, becoming a major component of international relations theory through the influence of realism. It nevertheless gained greater prominence from the 1970s onwards through the rise of neorealism or 'structural realism'. Neorealists shifted their attention from the state to the international system, and placed primary emphasis on the implications of anarchy. The characteristics of international life were thus taken to stem from the fact that states (and other actors) operate within a domain that has no formal central authority. Neorealists argue that international anarchy necessarily tends towards tension, conflict and the unavoidable possibility of war, for two main reasons. In the first place, as states are separate, autonomous and formally equal political units, they must ultimately rely on their own resources to realize their interest. International anarchy therefore results in a system of 'self-help', because states cannot rely on anyone else to 'take care of them'. Second, relationships between states are characterized by uncertainty and suspicion. This is best explained through the security dilemma. Uncertainty about motives therefore forces states to treat all other states as enemies, meaning that permanent insecurity is the inescapable consequence of living in conditions of anarchy.

ANIMAL RIGHTS

Animal rights are rights to which all animals, or certain categories of animals, are entitled. The idea underpinning animal rights is that the grounds for allocating rights to humans also applies to some or all non-human animals, and to deny rights to the latter amounts to 'speciesism', an arbitrary and irrational prejudice, akin to racism or sexism. As such, animal rights differ from 'special' rights, such as women's rights and minority rights, which belong only to a specific group, and are based on the particular needs and interests of that group. A distinction should nevertheless be drawn between the notion of animal welfare and the more radical idea of animal rights. Animal welfare reflects an altruistic concern for the well-being of other species, but does not necessarily place them on the same level as humans. To view all or some animals as rights-holders endows them with a moral status in their own right, and so goes beyond the desire to treat animals with dignity and respect, which stems from human moral sensibilities, notably compassion. The latter position may, at times, be compatible with killing and eating animals, or holding them captive, actions that would clearly be ruled out by the former position.

Significance

The notion of animal rights surfaced in the early 1960s, alongside burgeoning interest in 'green' or environment issues. It gained particular prominence through the growth of the animal liberation movement (sometimes called the animal rights movement), which embraces a form of deep ecologism that extols the virtues of 'bio-equality' and rejects any form of anthropocentrism (human-centredness). The case for animal rights was put forward by Tom Regan (2004). In his view, all creatures that are 'the subject of a life' qualify for rights. This implies that, as the right to life is the most fundamental of rights, the killing of an animal, however painless, is as morally indefensible as the killing of a human being. Regan acknowledges, however, that in some cases rights are invested in human beings on very different grounds, notably that they, unlike animals, are capable of rational thought and moral judgement. Rights such as freedom of speech and freedom of worship, as well as the right to education or to political participation, would thus seem bizarre if they were invested in animals. Others nevertheless point out that, as we learn more about the capacity of higher primates in particular to reason and use language, the moral distinction between humans and animals becomes blurred.

Critics of animal rights tend to adopt one of two lines of attack. This first is that once we allow that the doctrine of rights can jump the species barrier, it is difficult to see how it can subsequently be confined. If the distinction between humans and animals is called into question, how adequate are the distinctions between mammals and fish, and between animals and trees and plants? Apart from anything else, if living is a sufficient basis for having, at a minimum, a right to life, it is difficult to see how the human species could long survive, or how rights could be denied to viruses and bacteria, say. The second line of attack is that, as human constructs, rights have been devised specifically to address predicaments that confront humans as morally self-conscious creatures, something that does not apply in the case of other species, despite the capacity they may possess to think and communicate. How meaningful is it, for example, to treat animals as rights holders when they are unaware that they possess such rights, have no ability to demand their rights, and cannot, in any reasonable sense, be expected to fulfil the duties that their rights may entail?

ANTI-POLITICS

Anti-politics refers to a rejection of, and/or alienation from, conventional politicians and political processes, especially mainstream political parties and established representative mechanisms. One aspect of anti-politics is a decline in civic engagement, as citizens turn away from **politics** and retreat into private existence. This is reflected most clearly in a fall in voter turnout and a decline in levels of both party membership and party activism, suggesting that political parties are failing in their traditional role as agents of popular mobilization and political participation. However, anti-politics does not only reflect a breakdown in trust between the public and the political elite; it has also spawned new forms of politics, which, in various ways, articulate resentment or hostility towards political structures and seek to offer more 'authentic' alternatives. These include 'fringe' parties, whose attraction is linked to their image as political 'outsiders' untainted by the exercise of power, and protest movements that embrace an activist-based style of politics, part of whose appeal is that they appear to resist compromise.

Significance

The rise of anti-politics is often seen as part of a malaise from which many, if not most, mature democracies have come to suffer. Evidence of this malaise can be found in a trend of declining political participation, particularly since the 1970s, in countries such as Canada and Japan, across much of Western Europe, and in parts of Latin America. The other manifestation of anti-politics is the emergence of populist leaders, movements and parties ('anti-party' parties) in many parts of the world, particularly since the early 2000s. However, even if anti-politics is taken to be a meaningful phenomenon in its own right, it is less clear why this is happening. Possible explanations or contributory factors include:

- The narrowing of the ideological divide between parties, meaning that modern politicians appear to lack vision and moral purpose, all of them looking the same and sounding the same.
- The tendency of the media to breed a climate of cynicism by 'hyping' political events (all 'problems' become 'crises'), in their attempt to make the coverage of politics 'sexy' and attention-grabbing.
- The flaw in electoral democracy that forces politicians to promise more in the campaign than they can deliver in office, thus ensuring inevitable dissatisfaction among voters.
- The fact that complex, modern societies are increasingly difficult to govern because of, among other things, the expanding power of corporate and other vested interests and an increasingly globalized economy.
- The emergence of a distinct political class whose members have little experience outside politics and so appear to be unable to relate to ordinary people.

ARMS RACE

An arms race is a concerted military build-up that occurs as two or more states acquire weapons or increase their military capacity in response to each other. Classic examples include the UK–German arms race that preceded World War I, and the US–Soviet nuclear arms race during the Cold War. Arms races may be fuelled by defensive calculations or miscalculations (the **security dilemma**), or they may occur as one or more states seek military advantage in order to pursue offensive policies. Arms races often take place in a context of technological innovation, as new or more sophisticated weapons or weapons systems become available. However, arms races are seldom 'pure', or seldom remain 'pure' for very long, in the sense that they are driven by an essentially military or technological dynamic, as they invariably become entangled with institutional, political, ideological and other factors.

Significance

The central debate about the significance of arms races concerns their relationship to **war**. While arms races may increase the likelihood of war, by heightening fear and paranoia, and strengthening **militarism** and aggressive **nationalism**, they may also help to maintain an overall **balance of power** and so to ensure **deterrence**. The spread of nuclear weapons during the Cold War period, either by their acquisition by more states or other actors (*horizontal* proliferation), or their accumulation by established nuclear states (*vertical* proliferation), is often used as an example of how arms races can promote peace and stability. Not only did the vertical proliferation of nuclear arms tend to preserve the balance of power, albeit through a 'balance of terror', but the technological innovations that enabled such devastating weapons to be developed also made them, in effect, 'unusable'. However, there was no guarantee that nuclear proliferation would preserve the Cold War balance of power, and the possibility that a temporary nuclear imbalance could have been exploited by an aggressive state could not have been ruled out. It is also possible that the dynamics usually associated with an arms race do not apply in the case of weapons of mass destruction (WMD).

AUTHORITARIANISM

Authoritarianism is a belief in, or the practice of, government 'from above', in which political rule is imposed on society regardless of its consent. Authoritarianism thus differs from authority. The latter rests on legitimacy, and in that sense arises 'from below'. Authoritarianism is a very broad classification of government. It can be associated with monarchical absolutism, traditional dictatorships and most forms of military rule; and left-wing and right-wing versions of authoritarianism can be identified, associated, respectively, with communism and capitalism. However, authoritarianism is usually distinguished from totalitarianism, on the grounds that it is primarily concerned with the repression of opposition and political liberty, rather than with the more radical goal of obliterating the distinction between the state and civil society. Authoritarian regimes may therefore tolerate a significant range of economic, religious and other freedoms.

Significance

Authoritarianism was the dominant political form in pre-constitutional and pre-democratic societies, usually taking the form of monarchical rule and aristocratic privilege. Theories of authoritarianism can be traced back to thinkers such as Joseph de Maistre (1753–1821), who argued that the belief in the principle of authority, as opposed to individual freedom, is the only reliable means of securing order. In modern politics, however, authoritarianism is usually viewed as a regime type that differs from both democracy and totalitarianism. The value of the term is nevertheless limited by the fact that, while authoritarian regimes rely on command and obedience, they exhibit a wide range of political and ideological features. For example, so-called 'old' authoritarian regimes, such as General Franco's Spain, were often conservative in that they set out to protect traditional elites and de-politicize the masses, while 'new' authoritarian regimes, commonly found in the developing world, aim to bring about economic mobilization and, to some extent, rely on political agitation. Indeed, such regimes may develop authoritarian-populist features which resemble Bonapartism (after Louis Napoleon's regime in France, 1848–70), a style of government that fused personal leadership with conservative nationalism, or Peronism (after Juan Peron's regime in Argentina, 1946–55), a dictatorship that based its support on the impoverished masses and the promise of economic and social progress.

However, the stark authoritarian/democratic distinction is often misleading because authoritarian traits can be identified in democratic regimes. Examples of this include the McCarthyite 'witch hunts' of the 1950s in the USA and Thatcherism in the UK – the latter a combination of neo-liberal economics and neo-conservative social policies that has been interpreted as a form of 'authoritarian populism' (Hall and Jacques, 1983). Finally, authoritarianism has also been viewed as a psychological or sociological phenomenon linked to a disposition to obey orders unthinkingly or a rigid insistence on obedience from subordinates. The classic contribution to this approach to authoritarianism was the idea of the 'authoritarian personality', developed by Adorno *et al.* (1950), which explains unquestioning obedience and rigidity of character in terms of an 'extreme intolerance to ambiguity'; in other words, it is a response to deep insecurities precipitated by uncertainty and choice.

AUTHORITY

Authority, in its broadest sense, is a form of power, sometimes thought of as 'legitimate power'. Whereas power is the ability to influence the behaviour of others, authority is the right to do so. Authority is therefore based on an acknowledged duty to obey rather than any form of coercion or manipulation. In this sense, authority is power cloaked in legitimacy or rightfulness. However, authority may be used as either a normative or a descriptive term. As a normative term, used by political philosophers, it refers to a 'right to rule' and takes the form of a moral claim. This implies that it is less important that authority is obeyed than that it *should be* obeyed. Leaders, for example, could in this sense continue to claim the right to rule, on the basis of election results, constitutional rules, divine right or whatever, even though the majority of the population does not recognize that right.

Political scientists and sociologists, on the other hand, treat authority as a descriptive term. Max Weber (1864–1920) defined authority simply as a matter of people's belief about its rightfulness, regardless of where that belief came from and whether it is morally justified. Authority, in this sense, is 'legitimate power'. Weber distinguished between three kinds of authority, based on the different grounds on which obedience can be established. *Traditional authority*, in this sense, is rooted in history and tradition; *charismatic authority* stems from the power of personality; and *legal-rational authority* is grounded in a set of impersonal rules associated with an office rather than the office holder. An alternative distinction can be made between de jure and de facto authority. *De jure* authority, or authority in law, operates according to a set of procedures or rules that designate who possesses authority and over what issues. People described as being 'in authority' can be said to possess de jure authority: their 'powers' can be traced back to a particular office. Both traditional and legal-rational authority can therefore be viewed as forms of de jure authority. *De facto* authority, or authority in practice, operates in circumstances in which authority is exercised but cannot be traced back to a set of procedural rules. This includes all forms of charismatic authority, and what is called expert authority, when a person is recognized as being 'an authority' by virtue of his or her specialist skills or knowledge.

Significance

Authority has been one of the most basic and enduring issues in political analysis. In a sense, all studies of government or the state are in fact examinations of the nature and workings of political authority. Indeed, probably no system of rule could survive long without exercising some measure of authority, since to rule through power alone involves such a great expenditure of coercive resources as to be unsustainable. Nevertheless, there are recurrent debates regarding both the nature of authority and its value. Liberals and socialists tend to view authority as being instrumental, believing that it arises 'from below' through the consent of the governed. From this perspective, authority is rational, purposeful and limited, a view reflected in a preference for legal-rational authority and public accountability. Conservatives, by contrast, see authority as arising from natural necessity, being exercised 'from above' by virtue of the unequal distribution of experience, social position and wisdom. Those who exercise authority do so for the benefit of others, but this does not set clear limits or checks on authority, and it may blur the distinction between authority and authoritarianism.

The justifications for authority include, most basically, that it is essential for the maintenance of order and is thus the only means of escape from the barbarity and injustice of the 'state of nature', a society without political rule. Authority also establishes common norms and values that bind society together, and thereby gives individuals a social identity and sense of rootedness. Critics of authority, including, in particular, libertarians and anarchists, point out that authority is by definition the enemy of freedom; that it threatens reason and critical understanding by demanding unquestioning obedience; and that it is psychologically, and perhaps morally, corrupting in that it accustoms people to controlling or dominating others.

AUTONOMY

Autonomy literally means self-rule or self-government. States, institutions or groups can be said to be autonomous if they enjoy a substantial degree of independence, though autonomy in this connection is sometimes taken to imply a high measure of self-government, rather than sovereign independence. Applied to the individual, autonomy is linked closely with freedom. However, since it suggests not merely being 'left alone' but being rationally self-willed, autonomy is best classified as a form of positive freedom. By responding to inner or 'genuine' drives, the autonomous individual is seen to achieve authenticity and personal fulfilment.

Significance

In international politics, autonomy is widely used as an index of sovereignty, autonomous states being independent and self-governing. However, it is now widely accepted that very few, if any, states are autonomous in this sense, and pluralist theorists in particular now use autonomy in a relative, not an absolute, sense. As a constitutional principle, referring to institutions or levels of government, autonomy is linked closely to decentralization. Autonomy in this context is justified through an essentially liberal belief in fragmenting power, though the checks and balances thus established imply interdependence as well as independence. The term is also used in the analysis of the state, the autonomy of the state implying that it articulates its own interests and is not merely an instrument or agent through which powerful groups act in society at large. Liberals have traditionally defended this image of state autonomy against the Marxist theory of the class state, even though modern Marxists are prepared to accept the 'relative autonomy' of the state. Finally, the ideal of personal autonomy can be seen as the underlying value of libertarian and anarchist thought, self-governing individuals needing little or no guidance in the form of political authority. Autonomy in this sense is often linked with democracy, but may nevertheless also limit the jurisdiction of democracy, as it emphasizes individuality rather than collective or majority rule.

BALANCE OF POWER

The term 'balance of power' has been used in a wide variety of political contexts, but it features most prominently in international relations, where it has been accorded a number of meanings. As a *policy*, the balance of power refers to a deliberate attempt to promote a power equilibrium, using diplomacy, or possibly war, to prevent any individual state from achieving a predominant position. As a *system*, it refers to a condition in which no single state predominates over others, tending to create general equilibrium and curb the hegemonic ambitions of all states. Although such a balance of power may simply be fortuitous, neorealists argue that the international system tends naturally towards equilibrium because states are particularly fearful of a would-be hegemon, or dominant power, The term is also sometimes use to refer to power relationships generally, unconnected with the idea of equilibrium. This makes it possible to talk, for example, about 'the changing balance of power'.

Significance

The idea of the balance of power has played a central role within realism, even being viewed by Kenneth Waltz (1979) as the theory of international relations. For realists, the balance of power is the principal means through which the tendencies within international politics towards conflict and war can be constrained. However, while classical realists treat the balance of power as a product of prudent statecraft, neorealists see it more as a consequence of structural interactions that take place within the international system, which are, in turn, shaped by the distribution of power (or capacities) between and among states. From the neorealist perspective, the likelihood of a balance of power, and therefore the prospect of war or peace, largely boil down to the number of great powers operating in the international system, or what is called polarity (the existence within a system of one or more significant actors, or 'poles'). Bipolarity, as typified by the superpower rivalry of the Cold War period, is usually taken to be more favourable for the emergence of a balance of power than is multipolarity, the latter being biased in favour of fluidity and increasing the scope for great-power conflict.

However, liberals have generally been critical of the idea of the balance of power, believing that it legitimizes and entrenches power politics and international rivalry.

This is because the basic premise of the balance of power is that other states, or coalitions of states, pose a threat to security, and this can only be contained through a build-up of power or the formation of a rival alliance. A balance-of-power mindset is therefore more likely to cause war than prevent it. Constructivists, for their part, have emphasized the extent to which any assessment of the balance of power is dependent on perception, ideas and beliefs. In short, paraphrasing Wendt's (1992) oft-quoted assertion about anarchy, the balance of power is what states make of it.

BEHAVIOURALISM

Behaviouralism is the belief that social theories should be constructed only on the basis of observable behaviour (as opposed to behaviourism, which is the school of psychology that holds that human behaviour can ultimately be explained in terms of conditioned reactions or reflexes). The behavioural approach to political analysis developed out of positivism, adopting its assertion that scientific knowledge can be developed only on the basis of explanatory theories that are verifiable or falsifiable. Behavioural analysis typically involves the collection of quantifiable data through research surveys, statistical analysis and the construction of empirical theories that have predictive capacity.

Significance

The so-called 'behavioural revolution' of the 1950s made behaviouralism the dominant force in US political science and a powerful influence elsewhere, notably in the UK. The attraction of behaviouralism was that it allowed political analysis to break away from its concern with constitutions and normative theory, and gave the study of politics, perhaps for the first time, reliable scientific credentials. This fuelled the belief, expressed by political analysts such as David Easton (1979), that politics could adopt the methodology of the natural sciences through the use of quantitative research methods in areas such as voting behaviour and the behaviour of legislators, lobbyists and municipal politicians. Behaviouralism, however, came under growing pressure from the 1960s onwards. In the first place, it constrained the scope of political analysis significantly, preventing it going beyond what was directly observable. While behavioural analysis produced, and continues to produce, invaluable insights in fields such as voting studies, a narrow obsession with quantifiable data threatens to reduce the discipline of politics to little else.

Moreover, the scientific credentials of behaviouralism were called into question, in that its claim to be objective, reliable and 'value-free' is compromised by a range of unstated biases. For example, if democracy is redefined in terms of observable behaviour, it means what goes on in so-called democratic political systems in the developed West, and is disengaged from ideas such as popular participation and public accountability. Behaviouralism has, finally, been criticized for treating human behaviour as predictable and determined by the interaction of objective factors, when in fact it is shaped by a variable mix of psychological, social, cultural and historical circumstances. The now more common stance of post-behaviouralism differs from behaviouralism in that it goes further in recognizing the role of theory in imposing meaning on data, and acknowledges the degree to which theoretical perspectives may impinge on seemingly objective observations.

BICAMERALISM

Bicameralism is the fragmentation of legislative power, established through the existence of two chambers or houses in the parliament. Bicameral systems are usually classified according to the role, powers and composition of the 'second' chamber or 'upper' house. Most second chambers are constitutionally and politically subordinate to the first chamber, which is usually seen as the locus of popular authority. This is particularly the case in parliamentary systems in which government is generally responsible to, and drawn, largely or wholly, from the lower house. Second chambers often also exercise limited legislative power, meaning that they function essentially as 'revising' chambers. Not uncommonly, such weaker versions of bicameralism reflect the restrictive representative basis of the upper house, which may be selected through indirect elections, partial elections, appointment or, though rarely, inheritance. A stronger version of bicameralism is found in assemblies with two popularly elected chambers that have broadly equal powers. The US Congress is perhaps the only example of a legislative body that has a dominant upper chamber (while all taxation must be introduced in the House of Representatives, the Senate alone exercises ratification and confirmation powers).

Significance

Bicameralism is usually seen as a central principle of liberal constitutionalism. The chief benefits of bicameralism are that second chambers can check the power of first chambers and prevent majoritarian rule; that bicameral assemblies check the power of the executive more effectively; that the existence of two chambers widens the basis of representation and interest articulation; that the legislative burden of the first chamber can be relieved and legislation can be more thoroughly scrutinized; and that the second chamber can act as a constitutional safeguard, preventing or delaying the passage of controversial legislation. The representative advantages of bicameralism may be particularly important in systems in which federalism or devolution operate, as the second chamber can help to overcome conflict between the centre and the periphery by representing provincial or regional interests at the national level.

However, there was a clear trend towards unicameralism in the post-1945 period (with second chambers being abolished in New Zealand, Denmark and Sweden), and bicameralism has been criticized for a number of reasons. Unicameral assemblies may be more efficient, because the existence of a second chamber can make the legislative process unnecessarily complex and difficult. Second chambers may act as a check on democratic rule, particularly when their members are non-elected or indirectly elected. Bicameral parliaments may be a recipe for institutional conflict in the parliament, and may make strong or effective government impossible. The existence of two co-equal chambers may narrow access to policy-making by forcing joint committees to make decisions when there is disagreement between the chambers. Finally, second chambers may introduce a conservative political bias by upholding existing constitutional arrangements and, sometimes, the interests of social elites.

BILL OF RIGHTS

A bill of rights is a legal document that specifies the privileges, rights and liberties of the individual. As such, it defines the relationship between the state and the citizen, and establishes the legal extent of civil liberty. Bills of rights may either be entrenched or statutory. An *entrenched bill of rights* has the status of 'higher' or constitutional law and often comprises part of a written constitution. The first ten amendments of the US Constitution, which specify a collection of individual rights and freedoms, thus came to be known as the Bill of Rights, with the Fourteenth, Fifteenth and Nineteenth Amendments subsequently being accorded the same status. Entrenched rights are binding on the legislature, can usually be introduced, amended or removed only through a complex, constitutional process, and are ulti-mately upheld by a supreme or constitutional court. *A statutory bill of rights* has the same legal status as any other legislature-made law and can therefore be changed through the normal legislative process. Sometimes called a statute of rights, such a bill of rights can operate in the absence of a written constitution and a constitu-tional court, as in the case of the Human Rights Act 1998 in the UK, which incor-porated the European Convention on Human Rights into British law. In other cases, *advisory bills of rights* may operate, which oblige government to consider individual rights formally in the process of policy formulation without being bound to respect them.

Significance

Bills of rights are often considered a valuable, and perhaps essential, means of guar-anteeing limited government and of protecting freedom. Not only does a bill of rights provide the individual with a means of defence against overbearing public authority, but it also has an educational value in heightening sensitivity towards individual rights within government, among the judiciary and, most important, among the public at large. Underlying this argument is often a belief in the doctrine of human rights, the idea that there are certain fundamental, inviolable human rights to which all human beings are entitled, and that these should enjoy the protection of both international and state law. Opponents of this view may either question the validity of the idea of human rights or suggest that rights are adequately protected by common law and, in relation to entrenched bills of rights, by statute law. Other criticisms are that bills of rights compromise the neutrality of judges and inevitably draw them into political disputes; that rights are better left in the hands of elected politicians rather than non-elected judges; and that bills of rights legally embed ideological biases (for example, in relation to property rights) that are difficult to remove and may precipitate conflict.

BUREAUCRACY

Bureaucracy (literally 'rule by officials') is, in everyday language, a pejorative term meaning pointless administrative routine, or 'red tape'. In the social sciences the concept of bureaucracy is used in a more specific and neutral sense, but refers to phenomena as different as rule by non-elected officials, the administrative machinery of government, and a rational mode of organization. Despite disagreement regarding its location and character, it is generally accepted that abstract organization and rule-governed professional administration are features of bureaucracy. There are fewer difficulties with the use of the term bureaucracy in the field of comparative government. Here, it refers to the administrative machinery of the state, bureaucrats being non-elected state officials or civil servants.

Significance

The core function of the bureaucracy is to implement or execute law and policy. The broadening of the responsibilities of government has therefore been accompanied by a general increase in the size of bureaucracies across the globe. However, the political significance of the bureaucracy largely stems from its role as the chief source of policy information and advice available to governments. The principal sources of bureaucratic power therefore include the ability of civil servants to control the flow of information and thus determine what their political masters know; the logistical advantages they enjoy as permanent and full-time public officials; and their status as experts and supposed custodians of the national interest. The growth in bureaucratic power since the early twentieth century is usually explained in terms of the increased premium put on expertise and specialist knowledge by the fact that the task of policy-making in modern societies has become increasingly complex and demanding. This has made the control of the bureaucracy an important issue in all political systems. The principal means through which this control is exerted include mechanisms of public accountability to ministers, assemblies, the courts or sometimes an ombudsman; the politicization (either formally or informally) of senior bureaucratic posts; and the construction of counter-bureaucracies that provide politicians with alternative sources of advice.

The political role and impact of bureaucracy has been the source of considerable debate. Max Weber's (1864–1920) classic account of bureaucracy portrayed it as a reliable, efficient and, above all, rational means of social organization characterized by rule-governed behaviour, an ordered hierarchy, the use of written documents and a filing system, and an impersonal authority system in which appointment and advancement are based on professional criteria. Socialists, and particularly Marxists, on the other hand, have viewed bureaucracy as a power-bloc that can resist political control and reflects broader class interests, through either the social composition of the senior civil service or structural links between government departments and business interests. However, as communist regimes demonstrated, bureaucracy cannot be viewed as a narrowly capitalist phenomenon. Public choice theorists have interpreted bureaucracy in terms of career self-interest on the part of civil servants. In this view, the growth of government intervention is essentially a manifestation of bureaucratic power and the extent to which top bureaucrats are able to resist political control.

CABINET

A cabinet is a committee of senior ministers who represent the various government departments or ministries (this should not to be confused with *cabinet*, as used in France and the EU to denote groups of policy advisers who support individual ministers). In presidential systems the cabinet usually exists to serve the president by acting as a policy adviser rather than a policy-maker. Such cabinets function largely as an administrative tool and a 'sounding board', but are constitutionally subordinate to the president, who monopolizes formal policy-making responsibility. In contrast, the cabinet, in theory at least, is the apex of the executive in states that respect the principle of cabinet government. 'Cabinet government' is characterized by two features. First, the cabinet constitutes the principal link between the legislative and executive branches of government; its members are drawn from and accountable to the parliament, but also serve as the political heads of the various government departments. Second, the cabinet is the senior executive organ and policy-making responsibility is shared within it, the prime minister being merely 'first' in name only. This system is usually underpinned by collective responsibility – all cabinet ministers (and sometimes non-cabinet ministers) are required to 'sing the same song' and support official government policy.

Significance

The widespread use of cabinets reflects the political and administrative need for collective procedures within the political executive. In the first place, cabinets enable government to present a collective face to parliaments and the public. Without a cabinet, government could appear to be a personal tool wielded by a single individual. Second, cabinets are an administrative device designed to ensure the effective co-ordination of government policy. In short, in the absence of a cabinet, government would consist of rival bureaucratic empires each bent on self-aggrandisement. The virtues of cabinet government are therefore that it encourages full and frank policy debate within the democracy of a cabinet meeting, subjecting proposals to wide and effective scrutiny; and that it guarantees the unity and cohesion of government, since the cabinet makes decisions collectively, and collectively stands by them. Cabinet government has nevertheless been criticized because it acts as a cloak for prime-ministerial power by forcing dissenting ministers to support agreed government policy in public, and because it makes government policy incoherent and inconsistent, as decisions tend to be based on compromises between competing ministers and departmental interests.

Whether cabinets are invested with formal policy-making responsibility or not, they have struggled to maintain their political role and status. This is largely a consequence of the growing prominence of the chief executive (whether a president or prime minister), resulting from the media's, and particularly television's, tendency to focus on personality and image, and the need for clear policy leadership in an era of complex and widespread government intervention and global interdependence. Cabinets have also been weakened by the increased size and importance of government departments and other agencies, meaning that policy proposals emerge pre-packaged, with meaningful debate and scrutiny having happened elsewhere. However, cabinets continue to fulfil a residual and irreducible function as a means of policy co-ordination, and, particularly when they contain members with significant party or public support or when the chief executive's authority is weak, they may exert decisive policy influence.

CAPITALISM

Capitalism is an economic system as well as a form of property ownership. Its central features include the following. First, it is based on generalized commodity production, a 'commodity' being a good or service produced for exchange – it has market value rather than use value. Second, productive wealth in a capitalist economy is predominantly held in private hands. Third, economic life is organized according to impersonal market forces, in particular the forces of demand (what consumers are willing and able to consume) and supply (what producers are willing and able to produce). Fourth, in a capitalist economy, material self-interest and profit maximization provide the main motivations for enterprise and hard work.

However, there is no such thing as a 'pure' capitalist system; that is, one not contaminated by socialist and other impurities, such as public ownership, economic management, or collective practices. Moreover, all economic systems are shaped by the historical, cultural and ideological context in which they operate. At least three types of capitalist system can therefore be identified in the modern world. *Enterprise capitalism*, or free-market capitalism (found in the USA and, since the 1980s, the UK), is characterized by faith in the untrammelled workings of market competition, minimal public ownership, safety-net welfare provision and weak trade unions. *Social capitalism*, or Rhine-Alpine capitalism (found throughout continental Europe, especially in Germany) is characterized by the idea of a social market; that is, it attempts to balance the disciplines of market competition against the need for social cohesion and solidarity guaranteed by economic and social intervention. *Collective capitalism*, or 'tiger' capitalism (found in East Asia generally, and increasingly in China) is characterized by what had been called 'relational markets': close connections between industry and finance, and between producers and government; and by an emphasis on collaborative effort sometimes dubbed 'peoplism'.

Significance

Capitalist economic forms first emerged in seventeenth-century and eighteenth-century Europe, developing from within predominantly feudal societies. Capitalist practices initially took root in the form of commercial agriculture orientated towards the market, and increasingly relied on waged labour rather than bonded serfs. Developed or industrial capitalism started to emerge from the mid-nineteenth century onwards, first in the UK but soon in the USA and across Europe, with the advent of machine-based factory production and the gradual shift of populations from the land to the expanding towns and cities. Having defied socialist predictions about its inevitable demise, and withstood the twentieth-century ideological battle against communism, capitalism has, since the Eastern European Revolutions of 1989–91, emerged as a global system without serious rivals. The dual secrets of its success have been its flexibility, which has enabled it to absorb non-capitalist 'impurities' and adapt to a variety of cultures, and its seemingly relentless capacity to generate technological development, which has enabled it to deliver widespread, if uneven, prosperity.

Few issues have polarized political debate so effectively as capitalism; indeed, the left/right ideological divide is commonly interpreted as a battle between anti-capitalist and pro-capitalist positions. Three broad stances have been adopted in relation to capitalism. The first, taken up by fundamentalist socialists, rejects capitalism out of hand on the grounds that it amounts to a system of mass exploitation. Karl Marx (1818–83) was undoubtedly the foremost exponent of this view, arguing that capitalism, like all other class societies, is doomed because it is based on a fundamental contradiction between oppressors (the bourgeoisie) and the oppressed (the proletariat). The second stance, adopted in different ways by parliamentary socialists, modern liberals and paternalist conservatives, can be summed up in the assertion that capitalism is a good servant but a bad master. This view accepts that capitalism is the most reliable, perhaps the only reliable, mechanism for generating wealth, but emphasizes that unregulated capitalism is chronically unstable and prone to high unemployment and wide material inequalities. Associated with the ideas of J. M. Keynes (1883–1946), this perspective suggests that the issue is not so much capitalism but how and to what extent the capitalist system should be reformed or 'humanized'. The third stance, adopted by classical liberals, the New Right and, in its most extreme form, by anarcho-capitalists, is that capitalism is a self-regulating mechanism and should therefore be encumbered as little as possible by external controls, an idea summed up in the principle of laissez-faire, literally meaning 'leave to do'. The earliest and most influential exponent of this view was Adam Smith (1723–90), who argued that the market is regulated by 'an invisible hand' and so tends towards long-run equilibrium.

CENTRALIZATION/DECENTRALIZATION

Centralization is the concentration of political power or government authority within central institutions. These institutions are normally considered to be central because they operate at the national level; however, the term centralization is sometimes used to describe the concentration of power or authority within the national level of **government**, as, for example, when **executives** dominate legislatures or **parliaments**, or when **cabinets** are subordinate to chief executives. Decentralization is usually understood to refer to the expansion of local **autonomy** through the transfer of powers and responsibilities away from national bodies. Centralization and decentralization thus highlight different territorial divisions of power within the **state** between central (national) and peripheral (regional, provincial or local) institutions.

Significance

All modern states contain territorial divisions. The nature of these divisions nevertheless varies enormously. The divisions are structured by the constitutional framework within which centre–periphery relationships are conducted; the distribution of functions and responsibilities between the levels of government; the means by which their personnel are appointed and recruited; the political, economic, administrative and other powers the centre can use to control the periphery; and the independence that peripheral bodies enjoy. What is clear, however, is that neither central nor peripheral bodies can be dispensed with completely. In the absence of central government, a state would not be able to function as an actor on the international stage.

The case for centralization is that:

- Central government alone articulates the interests of the whole rather than its various parts; that is, the interests of the **nation** rather than those of sectional, ethnic or regional groups.
- Only central government can establish uniform **laws** and public services which help people to move easily from one part of the country to another.
- Central government is able to rectify inequalities that arise as a result of the areas with the greatest social needs invariably being those with the least potential for raising revenue to meet them.
- Economic development and centralization are invariably found in close association; only a central authority, for example, can manage a single currency, control tax and spending policies with a view to ensuring sustainable growth, and provide an economic infrastructure.

The case for decentralization includes the following:

- Local or regional government is more effective than central government in providing opportunities for citizens to participate in the political life of their community, thus creating a better-educated and a more informed citizenry.
- Peripheral institutions are usually 'closer' to the people and are more sensitive to their needs.
- Decisions made at a local level are more likely to be seen as intelligible and therefore legitimate, whereas central government may appear to be remote, both geographically and politically.

- Decentralization protects freedom by dispersing government power and creating a network of checks and balances; peripheral bodies check central government as well as each other.

CHECKS AND BALANCES

Checks and balances are a network of tensions within a system, usually a governmental system, that results from the fragmentation of power. While such a system may involve independence, its crucial feature is interdependence, ensuring that each element in it is able to check the power of other elements. Checks and balances can be found in all liberal political systems, each exhibiting some measure of institutional fragmentation, but the principle has been applied most rigorously to the US governmental system, where it amounted to, in effect, a constitutional blueprint. Not only do checks and balances operate among the legislature, executive and judicial branches (the separation of powers) but also between the two houses of the legislature (bicameralism), and between the national/federal government and the fifty states (federalism).

Significance

The principle of checks and balances is a cornerstone of liberal constitutionalism. It is based on the assumption that, as human beings are inherently self-interested, all systems of rule are likely to become tyrannical and oppressive. The purpose of checks and balances is therefore to safeguard liberty by creating internal tensions within the governmental system, thereby reducing its capacity to interfere in citizens' private affairs. Individual freedom thus expands to the extent to which government is fragmented. Two main criticisms have been levelled at the principle of checks and balances. First, institutional checks and balances may lead to deadlock, preventing government from acting, even in areas where intervention is widely deemed to be legitimate or necessary. This can be seen in the recurrent tendency of the US system towards 'government gridlock'. Second, ideological reservations have been expressed about the widespread use of checks and balances, on the grounds that this tends to minimize the role of the state, and so serves the interest of untrammelled capitalism.

CHRISTIAN DEMOCRACY

Christian democracy is a political and ideological movement that advances a moderate and welfarist brand of conservatism. The origins of Christian democracy lie in Catholic social theory, which, in contrast to Protestantism's stress on individualism, emphasizes the importance of social groups, in particular the family, and highlights a harmony of interests among these groups. While Christian democracy is ideologically vague and has adapted itself to different national cultures and political circumstances, two major themes have been recurrent. The first is a concern about the effects of unregulated market capitalism, reflected in a willingness to embrace

Keynesian (see social democracy) and welfarist policies. The second is a fear of state control, reflected in a hostility to socialism in general and to communism in particular. The most influential of Christian democrat ideas, particularly associated with the German Christian Democratic Union (CDU), is the notion of the social market. A social market is an economy structured on market principles and largely free from government control, operating in the context of a society in which cohesion is maintained through a comprehensive welfare system and effective public services. The market is thus not so much an end in itself as a means of generating wealth to achieve broader social goals.

Significance

Christian democracy has been an important political movement in many parts of Europe in the post-World War II period. Its success has been associated in particular with the influence of Christian democratic parties in France during the Fourth Republic, Italy, Germany, Austria, Belgium and the Netherlands, and, to a lesser extent, in Latin America and post-communist Eastern Europe. The success of these parties stems partly from their centre-right political stance, which parallels that of paternalistic conservatism and consolidates middle-class support, but it is also because 'Christian' has served as a rallying cry against communism, while 'democracy' indicates a concern with the common good rather than with elite or aristocratic interests (thereby breaking with pre-war conservative parties). It is notable, for example, that Christian democratic parties generally resisted the New Right enthusiasms that characterized conservatism in the UK and the USA in the 1980s and 1990s. The chief threats to Christian democracy have come from the declining importance of religion as a source of political motivation; from the receding threat of communism since the Eastern European Revolutions of 1989–91; and from the ideological ambiguities and uncertainties of Christian democracy itself. Since it both praises and warns against government intervention, it sometimes appears to be little more than a vehicle for winning or retaining government power.

CITIZENSHIP

Citizenship is a relationship between the individual and the state, in which the two are bound together by reciprocal rights and duties. Citizens differ from subjects and aliens in that they are full members of their political community, or state, by virtue of the possession of basic rights. Citizenship is viewed differently depending on whether it is shaped by individualism or communitarianism. The former, linked to liberalism, advances the principle of a 'citizenship of rights', and places particular stress on private entitlement and the status of the individual as an autonomous actor. There are socialist and conservative versions of communitarianism, but each advances the principle of a 'citizenship of duty', highlighting the importance of civic responsibility. Such theories tend to portray the state as a moral agency, and to underline the need for community and the role of social existence.

Significance

The idea that citizenship is the proper end of **government** can be traced back to the political thought of Ancient Greece, and to the belief that an interest in public affairs is a basic feature of individual existence. Recurrent interest in citizenship therefore reflects an enduring concern for, and commitment to, the 'public' face of human life. Controversies about citizenship centre on the rights it implies and its value as a political principle. The political **right** tends to endorse a narrow view of citizenship that stresses only civil and political rights, the rights that are exercised within **civil society** and rights of participation. The political **left**, by contrast, tends to endorse 'social citizenship', the idea that citizens are entitled to a social minimum, expressed in terms of social and welfare rights. Opponents of the very idea of citizenship include libertarians who reject the notion that individuals have a broader social identity and responsibilities. Marxists may also criticize citizenship, on the grounds that it masks the reality of unequal class power, while feminists may do so because it does not take into account patriarchal oppression. Nevertheless, the rise of communitarianism and the emergence of 'new' **social democracy** has led to a revival of interest in citizenship, as an attempt to re-establish a 'rights and responsibilities' agenda and to counterbalance the market individualism of the New Right. This is usually associated with the idea of 'active citizenship', a notion that places particular emphasis on the social duties and moral responsibilities of citizens.

CIVIL DISOBEDIENCE

Civil disobedience is lawbreaking that is justified by reference to 'higher' religious, moral or political principles. Civil disobedience is an overt and public act; it aims to break the **law** to 'make a point', not to get away with illegal behaviour. Indeed, its moral force is based largely on the willing acceptance of the penalties that follow from lawbreaking. This both emphasizes the conscientious and principled nature of the act and provides evidence of the depth of feeling or commitment that lies behind it. In some cases, civil disobedience may involve the breaking of laws that are themselves considered to be wicked or unjust (such as those that uphold racial discrimination), while in other cases, it involves breaking the law to protest against a wider injustice, even though the law being broken may not in itself be objectionable. Finally, the moral character of civil disobedience is normally underlined by the strict avoidance of violence.

Significance

Civil disobedience has a long and respectable history, drawing as it does on the ideas of writers such as Henry David Thoreau (1817–62) and the example of political leaders such as Mahatma Gandhi (1869–1948) and Martin Luther King (1929–68). Under Gandhi's influence, non-violent civil disobedience (or *satyagraha*, literally meaning 'defence of the truth') became a powerful weapon in the campaign for Indian independence, finally granted in 1947. In the early 1960s, King adopted similar political tactics in the struggle for black civil rights in the Southern states of the USA. Since the 1960s, civil disobedience has become more widespread and politically acceptable.

Those who argue that civil disobedience is a legitimate political tactic maintain that there is a clear distinction between law and justice. At the heart of civil disobedience stands the belief that the individual, rather than government, is the ultimate moral authority; to believe otherwise would be to imply that all laws are just, and to reduce justice to mere legality. In the modern period, the distinction between law and justice has usually been based on the doctrine of human rights, asserting that there is a set of higher moral principles against which human law can be judged. Critics of civil disobedience hold that it brings with it a number of insidious dangers. The first of these is that, as civil disobedience becomes fashionable, it threatens to undermine respect for alternative, legal and democratic means of exerting influence. At a deeper level, the spread of civil disobedience may ultimately threaten the social order and political stability by eroding the fear of illegality. When people cease to obey the law automatically and only do so out of personal choice, the authority of the law itself is called into question.

CIVIL LIBERTY

Civil liberty is a 'private' sphere of existence that belongs to the citizen, not the state. Civil liberty therefore encompasses a range of 'negative' rights, usually rooted in the doctrine of human rights, which demand non-interference on the part of government. Classic civil liberties are usually thought to include the right to freedom of speech, freedom of the press, freedom of religion and conscience, freedom of movement, and freedom of association. Civil liberties are often confused with civil rights. The former are freedoms *from* government, while the latter are generally 'positive' rights, in the sense that they are rights of participation and access to power. Civil rights campaigns thus typically call for a widening of voting and political rights, and for an end to discrimination, rather than for a broadening of civil liberty.

Significance

The maintenance of key civil liberties is generally seen as being vital to the functioning of liberal-democratic societies, since they provide the individual with protection against arbitrary government. In many cases, the principle of civil liberty is given constitutional expression through documents such as a bill of rights, and it is widely seen as a basic justification for judicial independence and a strict separation between law and politics. The clarity with which civil liberties are defined, and the effectiveness with which they are upheld, are therefore the crucial index of individual freedom from the liberal perspective. Reservations about civil liberty have nevertheless been expressed by both conservatives and socialists. Conservatives have argued that the strengthening of civil liberties tends to weaken government and, in particular, hamper the maintenance of domestic order. Socialists, on the other hand, have warned that the doctrine of civil liberty, especially when applied to property rights, can serve as a defence of social inequality and class oppression.

CIVIL SOCIETY

Civil society has been defined in a variety of ways. Originally it meant a 'political community', a society governed by law, under the authority of a state. More commonly, civil society is distinguished from the state, and is used to describe a realm of autonomous groups and associations, such as businesses, pressure groups, clubs, families and so on. It thus consists of what Edmund Burke (1729–97) called the 'little platoons'. In this sense the division between civil society and the state reflects a 'private/public' divide; civil society encompasses institutions that are 'private' in that they are independent of government and organized by individuals in pursuit of their own ends. G. W. F. Hegel (1770–1831), on the other hand, distinguished civil society not only from the state but also from the family. He viewed civil society as a sphere of 'universal egoism' in which individuals place their own interests before those of others, whereas the state and the family are characterized by 'universal altruism' and 'particular altruism', respectively.

Significance

Civil society is widely used as a descriptive concept to assess the balance between state authority and private bodies and associations. For example, totalitarianism is defined by the abolition of civil society, and the growth of private associations and clubs, lobby groups and independent trade unions in post-communist societies is described as the re-emergence of civil society. In most cases, however, civil society is invested with normative and ideological significance. In the conventional, liberal view, civil society is identified as a realm of choice, personal freedom and individual responsibility. Whereas the state operates through compulsory and coercive authority, civil society allows individuals to shape their own destinies. This explains why a vigorous and healthy civil society is usually regarded as an essential feature of liberal democracy, and why classical liberals in particular have a moral preference for civil society over the state, reflected in a desire to minimize the scope of public authority and maximize the private sphere. In contrast, the Hegelian use of the term is negative in that it counterposes the egoism of civil society with the altruism that is fostered by the family and within the state. Marxists and socialists generally have viewed civil society unfavourably, associating it in particular with unequal class power and social injustice. Such views would justify either the overthrow of civil society as structured at present, or the contraction of civil society through the expansion of state control and regulation.

COALITION

A coalition is a grouping of rival political actors brought together either through the perception of a common threat, or the recognition that their goals cannot be achieved by working separately. *Electoral coalitions* are alliances through which political parties agree not to compete against one another with a view to maximizing their joint representation. Legislative coalitions are agreements between two or more parties to support a particular bill or programme. *Government coalitions* are formal agreements between two or more parties that involve a cross-party distribution of ministerial portfolios. A 'grand coalition' or 'national government' comprises all the major parties, but they are usually formed only at times of national crisis or economic emergency.

Significance

Most debate about the political impact of coalitions centres on the workings of government coalitions. These are usually formed to ensure majority control of the parliament, and are therefore usually found in political systems that employ proportional representation, or which have fragmented party systems. Coalitions have been criticized on the grounds that, as they do not command a unified parliamentary majority, they result in weak and ineffective government; that conflict between coalition partners tends to produce instability; and that they prevent the development of bold, if controversial, policy initiatives. However, coalition governments may have the advantage that they promote compromise and consensus-building across the political spectrum; that they command wide, if diverse, public support; and that they scrutinize policy proposals more rigorously and effectively. Successful coalition governments usually operate in the context of a broad ideological consensus, in which parties act as 'brokers' for particular interests and are accustomed to compromise and flexibility. Coalition government is often seen as being particularly appropriate for divided societies.

COLLECTIVE SECURITY

Collective security is the theory or practice of states pledging to defend one another to deter aggression or punish a transgressor if international order has been breached. Its key idea is that aggression can best be resisted by united action taken by a number of states, this being the only alternative to the insecurity and uncertainty of power politics. Collective security thus differs from 'national' security, the latter implying that states view security primarily in individual terms, with each state being responsible for maintaining its own security, and seeing other states as at least a potential threat to that security. An example of collective security can be found in Article 5 of the NATO Charter, which states that an attack on one or several members of the organization would be considered an attack on all.

Significance

Though the idea of collective or common security has a history that can be traced back to Ancient Greece, and can be found in the writings of thinkers such as Immanuel Kant (1724–1804) and Jeremy Bentham (1748–1832), the principle has only played a major role in the theory and practice of international relations since World War I. The goal of constructing a collective security system was a powerful factor underpinning the creation of both the League of Nations in 1919 and the United Nations in 1945. Collective security has two principal benefits. First, it promises to be more effective than national security in deterring war and expansionism, because potential aggressors are likely to be confronted by military resources greater than any single state could muster when acting alone. Second, by lowering states' emphasis on 'self-help', collective security counters the tendencies inherent in international anarchy; and in particular reducing the extent to which state policy is driven by fear and anxiety.

Successful collective security nevertheless depends on three conditions. First, the states should be roughly equal, or at least there must be no preponderant power. Second, all states must be willing, as well as able, to bear the cost of defending one another. Third, collective security depends on the existence of an international body that has the moral authority and military capacity to take effective action. The difficulty of achieving these conditions has meant that collective security systems have often performed poorly in practice. The ill-starred League of Nations was, for example, nothing more than a bystander in the 1930s, as Imperial Japan, Fascist Italy and Nazi Germany embarked on programmes of expansion leading to the outbreak of World War II. The UN has been more effective, but its capacity to enforce collective security has been severely limited because it is essentially a creature of its members: it can do no more than its member states, and in particular the permanent members of the Security Council, permit. For realist theorists, such difficulties reflect flaws in the notion of collective security and not merely defects in the workings of particular institutions. These flaws stem from state egoism, and imply that, regardless of their notional obligations within international organizations, states will always be deeply reluctant to incur military and other costs in order to protect other states.

COLLECTIVISM

Collectivism is, broadly, the belief that collective human endeavour is of greater practical and moral value than individual self-striving. It reflects the idea that human nature has a social core, and implies that social groups, whether social classes, nations, races or whatever, are meaningful political entities. However, the term is used with little consistency. Mikhail Bakunin (1814–76) used collectivism to refer to self-governing associations of free individuals, describing his form of anarchism as collectivist anarchism. More commonly, collectivism is treated as the opposite of individualism, on the grounds that it implies that collective interests should prevail over individual ones. Collectivism in this sense is often linked to the state, as the mechanism through which collective interests are upheld against the individual interests of civil society. This suggests, in stark contrast to Bakunin's use of the term, that the growth of state responsibilities marks the advance of collectivism. It also explains why collectivism is often confused with collectivization, the extension of state control over the economy (though collectivization may be seen as a means of advancing collectivist goals).

Significance

Collectivism has been one of the key components of socialist ideology. The socialist case for collectivism is both moral and economic. Morally, collective endeavour in the form of co-operation fosters social solidarity and a responsibility for fellow human beings, based on their common humanity. Economically, collectivism enables the collective energies of society to be harnessed in a rational and efficient fashion, by contrast with self-striving, which results in wasteful competition. This emphasis on collectivism is evident in a traditional socialist belief in equality, welfare and common ownership. Marxism indeed subscribes to a form of methodological collectivism, in that it treats social classes rather than individuals as the principal agents of historical change. However, collectivism is by no means linked exclusively to socialism, and forms of collectivism can be identified in, for example, nationalism, racialism and feminism. Two basic objections are usually made to collectivism, both rooted in the ideas of liberal individualism. The first is that collectivism stifles individuality and diversity by insisting on a common social identity and shared human interests. The second is that collectivism is necessarily, and not accidentally, linked to statism and the erosion of freedom, as there is no effective means to advance collective interests except through political authority.

COLLECTIVIZATION

Collectivization is a system in which property is owned and controlled by a collective body, usually through the mechanism of the state. Collectivization is therefore a comprehensive form of nationalization, in that it brings the entirety of economic life, and not merely selected industries, under state control. Collectivized economies are organized on the basis of planning rather than the market, and therefore seek to allocate resources on a rational basis in accordance with clearly defined goals.

Significance

The best examples of collectivization were found in orthodox communist states, such as the USSR, which operated a system of central planning. Collectivization was introduced in the USSR under Stalin through a series of Five Year Plans, the first of which was announced in 1928. All Soviet enterprises – factories, farms, shops and so on – were set planning targets, ultimately by Gosplan (the State Planning Committee), and these were administered by a collection of powerful economic ministries. The attraction of collectivization was that it promised to achieve an important range of socialist goals, notably to gear the economy to the wider needs of society, as opposed to private profit, and to ensure that material inequalities were abolished or substantially reduced. However, collectivization effectively collapsed with the Eastern European Revolutions of 1989–91 and, where communism survived, as in China and Cuba, it did so in part by abandoning collectivization. The major criticisms of collectivization are that it is inherently inefficient because it is not orientated towards profit and allows little scope for material incentives, and that it is implicitly totalitarian because state control of the economy is a fundamental threat to civil society, the absence of economic freedom imposing an inevitable threat to political freedom.

COMMITTEE

A committee is a small work group composed of members drawn from a larger body and charged with specific responsibilities. Whereas ad hoc committees are set up for a particular purpose, and disbanded when that task is completed, permanent or standing committees have enduring responsibilities and an institutional role. However, the responsibilities entrusted to committees range from formal decision-making (as in the case of some cabinets), policy analysis and debate, to administrative co-ordination and information exchange. Not uncommonly, committees operate within a larger committee system of specialist committees, co-ordinating committees and sub-committees.

Significance

Committee structures have become increasingly prominent in legislative and executive branches of government, as deliberative and consultative forums and as decision-making bodies. It is generally accepted that the wider and more formal use of committees has become an administrative necessity, given the size and complexity of modern government. The major advantages of committees include the following: they allow a range of views, opinions and interests to be represented; provide the opportunity for fuller, longer and more detailed debate; encourage decisions to be made more efficiently and speedily; and make possible a division of labour that encourages the accumulation of expertise and specialist knowledge. However, committees have also been criticized. For example, they can easily be manipulated by those who set up and staff them, and they can encourage centralization by allowing a chairperson to dominate proceedings behind a mask of consultation. Moreover, they may narrow the range of views and interests that are taken into account in decision-making, particularly as their members may become divorced from the larger body, creating a form of sham representation.

COMMUNISM

The term communism has been used in three different, if related, ways: as a political principle, as a social model or regime-type based on this principle, and as an ideological movement whose central purpose is to establish such a society or regime. As a political principle, communism stands for the communal organization of social existence and, in particular, the common or collective ownership of wealth. In *The Communist Manifesto* (Marx and Engels, 1848/1967), Karl Marx (1818–83) thus summed up the theory of communism as the 'abolition of private property'. There are two versions of communism as a social model or regime-type. The first of these is a model of a future society described in the writings of Marx and Friedrich Engels (1820–95). Marx predicted that after the overthrow of capitalism there would be a transitionary 'socialist' stage of development, characterized by the 'revolutionary dictatorship of the proletariat', which would, as class antagonisms abated, eventually lead to full communism. Although Marx refused to describe in detail this communist society, he envisaged that it would have the following features:

- It would be based on the common ownership of wealth and would thus be classless.
- It would be stateless in the sense that once the class system had been abolished the state would gradually 'wither away'.
- It would be geared not towards commodity production and the market, but to production-for-use and the satisfaction of human needs.
- It would lead to the further development of the 'forces of production' as technology is liberated from the constraints of class-based production.
- By fostering unalienated labour, it would release creative energies and allow for the full development of human potential.

The second version of communism as a social model is based on the regimes that communist parties established when they gained power in the twentieth century, for example in the USSR and Eastern Europe, and in China, Cuba, Vietnam and elsewhere. Communism in this sense came to mean 'actually existing socialism', sometimes seen as 'orthodox communism'. Orthodox communism amounted to a form of state socialism in which political control was in the hands of a monopolistic and hierarchical communist party, and the economy was organized on the basis of state collectivization and central planning.

As an ideological movement, communism is intrinsically linked to Marxism: the terms are either used interchangeably, or communism is viewed as operationalized Marxism, Marxism being the theory and communism the practice. However, communism in this sense is better linked to so-called orthodox Marxism, sometimes portrayed as 'dialectical materialism', because it was as much influenced by the ideas of Leninism and Stalinism as it was by the classical ideas of Marx. Just as Soviet communism became the dominant model of communist rule in the twentieth century, Marxism-Leninism became the ruling ideology of the communist world. Despite communist ideology being reinterpreted in different societies and by different leaders, it was characterized by a number of recurrent themes. The most important of these were a sometimes crude belief in the primacy of economics over other historical factors; strong support for revolution rather than reform; the identification of the proletariat as the revolutionary class; a belief in the communist party as the 'vanguard of the working class'; support for socialist or proletarian internationalism; and a belief in comprehensive collectivization.

Significance

Communism as the principle of common ownership long pre-dates Marx and can be found in the writings of Plato (427–347 BCE) and Thomas More (1478–1535);

however, its modern significance is associated almost entirely with the theory and practice of Marxism. As an ideological movement, communism was one of the most powerful political forces of the twentieth century, though its influence was largely confined to the period 1917–91. However, during this time, communism presented the chief alternative to capitalism: it provided the basis for political and social reconstruction in what became known as the communist East, and constituted the principal oppositional force in many parts of the capitalist West. The ideological potency of communism stemmed from its stress on social equality and the common good, and its promise to bring to an end what Marx called 'the exploitation of the many by the few'. Its political success was closely linked to its capacity to mobilize oppressed or disadvantaged classes in support of revolutionary leaders who were well organized and followed clear political strategies. Communism in power proved to be a formidable force: the construction of one-party states not only weakened 'class enemies' and opposition groups, but also allowed communist parties to operate as 'ruling' parties in the sense that they dominated all aspects of government, the military, the economy and the ideological apparatus. In practice, twentieth-century communism was largely a vehicle for modernization that was most successful in economically backward societies, where its success was ultimately judged in terms of its capacity to deliver social development.

Critics of communism have usually focused on the more unattractive aspects of orthodox communism, sometimes tracing these back to the classical ideas of Marx. In this light, communism is seen to be intrinsically dictatorial, if not implicitly totalitarian. The oppressive face of communism stems from the fact that it combines the ideas of concentrated political power and centralized state control (despite Marx's doctrine of 'withering away'), creating an all-powerful party-state apparatus, typically dominated by a charismatic leader. The dramatic collapse of communism in the Eastern European Revolutions of 1989–91, and the radical reforms that have occurred where communist parties have clung on to power, indicate a number of structural weaknesses within orthodox communism. The most important of these are the (arguably) inherent inefficiency of planning systems and the inability of communist states to match the economic prosperity enjoyed in capitalist states (and in particular, the failure to produce Western-style consumer goods); the tendency towards sclerosis in a political system that was dominated by entrenched party and bureaucratic interests; and the fact that communist political systems lacked the mechanisms through which elite groups could monitor and respond to popular pressures.

COMMUNITARIANISM

Communitarianism is the belief that the self or person is constituted through the community, in the sense that individuals are shaped by the communities to which they belong and thus owe them a debt of respect and consideration – there are no 'unencumbered selves'. Communitarianism is not an ideology in its own right, but is, rather, a theoretical position that has been adopted by a variety of ideological traditions. Left-wing forms of communitarianism link the idea of community to the notions of unrestricted freedom and social equality (for example, anarchism and utopian socialism). Centrist forms of communitarianism hold that community is grounded in an acknowledgement of reciprocal rights and responsibilities (for example, social democracy and Tory paternalism). Right-wing forms of communitarianism hold that community requires respect for authority and established values (for example, neo-conservatism and, in its extreme form, fascism). In the 1980s and 1990s, communitarianism developed into a school of thought that articulates a particular political philosophy. In this form, associated with theorists such as Alasdair MacIntyre (1981) and Michael Sandel (1982), it advances a specific critique of liberalism, which highlights the damage done to the public culture of liberal societies by their emphasis on individual rights and liberties over the needs of the community. So-called 'high' and 'low' forms of communitarianism are sometimes identified. The former engages primarily in philosophical debate, while the latter, whose best known figure is Amitai Etzioni (1995), is more concerned with issues of public policy.

Significance

The origins of communitarianism lie in the nineteenth-century socialist utopianism of thinkers such as Robert Owen (1771–1858) and Pyotr Kropotkin (1842–1921). Indeed, a concern with community can be seen as one of the enduring themes in modern political thought, expressed variously in the socialist stress on fraternity and co-operation, the Marxist belief in a classless communist society, the conservative view of society as an organic whole, and even the fascist commitment to an indivisible national community.

Modern communitarianism emerged as a late-twentieth-century reaction against the imbalances in modern society and political thought that have occurred through the spread of liberal individualism. Communitarians warn that, unconstrained by social duty and a moral responsibility, individuals have been allowed or encouraged to take into account only their own interests and rights. In this moral vacuum, society, quite literally, disintegrates. The communitarian project thus attempts to restore to society its moral voice and, in a tradition dating back to Aristotle (384–322 BCE), to construct a 'politics of the common good'. As a critique of laissez-faire capitalism, communitarianism has had a growing influence on modern liberalism and social democracy.

However, critics of communitarianism allege that it has both conservative and authoritarian implications. Communitarianism has a conservative disposition in that it amounts to a defence of existing social structures and moral codes. Feminists, for example, have criticized communitarianism for attempting to bolster traditional gender roles under the guise of defending the family. The authoritarian features of communitarianism stem from its tendency to emphasize the duties and responsibilities of the individual over his or her rights and entitlements.

COMMUNITY

A community, in everyday language, is a collection of people in a given location; that is, a village, town, city, or even country. As a political or social principle, however, the term community suggests a social group that possesses a strong collective identity based on the bonds of comradeship, loyalty and duty. Ferdinand Tönnies (1855–1936) distinguished between *Gemeinschaft*, or 'community', typically found in traditional societies and characterized by natural affection and mutual respect, and *Gesellschaft*, or 'association' – that is, the looser, artificial and contractual relationships typically found in urban and industrialized societies. Émile Durkheim (1858–1917) emphasized the degree to which community is based on the maintenance of social and moral codes. If these are weakened, this induces *anomie*, feelings of isolation, loneliness and meaninglessness, which Durkheim associated with the incidence of suicide.

Significance

An emphasis on community has been a recurrent theme in political thought and can be traced back to Aristotle's assertion that human beings are essentially 'political animals', though the idea of community has often remained vague and ill-defined. Socialists and traditional conservatives have placed particular emphasis on community. For socialists, it implies co-operation and social responsibility and, in its most radical form, it has led to a preference for small, self-managing communities, or communes. For conservatives, it is linked to the need to give individuals a secure social identity and sense of rootedness. In the late twentieth century, the cause of community was advanced explicitly through the rise of communitarianism, which sets out to redress the 'atomism' that has resulted from the spread of liberal and individualist values.

Critics of the principle of community point out that it is either politically dangerous or intellectually bogus. The danger of community is that it can lead to individual rights and liberties being violated in the name of the collective body. This was demonstrated most graphically through Nazism's emphasis on the *Völksgemeinschaft*, or 'national community', which aimed to dissolve individuality, and indeed personal experience, within the social whole. The intellectual limitations of community derive from its tendency to imply the existence of collective identities and social bonds which in fact do not exist. Liberals may therefore point out that there is no such thing as community, but only a collection of individuals. Terms such as 'gay community' and 'black community' have come in for particular criticism in this respect.

CONFLICT OF CIVILIZATIONS

The 'conflict of civilizations' thesis suggests that, in the post-Cold War world, conflict would not primarily be ideological but, rather, cultural in character. According to Samuel Huntington (1996), the emerging 'world of civilizations' would comprise nine major civilizations – Western, Sinic or Chinese, Japanese, Hindu, Islamic,

Buddhist, African, Latin American and Orthodox Christian. Crucial to the thesis, however, is the assumption that a stronger sense of cultural belonging can only lead to tension and conflict. This is because cultures and civilizations are incommensurate: they establish quite different values and meanings. In Huntington's view, cultural conflict is likely to occur at both 'micro' and 'macro' levels. 'Micro-level' conflict will emerge at the 'fault-lines' between civilizations, where one human 'tribe' clashes with another, possibly resulting in communal wars. In that sense, civilizations operate rather like 'tectonic plates' that rub up against one another at vulnerable points. At the 'macro' level, conflict may break out between the civilizations themselves, in all likelihood precipitated by clashes between their 'core' states.

Significance

The idea of a clash of civilizations attracted increasing attention during the 1990s, as international politics was shaken by an upsurge in ethnic conflict in the former Yugoslavia, Rwanda and elsewhere. However, the thesis had its greatest impact after 11 September 2001 (subsequently known as '9/11'), when it was widely used as an explanation of the changing nature of world order, and global terrorism was seen as a symptom of an emerging clash between Islam and the West. From the perspective of the clash of civilizations thesis, the origins of Islamic militancy derive from a basic incompatibility between Islamic values and those of the liberal-democratic West. Such thinking was evident both in the militant Islamist belief that the 'godless' West and Western values are corrupt and corrupting, and in the tendency of neo-conservatives in the USA and elsewhere to view Islam as inherently totalitarian as a result of its belief that social life and politics, and not just personal morality, should conform to Islamic values.

This account of emerging and seemingly irresistible civilizational conflict has been severely criticized, however. For example, Huntington's 'tectonic' notion of civilizations presents them as being much more homogeneous, and therefore distinct from one another, than is in fact the case. In practice, civilizations have always interpenetrated one another, giving rise to blurred or hybrid cultural identities. Furthermore, in being founded on 'culturalism', which treats culture as the universal basis for personal and social identity, the thesis fails to recognize the extent to which cultural identities are shaped by political, economic and other circumstances. What appears to be a cultural conflict may therefore have a quite different, and more complex, explanation. The rise of militant Islamism may thus be better explained by tensions and crises in the Middle East in general, and in the Arab world in particular, linked to factors such as the inheritance of colonialism, the Arab–Israeli conflict, the survival of unpopular but often oil-rich autocratic regimes, and urban poverty and unemployment, rather than by cultural incompatibility between Western and Islamic value systems.

CONFUCIANISM

Confucianism is a system of ethics formulated by Confucius (Kong Fuzi) (551–479 BCE) and his followers that was outlined primarily in the *Analects*.

Confucian thought has concerned itself with the twin themes of human relations and the cultivation of the self. The emphasis on *ren* ('humanity' or 'love') has usually been interpreted as implying support for traditional ideas and values, notably filial piety, respect, loyalty and benevolence. The stress on *junzi* (the virtuous person) suggests a capacity for human development and potential for perfection, realized, in particular, through education. Confucianism offers the vision of a hierarchical society in which there is a well-defined role for every member. This is based on the belief that there are three categories of people – sages (who embody and transmit wisdom, but are very few in number); nobles or 'gentlemen' (who predominate in 'dealings with the world' and constantly strive to follow the path of self-cultivation); and the 'small men' (the mass of society, who have little concern for morality but will diligently follow the exemplary ruler). However, while this hierarchical model reflects the essentially conservative idea that moral responsibility increases with social status, it is founded on strictly meritocratic principles: Confucius believed that people are equal at birth and advocated a system of education that was open to all.

Significance

Confucianism was the dominant philosophical tradition in imperial China, shaping social structures, politics and almost every aspect of Chinese education until the early twentieth century. While Confucianism is often portrayed as one of the three great philosophical traditions in imperial China, the others being Buddhism and Daoism, there is little doubt that it was the most influential, even being seen by some as coexistent with Chinese civilization itself. Confucianism nevertheless came under attack from the Taiping Rebellion (1850–64) onwards, with criticism sharpening as a result of the rise of the May Fourth Movement (1915–19). Confucian thought was viewed increasingly as the source of China's social and cultural stagnation, having been made an easier target by its association with complex but ultimately meaningless ritual and unquestioning obedience to authority. This line of criticism was intensified once the Chinese Communist Party came to power in 1949, as Confucianism was taken to be starkly incompatible with Marxism-Leninism. However, interest in Confucianism was revived during the 1980s and 1990s, through its link to the idea of 'Asian values', such as social harmony, respect for authority and a belief in the family, which supposedly underpinned that rapid economic emergence of Japan and the so-called Asian 'tiger' economies – Hong Kong, South Korea, Thailand and Singapore. Confucianism has also gained greater respectability within China alongside the process of 'modernization' since the 1980s, leading some to proclaim a 'Confucian revival', at least within academic and intellectual circles.

CONSENSUS

A consensus is an agreement, but it is an agreement of a particular kind. Consensus implies, first, a broad agreement, the terms of which are accepted by a wide range of individuals or groups. Second, it implies an agreement about fundamental or underlying principles, as opposed to a precise or exact agreement. In other words, a consensus permits disagreement on matters of emphasis or detail. The term 'consensus politics' may be used in two ways. A *procedural* consensus is a willingness to make decisions through consultation and bargaining, either between political parties or between government and major interests. A *substantive* consensus is an overlap in the ideological positions of two or more political parties, reflected in agreement about fundamental policy goals (as in the UK's post-1945 social-democratic consensus, and Germany's social-market consensus).

Significance

Consensus is often portrayed as the very stuff of politics. This is because politics, in one sense at least, is a specifically non-violent means of resolving conflict. Given that the differing interests of individuals and groups are a permanent feature of human life, peaceful coexistence can be achieved only through a process of negotiation, conciliation and compromise; in short, through consensus-building. Procedural consensuses therefore reflect the recognition that the alternative to bargaining and compromise is open conflict and possibly violence. Consensus politics is likely to be a feature of mature pluralist democracies, substantive consensuses often occurring in political systems in which electoral alliances and coalitions are commonplace. Consensus politics can nevertheless be criticized on the grounds that it fosters unprincipled compromise; that it discourages consideration of bold but controversial policy initiatives; and that it tends to entrench centrist ideological priorities.

CONSENT

To consent means to agree or to grant permission. As a political principle, consent is normally linked to authority, as a means through which people agree to be governed and thus to be bound by political obligation. In practical terms consent is often associated with elections. However, voters are generally thought to have consented to be governed not specifically through voting for the winning party or candidate, but through having participated in the electoral mechanism and thereby having accepted it as a legitimate means for selecting leaders or establishing a government.

Significance

Consent is an important principle of liberalism. In the liberal view, authority and social relationships should always be based on consent, representing the voluntary actions of free individuals. This ensures that authority arises 'from below', and is always grounded in legitimacy. The classic expression of this doctrine is that government must be based on the 'consent of the governed'. Consent therefore disposes liberals to favour representation and democracy. However, they also believe that social bodies and associations should be based on consent, in that they are formed through contractual agreements entered into willingly by individuals

intent on pursuing their own self-interest. In this light, political and other obligations are morally binding, because our voluntary agreement implies a promise to
uphold them. Objections to the principle of consent stem from the grounds on
which it can be demonstrated and the extent to which individuals can be regarded
as free and self-willed actors. Is it, for example, reasonable to suggest that the act of
voting amounts to the granting of consent on the part of the governed? Are those
who vote obliged to respect their government and the laws it makes? Moreover,
the idea of consent ignores the capacity of ideology and government propaganda
to shape what people think, and thereby to influence their seemingly voluntary
behaviour.

CONSERVATISM

Conservatism, as a political attitude, is defined by the desire to conserve and is
reflected in a resistance to, or at least a suspicion of, change. However, while the
desire to resist change may be the recurrent theme within conservatism, what distinguishes conservatism as an ideology from rival political creeds is the distinctive
way in which this position is upheld. The central themes of conservative ideology
are tradition, human imperfection, organic society, authority and property. For a
conservative, tradition reflects the accumulated wisdom of the past, and institutions
and practices that have been 'tested by time'; it should be preserved for the benefit
of the living and for generations yet to come. Conservatives view human nature
pessimistically in at least three senses. First, human beings are limited, dependent
and security-seeking creatures; second, they are morally corrupt, tainted by selfishness, greed and a thirst for power; third, human rationality is unable to cope
with the infinite complexity of the world (hence conservatives' faith in pragmatism
and their preference for describing their beliefs as an 'attitude of mind' rather than
an ideology). The belief that society should be viewed as an organic whole implies
that institutions and values have arisen through natural necessity and should be
preserved to safeguard the fragile 'fabric of society'. Conservatives view authority as
the basis for social cohesion, arguing that it gives people a sense of who they are and
what is expected of them, and reflects the hierarchical nature of all social institutions. Conservatives value property because it gives people security and a measure
of independence from government, and encourages them to respect the law and the
property of others.

   However, there are significant divisions within conservative thought. *Authoritarian
conservatism* is starkly autocratic and reactionary, stressing that government 'from
above' is the only means of establishing order, and thus contrasts with the more
modest and pragmatic Anglo-American conservatism that stems from the writings
of Edmund Burke (1729–97). *Paternalistic conservatism* draws on a combination
of prudence and principle in arguing both that 'reform from above' is preferable
to 'revolution from below', and that the wealthy have an obligation to look after
the less well-off, duty being the price of privilege. Such ideas were expressed most
influentially by Benjamin Disraeli (1804–81). This tradition is developed most fully

in the form of One Nation conservatism, which advocates a 'middle way' approach to state–market relations, and gives qualified support to economic management and welfarism. *Libertarian conservatism* advocates the greatest possible economic liberty and the least possible government regulation of social life, echoing laissez-faire liberalism, but harnesses this to a belief in a more traditional, conservative social philosophy that stresses the importance of authority and duty. This tradition provided the basis for New Right theories and values.

Significance

Conservative ideas and doctrines first emerged in the late eighteenth and early nineteenth centuries, arising as a reaction against the growing pace of economic and social change, which was in many ways symbolized by the French Revolution, which began in 1789. In trying to resist the pressures unleashed by the growth of liberalism, socialism and nationalism, conservatism stood in defence of an increasingly embattled traditional social order. Authoritarian conservatism took root in continental Europe but was marginalized increasingly by the advance of constitutionalism and democracy, and eventually collapsed with the fall of fascism, with which it had often collaborated. The Disraelian form of conservatism ultimately proved to be more successful. Using Burke's notion of 'change in order to conserve', it allowed conservatism to adapt values such as tradition, hierarchy and authority to the emerging conditions of mass politics, thereby broadening its social and electoral base. Conservatism's remarkable resilience stems from its ideological caution and political flexibility, enabling it, at different times, to embrace welfarist and interventionist policies as manifestations of the One Nation ideal, and to advocate 'rolling back the state' as recommended by the New Right.

Conservative thought, however, has always been open to the charge that it amounts to nothing more than ruling-class ideology. In proclaiming the need to resist change, it legitimizes the status quo and defends the interests of dominant or elite groups. Other critics allege that divisions between traditional conservatism and the New Right run so deep that the conservative tradition has become entirely incoherent. In their defence, conservatives argue that they merely advance certain enduring, if at times unpalatable, truths about human nature and the societies we live in. That human beings are morally and intellectually imperfect, and seek the security that only tradition, authority and a shared culture can offer, merely underlines the wisdom of 'travelling light' in ideological terms. Experience and history, conservatives warn, will always provide a sounder basis for political action than will abstract principles such as freedom, equality and justice.

CONSOCIATIONALISM

Consociationalism is a form of government that contrasts with the majoritarianism of Westminster-style systems and is particularly suited to the needs of divided or plural societies. Lijphart (1977) identified two major features of what he called 'consociational democracy'. The first is executive power-sharing, usually through a grand coalition that represents all significant segments of society, though in presidential systems this may be accomplished through the distribution of other high offices. The second is that the various segments of society enjoy a large measure of autonomy, guaranteed, for example, by territorial divisions such as federalism or devolution. Two more minor features may also be present. These are, first, representative mechanisms that ensure proportionality and guarantee that minorities have a political voice; and second, a minority veto to prevent the vital interests of small sections of society being violated by the will of the majority.

Significance

Consociationalism has been practised widely, particularly in continental Europe since 1945. Examples include Austria in the 1945–66 period, Belgium since 1918, Netherlands and Luxembourg in the 1917–67 period, and, in certain respects, modern-day Israel and Canada. The conditions that particularly favour consociationalism are the existence of a relatively small number (ideally between three and five) of roughly equal-sized and geographically concentrated segments; a disposition to seek national consensus based on overarching loyalties; the absence of major socio-economic inequalities; and a relatively small total population.

The strength of consociationalism is that it offers an institutional solution to the problems of divided societies that is both stable and democratic. This it achieves by balancing compromise against autonomy: matters of common or national concern are decided jointly by representatives of all key segments, while allowing the segments the greatest possible independence in relation to other concerns. Two main criticisms have been advanced of consociationalism. First, the combination of conditions that favour it is so complex that it is appropriate only to very particular societies, and for limited periods of time. In other words, it may not be a solution that is suitable for all divided societies. Second, consociationalism has been criticized as being inherently unstable, as its emphasis on power-sharing and the protection of minority interests has the potential to create an arena for struggle among rival segments rather than provide a basis for compromise.

CONSTITUTION

A constitution is, broadly, a set of rules that seek to establish the duties, powers and functions of the various institutions of government, regulate the relationships between them, and define the relationship between the state and the individual. Constitutions thus lay down certain meta-rules for the political system; in effect, these are rules that govern the government. Just as government establishes ordered rule in society at large, a constitution brings stability, predictability and order to the actions of government. The most common way of classifying constitutions is to distinguish between codified and uncodified, or written and unwritten, constitutions. *Codified constitutions* draw together key constitutional provisions within a single, legal document, popularly known as a 'written' constitution or 'the constitution'. These documents are authoritative in the sense that they constitute 'higher' law – indeed, the highest law of the land. This, in turn, entrenches the provisions of the constitution, in that they can only be amended or abolished using a process more complicated than that employed for statute law. Finally, the logic of the codification dictates that, as the constitution sets out the duties, powers and functions of government institutions in terms of 'higher' law, it must be justiciable, meaning that all political bodies must be subject to the authority of the courts, and in particular a supreme or constitutional court.

Uncodified constitutions are now found in only two liberal democracies (Israel and the UK) and a handful of non-democratic states. In the absence of a 'written' constitution, uncodified constitutions draw on a variety of sources (in the UK these include statute law, common law, conventions, works of authority and EU law). Laws of constitutional significance are thus not entrenched: they may be changed through the ordinary legislative process. Most important, this means that sovereignty, or unchangeable legal authority, is vested in the parliament. The parliament has the right to make or unmake any law, and no body, including the courts, has the ability to override or set aside its laws. Alternative ways of classifying constitutions deal with the ease with which the constitution can be changed (whether it is rigid or flexible), the degree to which the constitution is observed in practice (whether it is effective, nominal or a façade constitution), or the basis of its contents (whether it is monarchical or republican, federal or unitary, parliamentary or presidential).

Significance

While the evolution of the British constitution is sometimes traced back to the Bill of Rights of 1689, or even the Magna Carta of 1215, it is more helpful to think of constitutions as late-eighteenth-century creations. The 'age of constitutions' was initiated by the enactment of the first 'written' constitutions: the US Constitution in 1787 and the French Declaration of the Rights of Man and the Citizen in 1789. Constitutions play a number of vital roles in the workings of modern political systems. The most basic of these is that they mark out the existence of a state and make claims concerning its sphere of independent authority. Constitutions also establish, implicitly or explicitly, a broader set of political values, ideals and goals (in the case of 'written' constitutions, this is usually accomplished in preambles that serve as statements of national ideals). Moreover, by serving as 'organizational charts' or 'institutional blueprints', constitutions introduce a measure of stability and predictability to the workings of government and enable conflicts to be resolved more speedily and efficiently.

However, constitutions are chiefly valued because they are a means of constraining government and protecting freedom. By laying down the relationship between the state and the individual, often through a bill of rights, they mark out their respective spheres of government authority and individual liberty. Nevertheless, the mere existence of the constitution does not guarantee constitutionalism. Constitutions are only a device of limited government when they fragment government authority and create effective checks and balances throughout the political system, and when, through whatever means, they ensure that civil liberty is clearly defined and legally upheld.

Other debates about the constitution focus on the implications of codification. Codified or written constitutions are seen to have the following strengths:

- As major principles and key constitutional provisions are entrenched, they are safeguarded from interference by the government of the day.
- The legislature is denied sovereignty and is thus unable to extend its own power at will.
- Non-political judges are able to police the constitution to ensure that its provisions are upheld by other public bodies.
- Individual liberty is protected more securely by an entrenched bill of rights.
- The codified document has a wider educational value, in that it highlights the central values and overall goals of the political system.

However, codification may also have drawbacks, the most important of which include the following:

- A codified constitution is rigid, and may therefore be less responsive and adaptable to changing circumstances than an uncodified one.
- Constitutional supremacy ultimately resides with non-elected judges rather than democratically accountable politicians.
- As constitutional documents are inevitably biased, they may either promote ideological hegemony or precipitate more conflicts than they resolve.
- Establishing a codified constitution requires that all major parties agree about important features of the political system, which may not be the case.

CONSTITUTIONALISM

Constitutionalism, in a narrow sense, is the practice of limited government brought about through the existence of a constitution. Constitutionalism in this sense can be said to exist whenever government institutions and political processes are constrained effectively by constitutional rules. More broadly, constitutionalism refers to a set of political values and aspirations that reflect the desire to protect freedom through the establishment of internal and external checks on government power. Constitutionalism is typically expressed in support for constitutional provisions that establish this goal, notably a codified constitution, a bill of rights, the separation of powers, bicameralism, and federalism or decentralization.

Significance

Constitutionalism is one of the basic political values of liberalism and one of the key components of liberal democracy. Its importance rests on the underlying fear that government is always liable to become a tyranny against the individual, because power in itself is corrupting. Constitutionalism is thus a vital guarantee of liberty. The forms it takes may nevertheless vary considerably. Liberal constitutionalism is usually associated with a written or codified constitution, a system of checks and balances among government institutions, and formal, and usually entrenched, guarantees of civil liberty. Nevertheless, the UK system of government has sometimes been regarded as constitutional even though it has traditionally lacked each of these three features. Critics of constitutionalism have pointed out that it pays attention only to the formal and usually legal organization of government. For example, constitutions and institutional fragmentation may be less important in maintaining individual liberty than party competition and democracy. Constitutionalism has also been criticized by socialists as a means of constraining government power and thus of preventing meaningful reform of the capitalist system.

CONSTRUCTIVISM

Constructivism (sometimes called 'social constructivism') is an approach to social and political analysis that has been particularly influential in the field of international relations. Constructivism is based on the belief that there is no objective social or political reality independent of our understanding of it. Constructivists do not therefore regard the social world as something 'out there', in the sense of an external world of concrete objects; instead, it exists only 'inside', as a kind of inter-subjective awareness. In the final analysis, people, whether acting as individuals or as social groups, 'construct' the world in which they live and act according to those constructions. People's beliefs and assumptions become particularly significant when they are widely shared, especially when they serve to give people, or a community, a sense of identity and distinctive interests. However, constructivist analysis in international relations can be *systemic* (focusing on the interaction of states in the international system); *unit-level* (focusing on how domestic social and legal norms shape the interests and identities of states); or *holistic* (focusing on the entire range of factors conditioning the identities and interests of states).

Significance

As an approach to international theory, constructivism has been paid significantly greater attention since the end of the Cold War. The failure of mainstream realist and liberal approaches to explain adequately why the Cold War ended, highlighted, in a sense, a missing dimension in international relations theory: the role played by ideas and perceptions, and in this case the changing social identity of the USSR. Instead of following mainstream theorists in treating political actors as though they have fixed or objective interests or identities, constructivists argue that these interests and ideas are fashioned by the traditions, values and sentiments that prevail in any given context. State interaction cannot therefore be explained essentially in terms of the rational pursuit of national interests (as some realists argue) or primarily in terms of interdependencies that operate at the international level (as some liberals argue).

However, the relationship between constructivism, on the one hand, and realism and liberalism, on the other, is a matter of debate. While 'critical' constructivism clearly goes beyond the positivism of mainstream theory in either denying the existence of the real world 'out there' (in common with postmodernism), or in arguing that it is buried under so many layers of conceptual and contextual meaning that we can never gain access to it, 'conventional' constructivism seeks to probe the inter-subjective content of events and episodes, but within a social-scientific methodology. As the latter position embraces only a weak form of post-positivism, it allows constructivism to be viewed as a means of refining or expanding mainstream analysis, rather than rejecting it. Critics of constructivism have nevertheless argued that it fails to recognize the extent to which beliefs are shaped by social, economic and political realities. In the final analysis, ideas do not 'fall from the sky' like rain. They are a product of complex social realities, and reflect an ongoing relationship between ideas and the material world.

CONSUMERISM

Consumerism is a psychic and social phenomenon whereby personal happiness is equated with the acquisition of material possessions. It is often associated with the emergence of a 'consumer society' or of 'consumer capitalism'. Consumer capitalism was shaped by the development of new advertising and marketing techniques that took advantage of the growth of the mass media and the spread of mass affluence. A consumer society is one that is organized around the consumption rather than the production of goods and services, a shift that has important socio-economic and cultural implications. Whereas 'productionist' societies emphasize the values of discipline, duty and hard work (the Protestant work ethic, for example), consumer societies emphasize materialism, hedonism and immediate rather than delayed gratification.

Significance

Consumerism has become an increasingly prominent feature of capitalist economies since the 1950s, reflecting the recognition that business growth and the expansion of corporate profits are reliant on ever-higher levels of consumption. Devices and strategies therefore had to be devised to ensure that consumers consume. Goods, for example, were transformed into 'brands', symbolic constructs, typically consisting of a name, logo or symbol, which conveys the promise, 'personality' or image of a product or group of products. This process was considerably boosted by the advent of globalization and the emergence of global goods and global brands, which came to dominate economic markets in more and more parts of the world. Global consumerism gave rise to what Benjamin Barber (2003) called 'McWorld', a world of 'fast music, fast compters and fast food – MTV, Macintosh and McDonald's – pressing nations into one homogeneous theme park'.

However, there is significance disagreement over the nature and implications of consumerism. The desire for wealth and the pleasure derived from material acquisition have been viewed as nothing more than expressions of human nature. For example, utilitarianism, the most widely accepted tradition of moral philosophy, assumes that individuals act to maximize pleasure and minimize pain, these being calculated in terms of utility or use-value, usually seen as satisfaction derived from material consumption. The global spread of consumerist ethics is therefore merely evidence of deep-seated material appetites on the part of humankind. Consumerism has nevertheless become one of the key targets of anti-corporate or anti-globalization criticism. The core theme of anti-consumerism is that advertising and marketing in their myriad forms create 'false' needs that serve the interests of corporate profit, and often, in the process, undermining psychological and emotional well-being. By creating ever-greater material desires, they leave consumers in a constant state of dissatisfaction because, however much they acquire and consume, they always want more. Consumerism thus works not through the satisfaction of desires, but through the generation of new desires, keeping people in a state of constant neediness, aspiration and want. A further criticism of consumerism is that it poses major environmental challenges, particularly through fuelling ecologically unsustainable levels of economic growth. Some would nevertheless argue that the image of consumerism as a tyrannical and unchecked force should be modified in the light of the progress made by consumer movements in recent decades in securing legal and regulatory protections for consumers.

CORPORATISM

Corporatism, in its broader sense, is a means of incorporating organized interests into the processes of government. The core bases of corporatism are therefore a recognition of the political significance of functional or socio-economic divisions in society, and the notion that these divisions can be reconciled through institutions that aim to map out a higher national interest. However, there are two faces of corporatism: authoritarian and liberal. *Authoritarian corporatism* (sometimes termed state corporatism) is an ideology or economic form closely associated with Italian fascism. It set out to establish what Mussolini called a 'corporate state', which claimed to embody the organic unity of Italian society but, in practice, operated through the political intimidation of industry and the destruction of independent trade unions. *Liberal corporatism* (sometimes termed 'societal' corporatism or neo-corporatism) refers to the tendency found in mature liberal democracies for organized interests to be granted privileged and institutionalized access to policy formulation. The mechanisms through which this form of group politics is achieved vary considerably, as does the degree of integration between groups and government. In contrast to its authoritarian variant, liberal corporatism is often viewed as a 'bottom-up' form of corporatism that strengthens groups in relation to government, not the other way round.

Significance

The idea of corporatism originated in Benito Mussolini's Italy and was associated with a fascist version of Catholic social theory. This emphasized the importance of groups rather than individuals, and stressed the need for social balance or harmony.

In practice, however, fascist corporatism amounted to little more than a means through which the Mussolini state could exercise control over the Italian economy. Attempts to export this authoritarian model of corporatism to António Salazar's Portugal or to post-1964 Brazil, Mexico and Peru proved to be similarly short-lived and unsuccessful, at least in terms of promoting economic growth.

Liberal corporatism, on the other hand, proved to be politically much more significant, especially in the early post-1945 period. Some commentators regard corporatism as a state-specific phenomenon, shaped by particular historical and political circumstances. They thus associated it with countries such as Austria, Sweden and the Netherlands and, to some extent, Germany and Japan, in which the government has customarily practised a form of economic management. Others, however, view corporatism as a general phenomenon that stems from tendencies implicit in economic and social development, and therefore believe that it is manifest, in some form or other, in all advanced industrial societies. From this perspective, corporatist tendencies may merely reflect the symbiotic relationship that exists between groups and government. Groups seek 'insider' status because it gives them access to policy formulation, which enables them to better defend the interests of their members. Government, for its part, needs groups both as a source of knowledge and information, and because the compliance of major economic interests is essential if policy is to be workable. Supporters of corporatism have thus argued that a close relationship between groups and government facilitates both social stability and economic development.

However, the general drift towards corporatism in advanced capitalist states has been reversed since the 1970s, with corporatist ideas and structures being subject to growing criticism. Concerns about corporatism have been many and various. It has been criticized for narrowing the basis of representation by leading to a form of tripartitism that binds together government, business and the unions, but leaves consumer and promotional groups out in the cold and restricts institutionalized access to so-called 'peak' associations. A second problem is that the distinction between liberal and authoritarian corporatism may be more apparent than real, in that the price that group leaders pay for privileged access to government is a willingness to deliver the compliance of their members. Third, corporatism may weaken the formal processes of representation by allowing decisions to be made outside the reach of democratic control and through a process of bargaining that is in no way subject to political scrutiny. Finally, New Right theorists argue that corporatism is responsible for the problem of government 'overload', in which government is effectively 'captured' by consulted groups and is unable to resist their demands. Corporatism thus fuels interventionism, which, in turn, stifles competition and the natural vigour of the market.

COSMOPOLITANISM

Cosmopolitanism literally means a belief in a *cosmopolis* or 'world state'. *Moral cosmopolitanism* is the belief that the world constitutes a single moral community, in that people have obligations towards (potentially) all people in the world, regardless of nationality, religion, ethnicity and so on. *Political cosmopolitanism* (sometimes called

'legal' or 'institutional' cosmopolitanism) is the belief that there should be global political institutions, and possibly a world government. However, most modern political
cosmopolitans tend to favour a system in which authority is shared between global,
state and sub-state levels, with no single level enjoying dominance over the others.

Cosmopolitan thinking has drawn, variously, on Kantianism, utilitarianism and
the doctrine of human rights. For Kant (1724–1804), the categorical imperative to
treat people as 'ends in themselves' and not merely as means for the achievement
of the ends of others implies that we have a universal duty of hospitality towards
foreigners, recognizing that, as citizens of the world, we should treat every human
being with consideration and respect. The cosmopolitan implications of utilitarianism derive from the belief that, in making moral judgements on the basis of maximizing happiness, 'everybody counts as one, nobody as more than one'. The principle
of utility is therefore no respecter of borders, a stance that has, for example, underpinned calls for the eradication of world poverty. Most contemporary cosmopolitan
theorizing is nevertheless based on the doctrine of human rights. Human rights have
cosmopolitan implications because they emphasize that rights are fundamental and
universal. Such thinking has, among other things, underpinned the idea of global
justice, and provided a justification for humanitarian intervention.

Significance

Cosmopolitanism can be traced back to the Cynic movement in Ancient Greece, and
the assertion by Diogenes of Sinope (400–323 BCE) that he was a 'citizen of the world'.
Interest in cosmopolitan themes revived during the Enlightenment and was expressed
most influentially in Kant's *Perpetual Peace* (1795/1970), which outlined the proposal
for a 'league of nations'. While contemporary cosmopolitanism has primarily a
moral orientation, it also deals with political and institutional themes, not least the
need to reform the existing system of global governance to bring it into line with
cosmopolitan moral principles. As such, cosmopolitanism provides the anti-globalization or anti-corporate movement with its core moral and ideological orientation.
Cosmopolitanism has many detractors, however. For example, communitarians and
others have taken issue with the moral universalism that underpins cosmopolitanism,
arguing that moral systems are only workable when they operate within a cultural or
national context. From this perspective, any assistance that is provided to 'strangers'
is based on charity alone and cannot be viewed as a moral obligation. Others have
argued that moral cosmopolitanism amounts to little more than 'wishful thinking' in
a world that lacks an institutional framework capable of upholding its principles. This
problem is compounded by the fact that it is difficult to see how such a framework,
even if it could be established, could either enjoy a meaningful degree of democratic
legitimacy or avoid turning into an emergent world government.

CRIMES AGAINST HUMANITY

The 1945 Nuremberg Charter outlined three characteristics of crimes against
humanity. These crimes must:

- Target civilians
- Be widespread or systematic, and repeated
- Be committed intentionally.

The Charter also distinguished between war crimes ('violations of the laws and customs of war') and crimes against humanity. Nevertheless, the most detailed and ambitious attempt to codify the crimes that can be categorized as crimes against humanity was undertaken in the 1998 Rome Statute, which established the International Criminal Court (ICC). This highlights crimes including murder, extermination, enslavement, deportation, torture, rape or sexual slavery, racial and other forms of persecution, and the crime of apartheid. Though genocide (the attempt to destroy, in whole or in part, a national, ethnic, racial or religious group) is clearly a crime against humanity in a general sense, it is treated as a separate category of crime, indeed as the 'crime of crimes', by the Genocide Convention (1948) and in the Rome Statute.

Significance

The idea that heinous or inhuman acts might be considered crimes first emerged in response to what was later called the 'Armenian genocide' (1915–17) and was subsequently extended in response to the atrocities that took place during World War II. The virtue of incorporating the concepts of crimes against humanity and genocide into international law is that they attempt to deal with the issue of widespread cruelty and barbarity by establishing individual responsibility for actions that may not conform to the conventional notion of a war crime. The concept of crimes against humanity is underpinned in particular by a form of moral cosmopolitanism which holds that the proper stance towards humanity is one of respect, protection and succour, humanity being indivisible. Critics of the concept have nevertheless questioned whether such a broad category of crime can ever be meaningful, and have also raised doubts about the supposedly universal moral principles on which it is based. These and other concerns about international humanitarian law have become more acute as a result of steps to anchor individual responsibility for war crimes, crimes against humanity and genocide through establishing international criminal tribunals for former Yugoslavia, Rwanda and elsewhere, and the ICC.

CRITICAL THEORY

Critical theory (sometimes called 'Frankfurt School critical theory') is a broadly Marxist-inspired approach to social and political theorizing. While critical theory does not constitute, and has never constituted, a unified body of work, it tends to be distinguished by certain general themes. The original intellectual and political inspiration for critical theory was Marxism. However, critical theorists were repelled by Stalinism, criticized the determinist and scientistic tendencies in orthodox Marxism, and were disillusioned by the failure of Marx's predictions regarding the inevitable collapse of capitalism. Critical theorists developed a form of neo-Marxism that focused more heavily on the analysis of ideology than on economics, and no longer treated the proletariat as the revolutionary agent. Critical theory is characterized by the attempt to extend the notion of critique to all social practices by linking substantive social research to philosophy. In doing so, it does not merely look beyond the classical principles and methodology of Marxism but also cuts across a range of traditionally discrete disciplines, including economics, sociology, philosophy, psychology and literary criticism.

While early Frankfurt thinkers were concerned primarily with the analysis of discrete societies, later theorists have often applied critical theory to the study of international politics, in at least three ways. First, critical theorists have underlined the linkage between knowledge and politics in international affairs, emphasizing the extent to which theories and understandings are embedded in a framework of values and interests. Second, critical theorists have adopted an explicit commitment to emancipatory politics: they are concerned to uncover structures of oppression and injustice in world politics in order to advance the cause of individual or collective freedom. Third, critical theorists have questioned the conventional association within international theory between political community and the state, and in doing so opened up the possibility of a more inclusive, and perhaps even cosmopolitan, notion of political identity.

Significance

Critical theory originated in the thinking of the so-called Frankfurt School, the Institute of Social Research, which was established in Frankfurt in 1923, relocated to the USA in the 1930s, and was re-established in Frankfurt in the early 1950s. The Institute was dissolved in 1969. Two phases in the development of critical theory can be identified. The first was associated with the theorists who dominated the Institute's work in the pre-war and early post-war period, notably Max Horkheimer (1895–1973), Theodor Adorno (1903–69) and Herbert Marcuse (1889–1979). The second phase stems from the work of the major post-war exponent of critical theory, Jürgen Habermas (1929–).

Critical theory has brought about important political and social insights through the cross-fertilization of academic disciplines and by straddling the divide between Marxism and conventional social theory. It has also provided a continuing fertile and imaginative perspective from which the problems and contradictions of existing society can be explored. During the 1960s and early 1970s, together with anarchism, critical theory played a major role in shaping New Left thinking and, through this, had an impact on the emergence of the 'new' social movements of the period. Since the end of the Cold War, critical theory has developed into one of the most influential currents of Marxist-inspired international theory. Critical theory has also attracted criticism, however. 'First-generation' Frankfurt thinkers in particular were criticized for advancing a theory of social transformation that was often disengaged from the ongoing social struggle. Moreover, they were accused of over-emphasizing the capacity of capitalism to absorb oppositional forces, and thus of underestimating the crisis tendencies within capitalist society.

CROSS-GENERATIONAL JUSTICE

Cross-generational justice is the idea that that the present generation (the living) have obligations towards future generations (those who are yet to be born). Justice should therefore be extended to take into account 'futurity', a concern about the future, implying that moral judgements about actions in the present should take into account their impact on posterity. 'Futurity' has been justified in different ways. Care for and obligations towards future generations have sometimes been seen as a 'natural duty', an extension of a moral concern for our children and, by extension, their children, and so on. A concern for future generations has also been linked to the idea of 'stewardship'. This is the notion that the present generation is merely the 'custodian' of the wealth and resources that have been generated by past generations and so should be conserved for the benefit of future generations. The most radical basis for cross-generational justice is nevertheless that future generations are entitled to rights on essentially the same grounds as people who are currently alive; their only problem is that they are unable to secure these rights themselves.

Significance

The idea that, in deciding how we should act, we should take into account the needs and interests of people who have not yet been born became politically prominent only with the emergence of green or environmental concerns in the 1960s. It has received particular attention since the 1990s, however, through a rising concern about the issue of climate change. This has occurred because it is in the nature of environmental matters that many of the consequences of our actions might well not be felt for decades, or even centuries. Industrialization, for example, had advanced for some 200 years before concerns were raised about the depletion of finite stocks of oil, gas or coal resources, or about the increase in greenhouse gas emissions. This creates the problem that each successive generation can act as a 'free rider', able to enjoy the benefits of economic growth, while leaving future generations to deal with its consequences. Apart from the stark inter-generational unfairness that this implies, such a situation is clearly unsustainable in the long run.

However, the idea of cross-generational justice has also been criticized. Some argue that all rights depend on reciprocity (rights are respected because of something that is done, or not done, in return), in which case it is absurd to endow people who have yet to be born with rights that impose duties on people who are currently alive. Moreover, in view of the potentially unlimited size of future generations, the burdens imposed by 'futurity' are, in practical terms, incalculable. Present generations may either be making sacrifices for the benefit of future generations that may prove to be much wealthier, or their sacrifices may be entirely inadequate to meet future needs.

DEMOCRACY

Democracy literally means rule by the *demos* or people (though the Greeks originally used *demos* to mean 'the poor' or 'the many'). However, the simple notion of 'rule by the people' is vague and has been subject to a bewildering variety of interpretations (indeed, democracy may equally be treated as a 'contested' value or be taken to stand for a variety of systems). Perhaps a more helpful starting point is Abraham Lincoln's Gettysburg Address, delivered in 1863, which extolled the virtues of what he called 'government of the people, by the people and for the people'. This highlights the importance of three core features of democracy. First, the stress on 'the people' implies political equality, an equal distribution of political power and influence. Second, government 'by' the people emphasizes the importance of popular participation. Third, government 'for' the people highlights the fact that democracy suggests ruling in the public interest.

However, there are a number of models of democracy. The most important distinction is between direct and representative democracy. *Direct democracy* (a term that overlaps with classical democracy, radical democracy and participatory democracy) is based on the direct, unmediated and continuous participation of citizens in the tasks of government. Direct democracy thus obliterates the distinction between government and governed, and between the state and civil society; it is a system of popular self-government. It was achieved in ancient Athens through a form of government by mass meeting (Athenian democracy), and its most common modern manifestation is in the use of referendums. *Representative democracy* (whose most common form is liberal democracy) is a limited and indirect form of democracy. It is limited in that popular participation in government is infrequent and brief, being restricted to the act of voting every few years, and it is indirect in that the public do not exercise power themselves; they merely select those who will rule on their behalf. This form of rule is democratic only in so far as representation establishes a reliable and effective link between government and governed. This is sometimes expressed in the notion of an electoral mandate.

Significance

The mass conversion of politicians and political thinkers to the cause of democracy was one of the most dramatic and significant events in political history. Well into the nineteenth century the term continued to have pejorative implications, suggesting a system of 'mob rule'. Now, however, we are all democrats. Liberals, conservatives, socialists, communists, anarchists and even fascists are eager to proclaim the virtues of democracy and to demonstrate their democratic credentials. Indeed, 'end of history' theorists interpreted the collapse of communism in the late twentieth century as implying the worldwide, and final, triumph of liberal democracy. Democratic processes and practices have displaced authoritarianism, basically because political stability in complex, and highly differentiated modern societies can be maintained only through a diffusion of power, a tendency that is strengthened by the development of a better-educated, better-informed and more politically sophisticated citizenry. Overwhelmingly, where democracy has triumphed it has done so in its more practicable, representative form; however, developments in information technology have increasingly made direct democracy more viable, particularly in small communities.

Most of the debates about democracy stem from rivalries between different theories or models of democracy, and concern how, and to what extent, democratic practices should be applied. The most common of these deal with the adequacy of representative democracy and, in particular, the link between elections and democracy, and whether democratic principles should be confined narrowly to political matters or extended more widely to cover, say, the family, the workplace and the distribution of economic power. Nevertheless, key debates regarding the virtues and vices of democracy remain relevant. Among the advantages that have been claimed for democracy are:

- It protects the individual from government, and so defends freedom, by ensuring that power is constrained and subject to popular consent.
- It promotes education and personal development by allowing citizens, through political participation, to gain an insight into how their society operates.
- It strengthens community and social solidarity by giving all people a stake in society by virtue of having a voice in its decision-making processes.
- It widens social and personal well-being by ensuring that government policies reflect the interests of citizens at large.
- It guarantees political stability by bringing the 'outputs' of government into line with popular 'inputs', so generating equilibrium.

Among the criticisms that have been made of democracy are:

- As wisdom and knowledge are distributed unequally in society, democracy leads to rule by the ignorant and poorly informed masses.
- It amounts to a 'tyranny of the 51 per cent', because it means that individual liberty and minority rights can be crushed by the majority, in the name of the people.
- It results in excessive government and state control because it articulates the interests of the collective body rather than those of the individual.
- It may result in dictatorship and repression because it allows demagogues to come to power by appealing to the basest instincts of the masses.

DEMOCRATIC PEACE

The 'democratic peace' thesis is a notion that there is an intrinsic link between peace and democracy, in particular in the sense that democratic states do not go to war against one another. Such thinking is grounded in a tradition of republican liberalism that can be traced back to Woodrow Wilson (1856–1924), if not to Immanuel Kant (1724–1804), which holds that the external behaviour of a state is crucially influenced by its political and constitutional make-up. In particular, while autocratic or authoritarian states are seen as being inherently militaristic and aggressive, democratic states are viewed as being naturally peaceful, especially in their dealings with other democratic states (Doyle, 1986).

Significance

The democratic peace thesis resurfaced with particular force in the aftermath of the collapse of communism, as the wider acceptance of liberal-democratic principles and structures was seen to promise the emergence of a more stable and peaceful global order (Fukuyama, 1992). Much of the basis for this view derives from empirical analysis. The advance of democratization has led to the emergence of 'zones of peace', in which military conflict has become virtually unthinkable. This certainly applies to Western and Central Europe (previously riven by war and conflict), North America and Australasia. Such a development has been explained in at least three ways. First, liberals have argued that states become less warlike to the extent that their governments are subject to popular control, as it is the citizens themselves who are likely to be war's victims. Second, democratic states operate on the basis of non-violent means of conflict resolution, and are inclined to apply these to foreign as well as domestic policy. Third, cultural ties tend to develop among democratic states, which encourages the states to view each other as friends rather than enemies.

However, realists and others have cast doubt on the notion of democratic peace. For example, the idea that democracies are inherently peaceful is undermined by continued evidence of war between democratic and authoritarian states. Moreover, empirical evidence to support the thesis is bedevilled by confusion over which states qualify as 'democracies'. If, for example, universal suffrage and multi-party elections are the features of democratic governance, NATO's bombardment of Serb forces in Kosovo in 1999, and Russia's invasion of Georgia in 2008, are both exceptions to the democratic peace thesis. Realists argue, moreover, that the thesis significantly over-estimates the degree to which a state's constitutional make-up affects its external actions, as these are shaped more by the fear and suspicion that are the consequence of international anarchy. Finally, if there is a tendency towards peace between democracies, it may be better explained by factors such as the economic interdependence that results from free trade, than by any political and constitutional similarities these states may have.

DEMOCRATIZATION

Democratization refers to the process of transition from authoritarianism to liberal democracy. Democratization encompasses three sometimes overlapping processes:

- The breaking down of the old regime – this usually involves a loss of legitimacy and the faltering loyalty of the military and the police.
- Democratic transition – this witnesses the construction of alternative liberal-democratic structures and processes.
- Democratic consolidation – this sees the new structures and processes becoming so embedded in the minds of both elites and the masses that democracy becomes 'the only game in town' (Przeworski, 1991).

Significance

Since the early nineteenth century, the process of democratization has transformed the political complexion of the world to such an extent that, by 2003, 63 per cent of states, accounting for about 70 per cent of the world's population, exhibited some of the key features of liberal-democratic governance. This is often seen as having occurred through three 'waves of democratization' (Huntington, 1991). The first took place between 1828 and 1926, and involved countries such as the USA, France and the UK; the second occurred between 1943 and 1962, and involved countries such as West Germany, Italy, Japan and India; and the third began in 1974 with the overthrow of right-wing dictatorships in Greece, Portugal and Spain, and the retreat of the generals in Latin America, but was greatly accelerated by the fall of communism during 1989–91. This process has not merely altered governance arrangements across most of the globe, but it has also been claimed to have had wider ramifications, including extending the scope for market-based economics (on the grounds that liberal democracy and capitalism are intrinsically linked), weakening traditional social bonds (on the grounds that democratic societies tend to strengthen individualism) and leading to a decline in large-scale state war (on the grounds of the democratic peace thesis).

Some have portrayed democratization as an inevitable process that is destined to continue, based on the belief that democracy is the highest form of human governance. The unique strength of democracy, from this viewpoint, is that it is able to address the central challenge of politics – the existence of rival views and interests within the same society – while containing the tendency towards bloodshed and violence. In short, only democratic societies are enduringly stable and peaceful. Further advantages of democracy include that, in being based on popular accountability and a system of checks and balances, it keeps tyranny at bay and widens the realm of freedom. However, democratization has also been viewed in a more pessimistic light. For example, far from delivering peace and harmony, democratization may deepen tribal, regional and ethnic tensions, and strengthen the tendency towards charismatic leadership and authoritarianism. Democratization therefore does not operate on the basis of a remorseless logic, as many 'transition states' have demonstrated in routinely allowing oppositional forces to be intimidated and basic freedoms to be curtailed despite that persistence of electoral democracy.

DETERRENCE

Deterrence is a theory of social control in which punishment is used to shape the future conduct of others. As a simple, two-person relationship, it involves A threatening to punish B should B act in an unacceptable fashion. As such, deterrence has a number of features. First, as it is based on the ability to provoke fear and inflict harm, it is a negative form of social control. Second, it operates on the basis of an unequal relationship between the parties concerned, in that (using the terminology above) A must have a greater capacity to cause harm than does B. Third, A must not only have the ability to impose its will on B but also be willingness to do so;

threats must be credible. Fourth, deterrence relies on rational decision-making, and especially on the ability of B to calculate, and act in accordance with, its own best interests.

Significance

The idea of deterrence has been applied in circumstances ranging from child-rearing to criminal justice, but it has received the greatest attention within the field of international relations. In an international context, deterrence is a tactic or strategy designed to prevent aggression by emphasizing the scale of the likely military response. The cost of the attack must therefore be greater than any benefit it may bring. However, if a military build-up designed to deter aggression is itself perceived as being aggressive, such a deterrence strategy may be counter-productive, provoking an arms race and increasing the chance of war. Such a possibility is highlighted by the security dilemma. A further limitation of deterrence theory is that international relations cannot always be relied on to operate on the basis of rational calculation. Not only may international actors fall prey to expansionist and aggressive political doctrines that blind them to the likely consequences of their actions, but as deterrence sets out to provoke fear, it may simply generate stress or anxiety among policy-makers, thus impairing their ability to make sober and balanced decisions.

The advent of nuclear weapons in 1945 gave debates about deterrence a sharper focus. This is because nuclear weapons have sometimes been seen as being especially well-suited to a deterrence role, both because of their enormous destructive potential and because they are relatively ineffective as defensive weapons. During the Cold War, the USA and the USSR both quickly developed a massive 'first-strike' nuclear capability, but they also acquired 'second-strike' capabilities that would enable them to withstand an enemy attack and still destroy major strategic targets and population centres. By the early 1960s, both superpowers had an invulnerable 'second-strike' capability, which ensured that nuclear war would result in mutually assured destruction (MAD). This system of nuclear deterrence led to a 'balance of terror' that some have viewed as being the key factor behind the 'long peace' of the Cold War era. The theory of nuclear deterrence nevertheless has its drawbacks. These include the fact that the awesome destructive power of nuclear weapons means that they are widely seen as 'unusable', and so cannot be a credible deterrent.

DEVELOPMENT

Development, in its simplest sense, means growth – the act of improving, enlarging or refining. In political analysis, development is conventionally understood in economic or material terms; and as such, it implies that the primary difference between 'under-developed/developing' countries or regions and 'developed' ones is their level of wealth or affluence. The process of development is therefore closely linked to the alleviation of poverty. However, the concept of development is contested and contro-versial. Not only are there variant forms of the term, associated, for example, with ideas such as **human development** and **sustainable development**, but the notion of development is invariably enmeshed in ideological assumptions, especially about its relationship to a distinctively Western form of modernization.

Significance

Development has featured with increasing prominence on the international political agenda since 1945, as concern has focused on the plight of what used to be called the 'Third World' (by contrast with the rich, capitalist 'First World' and the less rich, communist 'Second World'), and is now more commonly dubbed the 'global South' (from the 'North–South divide' – a term popularized by the Brandt Report (1980)). Since the 1960s, development and poverty reduction have been a major responsibility of the World Bank, and a growing concern of the United Nations. The 'mainstream' or 'orthodox' view of development is rooted firmly in the ideas of economic **liberalism**. From this perspective, the key to development is the ability to foster economic growth through market reform (privatization, financial deregulation, labour flexibility, tax cuts and so on) and the integration of the national economy into the global capitalist economy (free trade and an open economy). Despite the orthodox view dominating thinking on matters related to poverty and development since 1945, its influence has expanded through the conversion, from the 1980s onwards, of the institutions of global economic governance and a growing number of states, led by the USA, to a pro-market economic agenda, often called the 'Washington Consensus'.

Very different thinking has nevertheless emerged from the 'critical' or 'alternative' view of development, which has become more prominent since the 1980s. Much of this has been based on neo-Marxist theories that portray the global capitalist system not as the solution to the problem of development but as an obstacle to it. Dependency theorists have thus argued that, despite the advance of decolonization, states in the developing world continue to be subject to economic dependency through, for example, unequal trade relations, the impact of **transnational corporations**, and biases that operate within bodies such as the International Monetary Fund (IMF) and the World Bank that favour the interests of industrially advanced states. World-system theorists, for their part, explain global inequality in terms of the division of the world into 'core', 'peripheral' and 'semi-peripheral' areas. In this, economically advanced and politically stable core areas dominate and exploit peripheral areas that are characterized by low wages, rudimentary technology and a dependence on agriculture or primary production.

DEVOLUTION

Devolution is the transfer of power from central **government** to subordinate regional institutions (to 'devolve' means to pass powers or duties down from a higher authority to a lower one). Devolved bodies thus constitute an intermediate level of government between central and local government. Devolution differs from **federalism** in that, while their territorial jurisdiction may be similar, devolved bodies have no share in **sovereignty**; their responsibilities and powers are devolved from, and are conferred by, the centre. In its weakest form, that of *administrative devolution*, devolution implies only that regional institutions implement policies decided elsewhere. In the form of *legislative devolution* (sometimes called 'home rule'), devolution involves the establishment of elected regional assemblies invested with policy-making responsibilities and, usually, a measure of fiscal independence.

Significance

Devolution, at least in its legislative form, establishes the greatest possible measure of decentralization within a unitary system of government; that is, one in which sovereign power is vested in a single, national institution. Devolved assemblies have usually been created in response to increasing centrifugal tensions within a state, and as an attempt, in particular, to conciliate growing regional and some-times nationalist pressures. Spain and France both adopted forms of devolved government in the 1970s and 1980s, and, in the UK, the Scottish Parliament, the Welsh Assembly and the Northern Ireland Assembly assumed devolved powers in 1999. Despite their lack of entrenched power, once devolved institutions acquire a political identity of their own, and possess a measure of democratic legitimacy; they are very difficult to weaken and, in normal circumstances, impossible to abolish. Northern Ireland's Stormont Parliament was suspended in 1972, but only when it became apparent that its domination by the predominantly Protestant Unionist parties prevented it from stemming the rising tide of communal violence in the province. The newly created Northern Ireland Assembly was also suspended temporarily in the early 2000s.

The central issue in evaluating devolution is its impact on the integrity of the state and the strength of centrifugal pressures. Its supporters argue that devolution satis-fies the desire of regional or ethnic groups or constituent nations for a distinctive political identity while (unlike federalism) upholding the larger unity of the state by maintaining a single source of sovereignty. Critics, however, warn that devolution may fuel centrifugal pressures by strengthening regional, ethnic and national identi-ties, leading to federalism or even to state breakdown. What is clear is that devolution is a process and not an event, in the sense that it sets in train a re-working of political identities and relationships whose ultimate shape may not emerge for several years or perhaps even generations. A further factor is the potential for institutionalized conflict between the national government and devolved bodies. While the constitu-tional supremacy of the centre ultimately enables it to resolve disputes in its favour, the fact that devolved bodies may exercise significant legislative and fiscal powers, and enjoy political entrenchment through their democratic legitimacy, means that the system as a whole may acquire a quasi-federal character, requiring the develop-ment of linking institutions to foster co-operation between the two levels.

DIALECTIC

A dialectic is a process of development brought about by conflict between two opposing forces. Plato's (427–347 BCE) method of developing a philosophical argument by means of a dialogue between Socrates and a protagonist is thus referred to as dialectical. G. W. F. Hegel (1770–1831) explained the process of reasoning and both human and natural history in terms of a theory of the dialectic. According to this, both thought and reality develop towards a determinant end-point through conflict between a 'thesis' and the negation it embodies, the 'antithesis', producing a higher stage of development, the 'synthesis', which, in turn, serves as a new 'thesis'. By contrast with Hegel's idealism, Karl Marx (1818–83) gave the dialectic a materialist interpretation in identifying the driving force of history as internal contradictions within class society that are manifest in the form of class conflict.

Significance

The strength of the dialectical method is that it draws attention to tensions or contradictions within belief systems and social structures, often providing important insights into the nature of change. In addition, in emphasizing relationships and interdependence, dialectics can feature as part of a holistic perspective and be used to analyse ecological processes. Nevertheless, dialectical thinking plays little part in conventional social and political analysis. Its main drawbacks are that, in always linking change to internal contradictions, it over-emphasizes conflict in society and elsewhere, and, as in the writings of Hegel and, later, Friedrich Engels (1820–95), the dialectic has been elaborated into a metaphysical system supposedly operating in nature as well as in human society. 'Dialectical materialism' (a term coined by the Russian Marxist, Georgi Plekhanov (1856–1918), not Marx), refers to a crude and deterministic form of Marxism that dominated intellectual life in orthodox communist states.

DICTATORSHIP

A dictatorship is, strictly, a form of rule in which absolute power is vested in a single individual; in this sense, dictatorship is synonymous with autocracy. Originally, the term was associated with the unrestricted emergency powers granted to a supreme magistrate in the early Roman Republic, which created a form of constitutional dictatorship. In the modern usage of the term, however, dictators are seen as being above the law and acting beyond constitutional constraints. More generally, dictatorship is characterized by the arbitrary and unchecked exercise of power, as in the ideas of the 'dictatorship of the proletariat', 'military dictatorship' and 'personal dictatorship'. A distinction is sometimes drawn between traditional and totalitarian dictatorships. *Traditional dictatorships* aim to monopolize government power and conform to the principles of authoritarianism, while *totalitarian dictatorships* seek 'total power' and extend political control to all aspects of social and personal existence.

Significance

Dictators have been found throughout political history. Classic examples include Sulla, Julius Caesar and Augustus Caesar in Rome; Oliver Cromwell after the dissolution of Parliament in 1653; Napoleon Bonaparte, Napoleon III and Otto von Bismarck in the nineteenth century, and in the twentieth century Adolf Hitler, Joseph Stalin and Mao Zedong. While all dictators depend on fear and operate through the control of coercive power, the modern phenomenon of dictatorship is often linked to charismatic leadership and the idea that the leader in some way embodies the destiny or 'general will' of the people. Totalitarian dictatorships may thus masquerade as 'perfect democracies' and enjoy a significant measure of popular support based, crucially, on strict control of the means of mass communication. However, the personal aspect of dictatorship should not be over-emphasized, as most modern dictatorships are usually military dictatorships or operate through a monopolistic party. In these cases, unrestrained power is vested in the armed forces or the party–state apparatus (or a combination of the two), with leadership sometimes being shared among a group of people, the classic example of which is the military junta. There are indications, nevertheless, that dictatorship as the principal alternative to democracy is of declining significance. Its impact on the twentieth century was linked to the, now largely spent, ideological forces of fascism and communism, meaning that dictatorship has become mainly a developing-world phenomenon. On the other hand, the rising power of China and Russia in the twenty-first century has sometimes been interpreted as evidence of the re-emergence of dictatorship as a serious rival to democracy (Kagan, 2008). The glaring moral defect of dictatorship is its link to repression and tyranny; its major structural defect is its inability to generate or deal with the pressures generated by social and economic development.

DIPLOMACY

The term diplomacy is sometimes (but unhelpfully) treated as being synonymous with foreign policy, in which case it covers attempts by governments to influence or manage events beyond their states' borders, usually, but not exclusively, through their relations with foreign governments. Diplomacy, however, is usually defined more narrowly: it is confined to peaceful means of securing foreign-policy goals (diplomacy thus differs from war), and it is conducted only by personnel who are official agents of a state or an international organization. In everyday language, diplomacy also implies the use of tact or subtlety ('the application of intelligence'), but diplomats who are tactless or unintelligent do not thereby cease to be diplomats (Bull, 2012).

Significance

A system of diplomatic relations (involving ambassadors, embassies and established rules, including 'diplomatic immunity') developed in a piecemeal fashion between the fifteenth and twentieth centuries, the core of traditional diplomacy being based in the official relationships between sovereign states. Diplomacy has five main functions:

- Communicating and exchanging information between the political leaders of states and other entities in world politics

- Negotiating international agreements
- Gathering intelligence or information about foreign countries
- Minimizing the effects of 'friction' in international relations
- Representing states in world affairs, including through international organizations.

Those who emphasize the importance of diplomacy highlight its capacity to uphold international order and to reduce the use of military power in world affairs. This stems from the ability of diplomatic relations to build trust between international actors and to prevent, or at least to minimize, misunderstanding or misperception. If 'friction' in international relations is unavoidable, diplomacy at least provides states with mechanisms through which they can negotiate and bargain, allowing them to explore non-violent ways of resolving conflicts. Realists nevertheless stress that the capacity of diplomacy to balance various national interests is restricted by the fact that world politics is a self-help system in which states must ultimately rely on their own military resources to achieve their ends. Finally, the traditional model of inter-state diplomacy has become less relevant as a result of the growing prominence of international organizations and the emergence of a system of global governance.

DISCOURSE

Discourse, in everyday language, refers to verbal communication, talk or conversation. However, discourse has been adopted as an analytical concept or theoretical approach by a variety of academic disciplines, including linguistics, literature, philosophy and, most enthusiastically, cultural studies. In its technical sense, a discourse is a specialist system of knowledge embodied in a particular language, a kind of mind-set that structures understanding and behaviour (examples could range from legal jargon and religious rituals to ideological traditions). Discourse theory thus uncovers meaning in objects and practices by recognizing their discursive character and analysing the part they play in particular discourses and within a wider framework of meaning. Following Michel Foucault (1926–84), an emphasis on discourse, or what he called 'discursive formation', reflects the belief that knowledge is deeply enmeshed in power, with truth always being a social construct.

Significance

Political and social theorists sympathetic to postmodernism have been attracted to discourse theory for a number of reasons. These include that it recognizes that meaning is not implicit in social objects and practices but is historically and politically constructed, and that it can uncover social antagonisms and struggles for hegemony that conventional theory ignores.

Criticisms of discourse theory are either philosophical or substantive. Philosophically, an emphasis on discourse may reduce everything to thought or language and deny that there is a reality independent of our ideas or conceptions. It may also imply that everything is relative because truth or falsity can be asserted only in relation to particular discourses. Substantive criticisms include that discourse theory limits or discourages the analysis of political and social institutions, and that, in so far as discourse displaces the concept of ideology, it shifts the attention of political analysis away from issues of truth and falsity.

ECOLOGISM

The central feature of ecologism is the belief that nature is an interconnected whole, embracing humans and non-humans as well as the inanimate world (the term 'ecology' means the study of organisms 'at home' or 'in their habitats'). A distinction is often drawn between ecologism and environmentalism. Environmentalism refers to a moderate or reformist approach to the environment that responds to ecological crises but without fundamentally questioning conventional assumptions about the natural world. It thus includes the activities of most environmental pressure groups and is a stance that may be adopted by a range of political parties. Ecologism, in contrast, is an ideology in its own right, in that it adopts an ecocentric or biocentric perspective that accords priority to nature or the planet, and thus differs from the anthropocentric or human-centred perspectives of conventional ideological traditions. Nevertheless, two strains of ecologism are normally identified. 'Deep ecology' completely rejects any lingering belief that the human species is in some way superior to, or more important than, any other species – or, indeed, nature itself. 'Shallow ecology', on the other hand, accepts the lessons of ecology but harnesses them to human needs and ends. In other words, it preaches that if we can serve and cherish the natural world, it will, in turn, continue to sustain human life.

A variety of hybrid forms of ecologism have emerged. *Eco-socialism*, usually influenced by modern Marxism, explains environmental destruction in terms of capitalism's rapacious quest for profit. *Eco-anarchism* draws parallels between natural equilibrium in nature and in human communities, using the idea of 'social ecology'. *Eco-feminism* portrays patriarchy as the chief source of environmental destruction, and usually believes that women are naturally ecological. *Reactionary ecologism* links the conservation of nature to the defence of the traditional social order, and was expressed most radically in the 'blood and soil' ideas of Nazism. However, 'deep' ecology rejects all conventional political creeds. It tends to regard both capitalism and socialism as examples of the 'super-ideology' of industrialism, characterized by large-scale production, the accumulation of capital, and relentless growth. It supports bio-centric equality, holding that the rights of animals have the same moral status as those of humans, and portrays nature as an ethical community within which human beings are merely 'plain citizens'.

Significance

Ecological or green political ideas can be traced back to the nineteenth-century backlash against the spread of industrialization and urbanization. Modern ecologism emerged during the 1960s, along with renewed concern regarding the damage done to the environment by pollution, resource depletion, over-population and so on. Such concerns have been articulated politically by a growing number of 'green' parties which now operate in most developed societies and, at least in the case of the Greens in Germany, have shared government power, and through the influence of a powerful environmentalist lobby whose philosophy is 'think globally, act locally'. Despite, in origin at least, green parties styling themselves as 'anti-party parties' and adopting radical ecological perspectives, environmental pressure groups generally practise 'shallow' ecologism.

However, the spread of ecologism has been hampered by a number of factors. These include the limited attraction of its anti-growth, or at least sustainable growth, economic model, and that its critique of industrial society is sometimes advanced from a pastoral and anti-technology perspective that is out of step with the modern world. Some, as a result, dismiss ecologism simply as an urban fad, a form of post-industrial romanticism. Ecologism nevertheless has at least two major strengths. First, it draws attention to an imbalance in the relationship between humans and the natural world that is manifest in a growing catalogue of threats to the well-being of both. Second, ecologism has gone further than any other ideological tradition in questioning and transcending the limited focus of Western political thought. In keeping with globalization, it is the nearest thing that political theory has to a world philosophy.

ELECTION

An election is a device for filling an office or post through choices made by a designated body of people, the electorate. Elections may nevertheless be either democratic or non-democratic. Democratic elections are conducted according to the following principles: universal adult suffrage (however 'adult' is defined); 'one person, one vote', 'one vote, one value'; the secret ballot; and electoral choice offered by competition between both candidates and political parties. Non-democratic elections may therefore exhibit any of the following features: the right to vote is restricted on grounds such as property ownership, education, gender or racial origin; a system of plural voting is in operation or constituency sizes vary significantly; voters are subject to pressure or intimidation; or only a single candidate or single party can contest the election.

There are, however, a variety of democratic electoral systems. These differ in a variety of ways. Voters may be asked to choose between candidates or between parties; they may either select a single candidate, or vote preferentially, ranking the candidates they wish to support in order; the electorate may or may not be grouped into electoral units or constituencies; constituencies may return a single member or a number of members; and the level of support needed to elect a candidate may vary from a plurality (the largest single number of votes or a 'relative' majority) to an overall or 'absolute' majority or a quota of some kind. However, the most common way of distinguishing between electoral systems is on the basis of how they convert votes into seats.

Majoritarian (or non-proportional) systems enable larger parties to win a significantly higher proportion of seats than the proportion of votes they gain in the election. This increases the chances of a single party gaining a parliamentary majority and being able to govern on its own. Examples of majoritarian systems include the simple plurality system ('first-past-the-post'), the second ballot system and the alternative vote (AV). *Proportional systems* guarantee an equal, or at least more equal, relationship between seats and votes. In a pure system of proportional representation (PR), a party that gains 45 per cent of the votes would win exactly 45 per cent of the seats. Examples of proportional systems include the party list system, single transferable vote (STV) and the additional member system (AMS).

Significance

Elections are often seen as nothing less than democracy in practice. The conventional view is that elections, when they are fair and competitive, are a mechanism through which politicians can be called to account and forced to introduce policies that in some way reflect public opinion. This emphasises the 'bottom-up' functions of elections. In this view, elections are the major source of political recruitment, a means of making governments and of transferring government power, a guarantee of representation, and a major determinant of government policy. On the other hand, the 'radical' view of elections portrays them as being largely a mechanism through which governments and political elites can exercise control over their populations. This view emphasizes the 'top-down' functions of elections. These are that they have the capacity to build legitimacy for the regime, to enable the government to 'educate' the electorate and shape public opinion, and to neutralize political discontent and opposition by channelling them in a constitutional direction. In reality, however, elections have no single character: they are neither simply mechanisms of public accountability nor a means of ensuring political control. Like all channels of political communication, elections are a 'two-way street' that provide the government and the people, the elite and the mass, with the opportunity to influence one another.

Much of the debate regarding elections centres on the merits of different electoral systems, and in particular the choice between majoritarian and proportional systems. Majoritarian systems have the advantage that they allow governments to be formed that have a clear mandate from the electorate. They also increase the likelihood of strong and effective government, in that a single party usually has majority control of the parliament, and produce stable government because single-party governments rarely collapse through internal disunity. In contrast, proportional systems are 'fairer' in that party representation is linked reliably to electoral support, and ensure that governments have broader and usually majority support among the electorate. Moreover, by increasing the likelihood of coalition government, they institutionalize checks on power and encourage policy to be made through a process of bargaining and consensus-building. Nevertheless, there is no such thing as a 'best' electoral system. The electoral systems debate is, at heart, a debate about the desirable nature of government, and the respective merits of 'representative' and 'effective' government. Finally, the impact of particular electoral systems will vary from state to state, and possibly over time, depending on factors such as the political culture, the nature of the party system and the economic and social context within which politics is conducted.

ELITISM

The term elite originally meant, and can still mean, the highest, the best or the most excellent. Used in a neutral or empirical sense, however, it refers to a minority in whose hands power, wealth or privilege is concentrated, justifiably or otherwise. Elitism is a belief in, or practice of, rule by an elite or minority. At least three forms of elitism can exist. *Normative elitism* is a political theory which suggests that elite rule is desirable, usually on the grounds that power should be vested in the hands of a wise or enlightened minority (in this sense, elitism could be regarded as a value or even an ideology). This implies that democracy is undesirable, and is, for example, evident in Plato's (427–347 BCE) belief in rule by a class of benign philosopher-kings. *Classical elitism* claimed to be empirical (though normative beliefs often intruded), and saw elite rule as being inevitable, an unchangeable fact of social existence. This implies that egalitarian ideas such as democracy and socialism are impossible. The chief exponents of this view were Vilfredo Pareto (1848–1923), Gaetano Mosca (1857–1941) and Robert Michels (1876–1936). *Modern elitism* has also developed an empirical analysis, but it is more critical and discriminating regarding the causes of elite rule, usually linking these to particular economic and political structures rather than the inevitable structure of society. Modern elitists, such as C. Wright Mills (1916–62) have often been concerned to highlight elite rule in the hope of both explaining and challenging it. What is called variously 'pluralist', 'competitive' or 'democratic' elitism is a development within modern elitism that acknowledges that modern elites are typically fractured or divided rather than unified and coherent, and that rivalry among elites can, to some extent, ensure that non-elite groups are given a political voice.

Significance

Normative elitism has largely been abandoned, given the advance of democratic values and practices, though representative democracy can be seen to embody residual elitist assumptions in that it ensures that government decisions are made by educated and well- informed professional politicians rather than by the public directly. Classical elitism has had a considerable impact on social and political theory, being used, among other things, to reject the Marxist idea of a classless, communist society. Mosca argued that the resources or attributes that are necessary for rule are always unequally distributed, and that a cohesive minority will always be able to manipulate and control the masses, even in a parliamentary democracy. Pareto linked elite rule to two psychological types: 'foxes', who rule by cunning and manipulation; and 'lions', who dominate through coercion and violence. Michels developed what he termed the 'iron law of oligarchy', the idea that in all organizations power is concentrated in the hands of a small group of leaders. However, such arguments have been criticized for generalizing on the basis of assumptions about human nature or organization, and because they are difficult to reconcile with modern democratic practices.

Modern elitism nevertheless offers an important critique of both pluralism and democracy. The democratic elitism of Joseph Schumpeter (1883–1950) offered a 'realistic' model of democracy, which emphasized that, while elections can decide which elite rules, they cannot change the fact that power is always exercised by an elite. This gave rise to the 'economic theory of democracy', which applies rational choice theories to politics by treating electoral competition as a political market. The 'power elite' model advanced by theorists such as Mills (1956) departed from Marxism in so far as it rejected the idea of an economically defined 'ruling class', but nevertheless drew attention to the disproportionate influence of the military–industrial complex. Attempts to provide empirical support for elite theory have been provided by a variety of community power studies. However, despite it still being influential in the USA in particular, the elitist position has its drawbacks. These include that it is less theoretically sophisticated than, say, Marxism or pluralism, and that empirical evidence to sustain elitist conclusions, especially concerning the distribution of power at the national level, is as yet unconvincing.

EMPIRICISM

Empiricism is the doctrine that sense-experience is the only basis of knowledge, and that therefore all hypotheses and theories should be tested by a process of observation and experiment. This was evident in John Locke's (1632–1704) belief that the mind is a *tabula rasa* (blank tablet) on which information is imprinted by the senses in the form of sense-data. For David Hume (1711–76), empiricism also implied a deep scepticism which, in its extreme form, should lead us to doubt the existence of objects independent of our perception of them – for example, does a tree exist if no one can see it, touch it and so on? Since the early twentieth century, empiricism has been closely associated with pragmatism, as an epistemological theory. Philosophical pragmatism is the belief that the only way of establishing truth is through practical application, by establishing 'what works out most effectively'. All forms of empiricism draw a clear distinction between 'facts', propositions that have been verified by experience, observation and experiment, and 'values', which as subjective beliefs or opinions are always to be distrusted.

Significance

An empirical tradition can be traced back to the earliest days of political thought. It can be seen in Aristotle's (384–22 BCE) attempt to classify constitutions, in Machiavelli's (1469–1527) realistic account of statecraft, and in C.-L. Montesquieu's (1689–1775) sociological theory of government and law. In many ways, such writings constitute the basis of what is now called comparative government, and gave rise to an essentially institutional approach to the discipline. The empirical approach to political analysis is characterized by the attempt to offer a dispassionate and impartial account of political reality. It is 'descriptive' in that it seeks to analyse and explain, whereas the normative approach is 'prescriptive' in the sense that it makes judgements and offers recommendations. Empiricism thus provided the basis for positivism and, later, behaviouralism. However, the high point of philosophical empiricism was reached in the early twentieth century and it has subsequently been subjected to considerable attack. Strict empiricism has been criticized because it is linked to a simplistic model of science that has been badly damaged by advances in the philosophy of science. It also fails to recognize the extent to which human perception and sense-experience are structured by concepts and theories, and is of limited value in dealing with matters that are ethical or normative in character.

EQUALITY

Equality is the principle of uniform apportionment; it does not imply identity or sameness. Equality, however, is meaningless unless we can answer the question: equal in what? The term equality has very different implications, depending on what is being apportioned. *Foundational equality* is the idea that human beings are 'born equal' in the sense that their lives are of equal moral value. *Formal equality* refers to the formal status of individuals in society in terms of their rights and entitlements; its clearest expression is in the form of legal equality ('equality before the law') and political equality (universal suffrage and one person, one vote; one vote, one value). *Equality of opportunity* means that everyone has the same starting point, or equal life chances. This distinguishes between inequalities that result from unequal social treatment (which are non-legitimate) and ones that result from an unequal distribution of merit, talent and the willingness to work (which are legitimate). *Equality of outcome* refers to an equal distribution of rewards; it is usually reflected in social equality, an equal distribution of income, wealth and other social goods. These different views of equality are sometimes mutually incompatible. For example, equality of opportunity may justify unequal social outcomes on the grounds of meritocracy and the need for incentives.

Significance

The idea of equality is perhaps the defining feature of modern political thought. Whereas classical and medieval thinkers took it for granted that hierarchy was natural or inevitable, few modern ones have not been willing to support equality in one of its various forms. In a sense we are all egalitarians now. The modern battle about equality is therefore fought not between those who support the principle and those who reject it, but between different views as to where and how equality should be applied. Despite foundational equality as a philosophical principle, and formal equality as a legal and political principle, being widely accepted, at least in liberal-democratic societies, deep controversy continues to surround the idea of equality of outcome or rewards. Indeed, many treat the left/ right political spectrum as a reflection of differing attitudes towards social equality, with left-wingers broadly supporting it, while right-wingers question or oppose it.

Among the arguments in favour of social or material equality are:

- It strengthens social cohesion and community by creating a common identity and shared interests.
- It promotes justice in that the most obvious forms of social inequality are the result of unequal treatment by society rather than unequal natural endowment.
- It enlarges freedom in the sense that it safeguards people from poverty and satisfies basic needs, enabling them to achieve fulfilment.
- It is the only meaningful form of equality, in that all other equalities rest on it: genuine legal and political equality require that people have access to equal social resources.

Among the arguments against social equality are:

- It is unjust because it treats unequals equally and therefore fails to reward people in line with their talents and capacities.
- It results in economic stagnation in that it removes incentives and caps aspirations, amounting to a process of 'levelling down'.
- It can be achieved only through state intervention and a system of 'social engineering', meaning that it always infringes on individual liberty.
- It results in drab uniformity; diversity is vanquished, and with it the vigour and vitality of society.

EXECUTIVE

The executive, in its broadest sense, is the branch of government responsible for the implementation of laws and policies made by the parliament. The executive branch extends from the head of government, or chief executive, to the members of enforcement agencies such as the police and the military, and includes both ministers and civil servants. More commonly, the term is now used in a narrower sense to describe the smaller body of decision-makers who take overall responsibility for the direction and co-ordination of government policy. This core of senior figures is often called the *political executive* (roughly equivalent to the 'government of the day', or, in presidential systems, 'the administration'), as opposed to the *official executive*, or bureaucracy. The term 'core executive' is sometimes used to refer to the co-ordinating and arbitrating mechanisms that lie at the heart of central government and straddle the 'political/official' divide by including the chief executive, the cabinet, senior officials in key government departments and the security and intelligence services, and networks of political advisers.

However, the organization of the political executive differs significantly depending on whether it operates in a parliamentary or a presidential system of government. *Parliamentary executives* have the following features:

- The personnel of the political executive are drawn from the parliament, usually on the basis of their status and position within the leading party or parties.

- The executive is directly accountable to the parliament (or at least its lower chamber), in the sense that it survives in government only as long as it retains the confidence of the parliament.
- The cabinet is often regarded as the formal apex of the executive, thereby upholding the idea of collective leadership.
- As the prime minister is a parliamentary officer, a separate head of state, in the form of a constitutional monarch or non-executive president, is required to fulfil ceremonial duties and carry out state functions.

Presidential executives are characterized by the following features:
- The president as chief executive is elected separately from the parliament, and there is a formal separation of personnel between the legislative and executive branches.
- The executive is invested with a range of independent constitutional powers and is not removable by the parliament.
- Executive authority is concentrated in the hands of the president; the cabinet and other ministers are merely advisers responsible to the president.
- The roles of head of state and head of government are combined in the office of the presidency.

Semi-presidential executives are headed by a separately elected president who presides over a government drawn from, and accountable to, the parliament. The balance of power between the president and the prime minister in such circumstances depends on factors such as the formal powers of the presidency, which may include the ability to dissolve the parliament, and the party composition of both institutions.

Significance

The executive is the irreducible core of government. Political systems can operate without constitutions, parliaments, judiciaries and even political parties, but they cannot survive without an executive branch. This is because the key function of the political executive is to direct and control the policy process, both in formulating government policy and ensuring that it is implemented. In short, the executive is expected to 'govern'. The political executive is expected, in particular, to develop coherent economic and social programmes that meet the needs of complex and politically sophisticated societies, and to control the state's various external relationships in an increasingly interdependent world. One important consequence of this has been the growth of the executive's legislative powers, and its encroachment on the traditional responsibilities of the parliament. Other important functions of the political executive include overseeing the implementation of policy and strategic control of the bureaucratic machinery of government, the provision of leadership in the event of either domestic or international crises, and the carrying out of various ceremonial and diplomatic responsibilities in which heads of state, chief executives and, to a lesser extent, senior ministers 'stand for' the state. Moreover, the popularity of the political executive, more than any other part of the political system, is crucial to the character and stability of the regime as a whole. The ability of the executive to mobilize support ensures the compliance and co-operation of the general public, and, more important, the political executive's popularity is a crucial determinant of the legitimacy of the broader regime.

Such is the potential power of executives that much of political development has taken the form of attempts to check or constrain them, either by forcing them to operate within a constitutional framework, or by making them accountable to a popularly elected parliament or democratic electorate. Nevertheless, as the source of political leadership, the executive's role has been greatly enhanced by the widening responsibilities of the state in both domestic and international realms, and the media's tendency to portray politics in terms of personalities. This, in turn, has led to contradictory shifts in the location of executive power. The official executive, as the source of expertise and specialist knowledge, has been strengthened at the expense of the political executive, but, regardless of the parliamentary/presidential distinction, power has also been concentrated in the hands of the chief executive as the popular face of modern politics. However, the hopes and expectations focused on executives may also prove to be their undoing. In many political systems, leaders are finding it increasingly difficult to 'deliver the goods'. This is linked both to the growing complexity of modern society and to the fact that, through the impact of globalization, the capacity of national governments to solve problems has declined.

FAILED STATE

A failed state (sometimes called a 'quasi-state' or a 'weak state') is a state that is unable to perform its key role of ensuring domestic order by monopolizing the use of legitimate force within its borders. (Technically, failed states cease to be states, since they lack meaningful sovereignty.) Some examples of failed states in the twentieth and twenty-first centuries include Haiti, Rwanda, Liberia, the Democratic Republic of the Congo, Somalia, Libya, Syria and Iraq. Failed states are no longer able to act as viable political units, in that they lack a credible system of law and order, often being gripped by civil war or warlordism (a condition in which, in the absence of a sovereign state, locally-based militarized bands vie for power). They are also no longer able to act as viable economic units, in that they are incapable of providing for their citizens and have no functioning infrastructure. While relatively few states collapse completely, a much larger number are barely functioning and dangerously close to collapse.

Significance

Failed states are characterized by recurrent civil strife, and even civil war, in line with the tendencies usually associated with anarchy. Failed states, nevertheless, are not only a domestic problem. They often have a wider impact through, for example, precipitating refugee crises; providing a refuge for drug dealers, arms smugglers and terrorist organizations; generating regional instability; and provoking external intervention to provide humanitarian relief and to keep the peace. The failure of such states stems primarily from the experience of colonialism. The colonial inheritance tends not only to include a lack of political, economic, social and educational development, but also deep ethnic, religious and tribal divisions. Nevertheless, colonialism does not, on its own, explain the weakness or failure of post-colonial states. Other sources of state failure include internal factors, such as the existence of social elites, backward institutions and parochial value systems that block the transition from pre-industrial, agrarian societies to modern industrial ones, and external factors such as the impact of transnational corporations and neo-colonialism.

The issue of how to deal with the problem of failed states has been no less troubling, especially in the light of attempts by the international community to intervene in order to promote 'state-building', as in Iraq and Afghanistan. To date, the record of state-building has been, at best, patchy, with at least three challenges standing in its way. The first is that new or reformed institutions and structures have to be constructed in a context of often deep political and ethnic tension and endemic poverty. Second, the democratization usually deemed necessary to invest these structures with legitimacy may both bring ethnic and other tensions to the surface and expose the flaws and failings of emergent institutions. Third, state-building may involve the imposition of an essentially Western model of political development that is unsuited to the needs of developing counties.

FASCISM

Fascism is a political ideology whose core theme is the idea of an organically unified national community, embodied in a belief in 'strength through unity'. The individual, in a literal sense, is nothing; individual identity must be entirely absorbed into the community or social group. The fascist ideal is that of the 'new man', a hero, motivated by duty, honour and self-sacrifice, prepared to dedicate his life to the glory of his nation or race, and to give unquestioning obedience to a supreme leader. In many respects, fascism constitutes a revolt against the ideas and values that dominated Western political thought from the French Revolution onwards; in the words of the Italian fascist slogan: '1789 is dead'. Values such as rationalism, progress, freedom and equality were thus overturned in the name of struggle, leadership, power, heroism and war. In this sense, fascism has an 'anti-character'. It is defined largely by what it opposes: it is anti-rational, anti-liberal, anti-conservative, anti-capitalist, anti-bourgeois, anti-communist and so on. Fascism represents the darker side of the Western political tradition, the central values of which it transformed rather than abandoned. For fascists, freedom means complete submission, democracy is equated with dictatorship, progress implies constant struggle and war, and creation is fused with destruction.

Fascism has nevertheless been a complex historical phenomenon, and it is difficult to identify its core principles or a 'fascist minimum'. For example, while most

commentators treat Mussolini's fascist dictatorship in Italy and Hitler's Nazi dictatorship in Germany as the two principal manifestations of fascism, others regard
fascism and Nazism as distinct ideological traditions. Italian fascism was essentially
an extreme form of statism that was based on unquestioning respect and absolute
loyalty towards a 'totalitarian' state. As the fascist philosopher, Giovanni Gentile
(1875–1944), put it, 'everything for the state; nothing against the state; nothing outside
the state'. German Nazism, on the other hand, was constructed largely on the basis
of racialism. Its two core theories were Aryanism (the belief that the German people
constituted a 'master race' and were destined for world domination) and a virulent
form of anti-Semitism that portrayed the Jews as inherently evil and aimed at their
eradication. *Neo-fascism* or 'democratic fascism' claims to have distanced itself from
principles such as charismatic leadership, totalitarianism and overt racialism. It is a
form of fascism that is often linked to anti-immigration campaigns and is associated
with the growth of insular, ethnically or racially based forms of nationalism that have
sprung up as a reaction against globalization and supranationalism.

Significance

While the major ideas and doctrines of fascism can be traced back to the nineteenth
century, they were fused together and shaped by World War I and its aftermath,
and in particular by a potent mixture of war and revolution. Fascism emerged most
dramatically in Italy and Germany, manifesting respectively in the Mussolini regime
(1922–43) and the Hitler regime (1933–45). Some historians regard fascism as a
specifically inter-war phenomenon, linked to a historically unique set of circumstances. These circumstances included World War I's legacy of disruption, lingering
militarism and frustrated nationalism; the fact that in many parts of Europe
democratic values had yet to replace older, autocratic ones; the threat to the lower
middle classes of the growing might of big business and organized labour; the fears
generated among propertied classes generally, and elite groups in particular, by
the Bolshevik Revolution in Russia; and the economic insecurity of the 1920s that
deepened with the full-scale world economic crisis of the early 1930s. According to
this view, fascism died in 1945 with the final collapse of the Hitler and Mussolini
regimes, and it has been suppressed ever since by a combination of political stability
and economic security. The late twentieth century nevertheless witnessed a renewal
of fascism in the form of neo-fascism. Neo-fascism has been particularly influential
in Eastern Europe, where it has sought to revive national rivalries and racial hatreds,
and has taken advantage of the political instability resulting from the collapse of
communism. However, it is questionable whether fascism can meaningfully adopt
a 'democratic' face, since this implies an accommodation with principles such as
pluralism, toleration and individualism.

FEDERALISM

Federalism (from the Latin *foedus*, meaning 'pact', or 'covenant') refers to the legal
and political structures that distribute power between two distinct levels of govern-

ment, neither of which is subordinate to the other. Its central feature is therefore the notion of shared sovereignty, under which each level of government exercises supreme and autonomous control over a specific range of issues. On the basis of this definition, 'classical' federations are few in number: the USA, Switzerland, Belgium, Canada and Australia. However, many more states have federal-type features. Federalism differs from devolution in that devolved bodies have no share in sovereignty, and it differs from confederations in that the latter are qualified unions of states in which each state retains its independence, typically guaranteed by a system of unanimous decision-making. Federalism also has an international dimension, in which case it is characterized by the 'pooling' of sovereignty in designated areas, meaning that supranational governance coexists with a delimited form of national sovereignty. The clearest example of this is found in the European Union (EU), though it is perhaps more accurate to talk of a 'federalizing Europe' than a 'federal Europe'.

There are differences within federalism, between federal states that operate a separation of powers between the executive and legislative branches of government (typified by the US presidential system), and parliamentary systems, in which executive and legislative power is 'fused'. The former tend to ensure that government power is diffused both territorially and functionally, meaning that there are multiple points of contact between the two levels of government. Parliamentary systems, however, often produce what is called *executive federalism* (notably in Canada and Australia) in which the federal balance is largely determined by the relationship between the executives of each level of government. In states such as Germany and Austria, so-called *administrative federalism* operates, in which central government is the key policy-maker, and provincial government is charged with the responsibility for the details of policy implementation.

Nevertheless, certain features are common to most, if not all, federal states (see Figure 1).

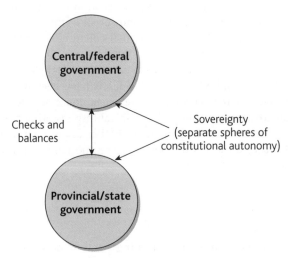

Figure 1   Federal states

- Both central government (the federal level) and regional government (the state level) possess a range of powers on which the other cannot encroach; these include at least a measure of legislative and executive authority, and the capacity to raise revenue and thus enjoy a degree of fiscal independence.
- The responsibilities and powers of each level of government are defined in a codified or written constitution, meaning that the relationship between the centre and the periphery is conducted within a formal legal framework that neither level can alter unilaterally.
- The formal provisions of the constitution are interpreted by a supreme court, which arbitrates in the case of disputes between the federal and state levels of government.
- Linking institutions foster co-operation and understanding between federal and state levels of government, giving the regions and provinces a voice in the processes of central policy-making (this is usually achieved through the second chamber of the bicameral national legislature).

Significance

It is widely argued that the federal principle is more applicable to some states than to others. In the first place, federations have often been formed by the coming together of a number of established political communities which nevertheless wish to preserve their separate identities and, to some extent, their autonomy. This clearly applies in the case of the world's first federal state, the USA, formed by former colonies that each possessed a distinctive political identity but jointly recognized their need for a new and more centralized constitutional framework. The second factor influencing the formation of federations is the existence of an external threat or a desire to play a more effective role in international affairs. Small, strategically vulnerable states, for example, have a powerful incentive to enter broader political unions. The drift towards the construction of a 'federal Europe' was thus, in part, brought about by a fear of Soviet aggression and by a perceived loss of European influence in the emerging bipolar world order. A third factor is geographical size. It is no coincidence that many of the territorially larger states in the world – the USA, Canada, Brazil, Australia, Mexico and India – have opted to introduce federal systems. The final factor encouraging the adoption of federalism is cultural and ethnic heterogeneity. Federalism, in short, has often been seen as an institutional response to societal divisions and diversity.

One of the chief strengths of federal systems is that, unlike unitary systems in which sovereignty is concentrated in a single, central body, they give regional and local interests a constitutionally guaranteed political voice. The states and provinces exercise a range of autonomous powers and enjoy some measure of representation in central government, usually through the second chamber of the federal legislature. The second advantage of federalism is that, in diffusing government power, it creates a network of checks and balances that help to protect individual liberty. Third, federalism has provided an institutional mechanism through which fractured societies maintain unity and coherence. In this respect, the federal solution may be appropriate only to a limited number of ethnically diverse and regionally divided societies; but in these cases it may be absolutely vital.

On the other hand, critics argue that federalism often proves to be an ineffective check on centralization, and may even foster the trend. This applies in the case of the USA, which, despite the principle of each state's rights being enshrined in the Tenth Amendment of the Constitution, has witnessed a steady growth in the powers of federal government, dating back to the 1930s. Eurosceptics, for their part, warn that 'pooled' sovereignty within the EU is a recipe for the progressive erosion of the autonomy of member states. A further charge made against federalism is that structures intended to create healthy tension within a system of government may, in practice, generate frustration and paralysis, making it difficult, if not impossible, for bold economic or social programmes to be implemented. At the heart of this criticism lies the belief that shared sovereignty is a contradiction in terms: sovereignty is only meaningful if it is single and indivisible.

FEMINISM

Feminism is a political movement and ideology that aims to advance the social role of women. Feminists have highlighted what they see as the political relationship between the sexes: the supremacy of men and the subjection of women in most, if not all, societies. Feminist ideology is therefore characterized by two basic beliefs. First, women and men are treated differently because of their sex; and second, this unequal treatment can and should be overturned. while most feminists therefore embrace the goal of sexual equality, it is misleading to define feminism in terms of this goal, as some feminists distinguish between liberation and equality, arguing that the latter implies that women should be 'like men'. The central concept in feminist analysis is patriarchy, which draws attention to the totality of oppression and exploitation to which women are subject. This, in turn, highlights the political importance of gender, understood to refer to socially imposed rather than biological differences between women and men. Most feminists view gender as a political construct, usually based on stereotypes of 'feminine' and 'masculine' behaviour and social roles.

Feminist theory and practice is highly diverse, however. Distinctive liberal, socialist/Marxist and radical forms of feminism are conventionally identified. *Liberal feminism* reflects a commitment to individualism and formal equality, and is characterized by the quest for equal rights and opportunities in 'public' and political life. *Socialist feminism*, largely derived from Marxism, highlights links between female subordination and the capitalist mode of production, drawing attention to the economic significance of women being confined to the family or domestic life. *Radical feminism* goes beyond the perspectives of established political traditions in portraying gender divisions as the most fundamental and politically significant cleavages in society, and in calling for the radical, even revolutionary, restructuring of personal, domestic and family life. Radical feminists proclaim that 'the personal is the political'. However, the breakdown of feminism into three traditions – liberal, socialist and radical – has become increasingly redundant since the 1970s, as feminism has become yet more sophisticated and diverse. Among its more recent forms have been black feminism, psychoanalytic feminism, eco-feminism and postmodern feminism.

Significance

The so-called 'first wave' of feminism was associated closely with the women's suffrage movement, which emerged in the 1840s and 1850s. The achievement of female suffrage in most Western countries in the early twentieth century meant that the campaign for legal and civil rights assumed a lower profile and deprived the women's movement of a unifying focus. The 'second wave' of feminism arose during the 1960s and expressed, in addition to the established concern with equal rights, the more radical and revolutionary demands of the growing women's liberation movement. Since the early 1970s, feminism has undergone a process of de-radicalization, leading some to proclaim the emergence of 'post-feminism'. This was undoubtedly linked to a growing backlash against feminism, associated with the rise of the New Right, but it also reflected the emergence of more individualized and conventionalized forms of feminism, characterized by an unwillingness to view women any longer as 'victims'. The term 'third-wave' feminism has increasingly been adopted since the 1990s by a younger generation of feminist theorists for whom the campaigns and demands of the 1960s and 1970s women's movement seem to be of limited relevance. This form of feminism has generally favoured a more radical engagement with the politics of difference, bringing into focus not only differences between women and men but also differences among women themselves.

The major strength of feminist ideology is that it has exposed and challenged the gender biases that pervade society, and which have been ignored by conventional political thought. As such, feminism has gained growing respectability as a distinctive school of political thought. It has shed new light on established concepts such as power, domination and equality, but also introduced a new sensitivity and language into politics related to ideas such as connection, voice and difference. Feminism has nevertheless been criticized on the grounds that its internal divisions are now so sharp that feminist theory has lost all coherence and unity. Postmodern feminists, for example, even question whether 'woman' is a meaningful category. Others suggest that feminism has become disengaged from a society that is increasingly post-feminist, in that, largely thanks to the women's movement, the domestic, professional and public roles of women, at least in developed societies, have undergone a major transformation.

FREE TRADE

Free trade refers to a condition in which the free flow of goods and services in international exchange is neither restricted nor encouraged by direct government intervention. Free trade thus requires the absence of tariffs (taxes on imports), quotas (restrictions on the quantity of imports), subsidies (aid designed to reduce the price of exports) or other forms of protectionism, such as regulatory barriers. Free trade can be promoted either by bilateral trade agreements or through the establishment of 'free trade areas' – areas within which states agree to reduce tariffs and other barriers to trade. Free trade is nevertheless a relative, rather than an absolute term, as all modern governments are involved, to some degree, in regulating foreign trade.

Significance

Advocates of free trade argue that it brings massive economic and political benefits. The key economic argument in favour of free trade, which can be traced back to Adam Smith (1723–90) and David Ricardo (1772–1823), is the theory of comparative advantage. This suggests that international trade benefits all countries because it allows each to specialize in the production of the goods and services it is best suited to produce (in view of its natural resources, climate, size of population and so on). Free trade thus draws economic resources, at the international level, to their most profitable use, and so delivers general prosperity. Other economic advantages of free trade include the fact that specialization allows production to be carried out on a larger scale, so allowing for economies of scale. Such thinking helps to explain the widespread belief that the success of the General Agreement on Tariffs and Trade (GATT), and of its successor, the World Trade Organization (WTO), founded in 1995, in countering protectionism has underpinned growth in the world economy since 1945. The central political argument in favour of free trade is that it promotes international peace and harmony, by generating economic interdependence and strengthening social intercourse, and therefore understanding, between states.

Nevertheless, free trade has its critics. Some, for example, argue that free trade benefits industrialized and economically advanced countries at the expense of poor and developing ones. The latter are locked into the production of food and raw materials (for which prices are volatile with value being added to them outside the producing country), thereby preventing them from making economic progress. In this way, free trade entrenches divisions between prosperous 'core' and poorer 'peripheral' areas. Similarly, the strategic use of protectionist measures may help to create a domestic economic environment more favourable to growth, particularly by ensuring that fragile economies and so-called 'infant' industries are not exposed to the full force of international competition, and so never develop further. Finally, the chief political argument against free trade is that national security requires countries to maintain their own agriculture and energy supply, in particular, for fear that foreign supplies of vital goods may be curtailed as a result of international crises or war.

FREEDOM

Freedom or liberty (the two terms are best used interchangeably) is, in its broadest sense, the ability to think or act as one wishes. An important distinction is nevertheless made between negative and positive freedom (Berlin, 1958). *Negative freedom* means non-interference: the absence of external constraints on the individual. The individual is thus 'at liberty' to act as he or she wishes. The clearest manifestations of negative freedom are in the form of freedom of choice, civil liberty and privacy. *Positive freedom* is linked to the achievement of some identifiable goal or benefit, usually personal development or self-realization, though Berlin defined it as self-mastery and linked it to democracy. For Berlin, the negative/positive distinction was reflected in the difference between being *free from* something and being *free to do* something. However, the 'freedom from' and 'freedom to' distinction is misleading, because every example of freedom can be described in both ways. For example, being free from ignorance means being free to gain an education. G. C. MacCallum (1991) proposed a single, value-free concept of freedom in the form: 'X is free from Y to do or be Z'. This suggests that the apparently deep question 'Are we free?' is meaningless, and should be replaced by a more complete and specific statement about what we are free from, and what we are free to do.

Significance

Freedom is often considered to be the supreme political value in Western liberal societies. Its virtue is that, attached to the idea that human beings are rationally self-willed creatures, it promises the satisfaction of human interests or the realization of human potential. In short, freedom is the basis for happiness and well-being. However, despite its popularity, different political thinkers and traditions draw quite different conclusions from their belief in freedom. For classical liberals and supporters of the New Right, who view freedom in strictly negative terms, it implies rolling back the state and minimizing the realm of political authority. Indeed, for anarchists, who alone regard freedom as an absolute value, it is irreconcilable with any form of political authority. On the other hand, modern liberals and socialists have tended to subscribe to a positive view of freedom that justifies widening the responsibilities of the state, particularly in relation to welfare and economic management. The state is regarded as the enemy of freedom when it is viewed as an external constraint on the individual, but as a guarantee of freedom when it lays down the conditions for personal development and self-realization. Conservatives, for their part, have traditionally endorsed a weak view of freedom as the willing recognition of duties and responsibilities. This position is taken to its extreme by fascists, who portrayed 'true' freedom as unquestioning obedience to the leader and the absorption of the individual into the national community.

Nevertheless, with the exception of anarchism, freedom is not regarded as an unqualified blessing. This is reflected in the widely accepted distinction between liberty and licence, the former referring to morally acceptable forms of freedom, and the latter to the abuse of freedom or excessive freedom. As R. H. Tawney (1880–1962) put it, 'The freedom of the pike is death to the minnows.' Above all, freedom must be balanced against order, and the nature of this balance has been one of the central themes in political theory. Those who believe that this balance should favour freedom, such as liberals and socialists, generally regard human beings as rational and enlightened creatures, capable of making wise decisions in their own interests. Those, in contrast, who emphasize order over freedom, such as traditional conservatives, usually regard human beings as weak, limited or even corrupt creatures, who need authority to be exercised over them.

In addition to philosophical debates about freedom, political thinkers have sometimes discussed its psychological impact. In sharp contrast to the optimistic expectations of liberal thinkers such as J. S. Mill (1806–73) that freedom will result in human flourishing, writers such as Erich Fromm (1984) have drawn attention to the 'fear of freedom'. This is the idea that freedom entails psychological burdens in terms of choice and uncertainty, which at times of political instability and economic crisis may incline people to flee from freedom and seek security in submission to an all-powerful leader or totalitarian state. This has been used as an explanation for the rise of fascism and religious fundamentalism.

FUNCTIONALISM

Functionalism is the doctrine stating that social institutions and practices can be understood in terms of the functions they carry out in sustaining the larger social system. As functions are the actions or impacts that one thing has on other things, functionalism suggests that social and political phenomena should be understood in terms of their consequences rather than their causes. In the functionalist view, the whole is more than merely a collection of its parts, in the sense that the various parts are structured according to the 'needs' of the whole. A variety of political theories have adopted a functionalist methodology. These include the tendency of historical materialism to interpret the state, law and ideology in terms of their function in sustaining the class system, and the general systems theory approach to political analysis.

Significance

While a willingness to use aspects of a functional approach to understand political processes has a long heritage, functionalism has never enjoyed the academic status in political analysis that it did in sociology in the 1950s and 1960s, when it was accepted, in the USA in particular, as the dominant theoretical perspective. Nevertheless, an important application of functionalist thinking has been in the traditional conservative notion of an organic society. This is based on an organic analogy that draws parallels between society and living entities. In this view, society and social institutions arise out of natural necessity, and each part of society – family, church, business, government and so on – plays a particular role in sustaining the whole and maintaining the 'health' of society. Functionalism's impact on academic political analysis was greatest in the early post-1945 period, when it was linked to the application of the systems model of political interaction, and widely used in analysing institutional relationships and performance.

However, the star of functionalism has faded since the 1960s, in political analysis as in sociology. Functionalism has been criticized in two main ways. First, it has been accused of reductionism in that it appears to deprive the state and political institutions of meaning in their own right, and interprets them only in terms of their role in relation to the whole political system. Second, functionalism is implicitly, and sometimes explicitly, conservative. If what is important about institutions is their function in maintaining society, all existing institutions must play a worthwhile role in this respect and the value of maintaining the existing social order is taken for granted. For example, the very survival of the monarchy becomes its defence – it has survived because of its capacity to generate social cohesion, national unity or whatever, and it should therefore be preserved for the benefit of present society and future generations.

GAME THEORY

Game theory is a branch of mathematics that analyses competitive situations whose outcomes depend on choices made by all 'players', and these are, in turn, influenced by attempts to anticipate the choices of others. Game theory therefore focuses on a series of interdependent strategic calculations. The best known example of game theory is the prisoners' dilemma (PD). In this, two prisoners, held in separate cells, are faced with a choice of 'squealing' or 'not squealing' on one another. If one of them confesses, but provides evidence to convict the other, he will be released without any charge, while his partner will take the whole blame and be jailed for ten years. If both prisoners confess, they will be jailed for six years. If both refuse to confess, they will only be convicted of a minor crime, and they will each receive a one-year sentence. Figure 2 shows the options available to the prisoners and their consequences in terms of jail sentences.

Significance

Game theory has been used to inject increased analytical rigour into the study of political behaviour, most influentially in the field of international relations. Game theory has often been used to draw attention to the way in which individually rational strategies generate collectively irrational (or sub-optimal) outcomes. In the case of PD, for example, it is likely that both prisoners will confess (and jointly serve a total of 12 years in jail), fearing that if they do not the other will 'squeal' and they will receive the maximum sentence. Realist theorists have thus used game theory as a means of explaining the tendency towards conflict in an international system dominated by suspicion and distrust. Liberal institutionalists, by contrast, have argued

		Prisoner B			
		Confesses		Does not confess	
Prisoner A	Confesses	A: 6 yrs	B: 6 yrs	A: 0 yrs	B: 10 yrs
	Does not confess	A: 10 yrs	B: 0 yrs	A: 1 yr	B: 1 yr

Figure 2 Options in the prisoners' dilemma

that game theory can uncover a disposition towards co-operation, helping, in part, to explain the growing prominence of international organizations. Among other things, this is because, in economics and other areas, international relations may be a 'positive-sum' rather than a 'zero-sum' game (states achieving mutual benefit, rather than benefiting only at the expense of other states); international organizations serve to improve communication between states and thereby counter distrust; and, as games in international politics tend to be 'repeat-play', rather than 'single-play', games, states become more aware of the costs of 'defection' over time. Those who reject game theory completely tend to emphasize either that (as with rational choice theory, with which it has much in common) the assumption that behaviour is always rationally self-interested introduces an ideological bias into game theory, or that game theory is flawed because it ignores the processes through which interests and perceptions are determined.

GENDER

Gender refers to distinctions between males and females in terms of their social roles and status. While the terms gender and sex are often used interchangeably in everyday language, the distinction between them is crucial to social and political analysis. Gender highlights social or cultural differences between women and men, while sex denotes biological differences. Gender is thus a social construct and usually operates through stereotypes of 'femininity' and 'masculinity'.

Significance

Gender was largely ignored by political thinkers until the re-emergence of the women's movement and the revival of feminism in the 1960s. Since then, it has become a central concept in feminist theory and has received wider attention in mainstream political analysis. For most feminists, gender highlights that biological or physical differences between women and men ('sexual' differences) do not imply, or legitimize, their different social roles and positions ('gender' differences). In short, the quest for gender equality, which is basic to most forms of feminism, reflects the belief that sexual differences have no political or social significance; biology is not destiny. Radical feminists view gender divisions as the deepest and most politically significant of all social cleavages; gender is thus a 'political' category imposed by patriarchy and reproduced through a process of conditioning that operates mainly through the family. Gender, for radical feminists, plays a similar role as does social class in Marxist analysis, 'sisterhood' being equivalent to 'class consciousness'. Socialist feminists, on the other hand, argue that gender divisions are intrinsically linked to capitalism, and therefore treat gender and class as interrelated social cleavages. Liberal feminists and mainstream political analysts understand gender divisions less in terms of structural oppression and more as an unequal distribution of rights and opportunities that prevents the full participation of women in the 'public' realm. From this perspective, gender politics draws attention to issues such as women's rights and the under-representation of women in politics and in general professional and managerial positions.

GEOPOLITICS

Geopolitics is an approach to foreign policy analysis that understands the actions, relationships and significance of states in terms of geographical factors, such as location, climate, natural resources, physical terrain and population. The field of geopolitics was shaped significantly by Alfred Mahan (1840–1914), who argued that states that control the seas control world politics, and Halford Mackinder (1861–1947), who suggested, by contrast, that control of the land mass between Germany and central Siberia is the key to controlling world politics.

Significance

Though the subject of geopolitics has played a central role in mainstream inter-national relations, traditional approaches to the discipline have been shaped in significant ways by geopolitical assumptions. Thus, while the key elements of national power were, especially in realist analysis, taken to be military strength and economic development, these were underpinned by factors such as popula-tion and geography. For example, a large population has been seen as economi-cally and militarily beneficial, in that it gives a state a sizeable workforce and the potential to develop a large army. The geographical factors that have been accepted as bolstering state power have included access to the sea (for trading and military purposes); a temperate climate away from earthquake zones and areas where tropical storms are frequent; navigable rivers for transport, trade and energy production; arable land for farming; and access to mineral and energy resources. Critics of geopolitics have usually objected to geographical determinism, which appears to imply that in international politics 'geography is destiny'. The rise of globalization, geopolitics is also sometimes seen to have made geopolitics obsolete, geographical location being of limited importance in an era of 'time/space compression', in which social and economic interactions cease to be constrained by spatial barriers and distance. On the other hand, concerns about 'resource security' have helped to ensure that geopolitical considerations continue to remain relevant to modern world politics.

GLOBAL CIVIL SOCIETY

Global civil society refers to an arena in which transnational non-governmental groups and associations interact. Civil society groups are typically private, self-governing, voluntary and non-profit-making, setting them apart from transna-tional corporations (TNCs). However, the term 'global civil society' is complex and contested. In its 'activist' version, transnational social movements are seen as the key agents of global civil society, giving it an 'outsider' orientation and a strong focus on humanitarian goals and cosmopolitan ideals. In its 'policy' version, non-governmental organizations (NGOs) are viewed as the key agents of global civil society, giving it an 'insider' orientation and meaning that overlaps with the notion of global governance.

Significance

Interest in the idea of global civil society grew during the 1990s, as a mosaic of new groups, organizations and movements started to appear, which both sought to challenge or resist what was seen as 'corporate' globalization and articulate alternative models of social, economic and political development. This happened against a backdrop of the spread of demands for democratization around the world, in the aftermath of the Cold War, and in the light of the intensifying of the process of global interconnectedness. In some cases, these groups and organizations rejected globalization completely, styling themselves as part of an 'anti-globalization' movement, but in other cases they supported a reformed model of globalization, sometimes seen as 'social democratic' or 'cosmopolitan' globalization. The ideological orientation of most of these new groups and movements broadly favours a global justice or world ethics agenda, reflected in a desire to extend the impact and efficacy of human rights, deepen international law and develop citizen networks to monitor and put pressure on states and international organizations.

Optimists about global civil society argue that it has two main advantages. It provides a necessary counterbalance to corporate power. Until the 1990s, the advance of TNC interests met with little effective resistance, meaning that international organizations in particular fell too easily under the sway of a neoliberal agenda committed to free markets and free trade. In addition, global civil society is often seen as the basis for a fledgling democratic global politics. This has occurred because civil society bodies have articulated the interests of people and groups disempowered by the globalization process, acting as a kind of counter-hegemonic force. However, global civil society also has its critics. In the first place, the democratic credentials of NGOs and, for that matter, social movements, may be entirely bogus. For example, how can NGOs be in the forefront of democratization when they are entirely non-elected and self-appointed bodies? Second, the tactics of popular activism and direct action, so clearly associated with social movements and certain NGOs, have arguably alienated many potential supporters and given wider global civil society an image of recklessness and irresponsibility. Finally, NGOs and social movements tend to distort national and global political agendas through their fixation on gaining media attention, both as the principal means of exerting pressure and in order to attract support and funding.

GLOBAL GOVERNANCE

Global governance is a broad, dynamic and complex process of interactive decision-making at the global level that involves formal and informal mechanisms as well as governmental and non-governmental bodies. Nevertheless, being more a *field* than an object of study, global governance defies simple definitions or explanations. While it can be associated with particular institutions and identifiable actors (not least the international organizations that are currently in existence), global governance is essentially a process or a complex of processes, with the following features. First, global governance is multiple rather than singular: despite the UN's overarching role within the modern global governance system, it comprises different institutional frameworks and decision-making mechanism in different issue areas. Second, states and national governments retain considerable influence within the global governance system, reflecting international organizations' general disposition towards consensual decision-making and their usually weak powers of enforcement. Third, in common with governance at the national level, global governance blurs the public/private divide, in that it embraces non-governmental organizations and other institutions of so-called global civil society. Finally, global governance does not operate only at the global level; it also features interactions between groups and institutions at various levels (sub-national, national, regional and global), with no single level predominating over the others.

Significance

The notion of global governance emerged in the context of the growing importance, especially since 1945, of organizations such as the United Nations (UN), the International Monetary Fund (IMF), the Word Trade Organization (WTO), the European Union (EU) and so on. It has assumed particular prominence since the end of the Cold War, especially in response to, but also, to some extent, in an attempt to shape, the process of globalization. As the significance of international institutions expanded, the traditional assumption that international politics operates in a context of anarchy, with no authority being higher than the nation-state, became more difficult to sustain. On the other hand, global governance stops well short of world government, in which all of humankind is united under a common political authority. Global governance can thus be understood as the management of international politics in the absence of world government.

Global governance has nevertheless been at the heart of both empirical and normative debates. Empirical controversy focuses on its practical significance for global governance. Some argue that the unmistakable growth in the number and importance of international organizations since 1945 provides irrefutable evidence of a greater willingness among states to co-operate and engage in collective action. Others, however, suggest that, to the extent that states maintain sovereignty despite the paraphernalia of global governance, international anarchy continues to reign. In short, states pursue self-interest regardless of the context in which they operate. Normative debates have raged over whether the advance of global governance should be welcomed or feared. Liberals have supported global governance on the grounds that it provides a mechanism through which states can co-operate without, it seems, abandoning sovereignty, helping, in the process, to reduce levels of suspicion and distrust in the international system. Realists, by contrast, have warned that international organizations inevitably develop interests separate from those of their state members, in which case global governance amounts to a form of proto-world government.

GLOBAL JUSTICE

Global justice refers to a morally justifiable distribution of rewards and punishments at the global level, with particular reference to material or social rewards, such as wealth, income and social status. At the heart of global justice is the notion of universal rights and obligations stretching across the globe, establishing 'justice beyond borders'. However, two contrasting principles of global justice have been advanced. The first is grounded in humanitarianism and reflects a basic moral duty to alleviate suffering and attend to those in severe need. This 'humanitarian' model of social justice focuses on the limited, if politically pressing, task of eradicating poverty. The second conception of global justice is rooted in cosmopolitanism and goes beyond the problem of poverty by seeking to reduce, or perhaps remove, global inequality. The 'cosmopolitan' model of social justice is therefore linked to a substantial redistribution of wealth and resources from rich to poor countries.

Significance

Theories of justice have traditionally focused almost entirely on justice within particular states or communities. Since the 1980s, however, attempts have been made to extend arguments for justice, in particular social justice, originally conceived for the limited context of the nation-state, to the global arena. This has happened against the backdrop of 'accelerated' globalization, especially in view of the perception that economic globalization has deepened global inequality. Advocates of global justice, who claim that moral obligations extend to the whole of humanity, tend to base their claims on one of three arguments. The first uses the doctrine of human rights to demonstrate that there is just a single moral community, and that is humankind. Human rights are therefore fundamental and universal rights. The second focuses on the extent to which increased cross-border information and communication flows have globalized moral sensibilities by reducing the 'strangeness' and unfamiliarity of people on the other side of the globe. The third argument emphasizes that, thanks to globalization, we now live in a world of global cause and effect, in which our actions have moral consequences, potentially, for people everywhere.

The notion of global justice has attracted significant criticism, however. For example, some have dismissed the idea on the grounds that social justice is only meaningful if it is applied to a substantive political community, usually a nation-state. Rawls (1971) thus applied his theory of justice only to the state, on the grounds that it constitutes a closed and self-sufficient system of social co-operation. Moreover, even if global justice was deemed to be desirable, it is entirely unfeasible in that rich countries have never shown a willingness to make the sacrifices that it implies. Finally, the principle of global justice perpetuates the idea that poor countries are in some way 'victims' of global injustice, who need to be rescued by others, rather than being masters of their own destinies.

GLOBALIZATION

Globalization is the emergence of a complex web of interconnectedness which means that our lives are shaped increasingly by events that occur, and decisions that are made, at a great distance from us. The central feature of globalization is therefore that geographical distance is of declining relevance, and that territorial boundaries, such as those between nation-states, are becoming less significant. By no means, however, does globalization imply that 'the local' and 'the national' are subordinate to 'the global'. Rather, it highlights the deepening as well as the broadening of the political process, in the sense that local, national and global events (or perhaps local, regional, national, international and global events) constantly interact, as indicated in Figure 3. Globalization has nevertheless been interpreted in three ways:

- *Economic globalization* is the process through which national economies have, to a greater or lesser extent, been absorbed into a single global economy.
- *Cultural globalization* is the process whereby information, commodities and images that have been produced in one part of the world entering into a global flow that tends to 'flatten out' cultural differences between nations, regions and individuals.
- *Political globalization* is the process through which policy-making responsibilities have been passed from national governments to international organizations.

Significance

The term globalization is used to draw attention to a set of complex and multi-faceted changes that began to take place in the second half of the twentieth century. In the first place, global interdependence was one of the results of the superpower rivalry that characterized the Cold War period. The capabilities and resources of the post-1945 superpowers (the USA and the USSR) were so overwhelming that they were able to extend their influence into virtually every region of the world. Second, the spread of international trade and the transnational character of modern business organizations brought a global economy into existence. In particular, the collapse of communism gave impetus to the emergence of a global capitalist system. Third, globalization has been fuelled by technological innovation. This has affected almost every realm of existence, ranging from the development of nuclear weapons and the emergence of global pollution problems, such as acid rain and ozone depletion, to the introduction of international telephone links, satellite television and the internet. Fourth, globalization has an important politico-ideological dimension. One aspect of this has been

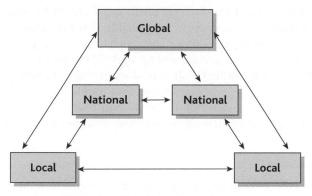

Figure 3 Global interdependencies

the spread of Western liberal political values, sometimes portrayed as the worldwide triumph of liberal democracy, but it is also linked to the growth of Islam as a transnational political creed and to burgeoning interest in green ideas and philosophies.

Much of the debate about globalization focuses on its impact on the state and its implication for national politics. Some have argued that globalization implies the 'death of politics' and the irrelevance of the state. If national economies have been absorbed effectively into a larger global economy, and if information and cultural exchanges are now routinely transnational, national government is perhaps an anachronism, even though effective supranational bodies have yet to emerge. The alternative interpretation is not that the state has become irrelevant, but that its functions have changed. In this view, economic globalization has fostered the emergence of 'competition states', states whose role is primarily to develop strategies for national prosperity in a context of intensifying transnational competition. Globalization is also significant because it has unleashed countervailing forces, in the form of ethnic politics and particularist nationalism. In an increasingly globalized world, ethnicity may replace nationality as the principal source of social integration, its virtue being that, whereas nations are bound together by 'civic' loyalties, ethnic and regional groups are able to generate a deeper sense of 'organic' identity.

Finally, there is debate about whether globalization should be embraced or resisted. Its supporters associate globalization with rising prosperity, the spread of democracy and the declining incidence of war; in this view, the only societies that suffer are those that do not participate in globalization. Its opponents nevertheless warn against the spread of capitalist values, the deepening of inequality and loss of identity. Some, indeed, suggest that globalization is largely a myth, exaggerated by politicians who wish to portray market-driven shifts in economic policy as being necessary or inevitable.

GOVERNANCE

'Governance' is a broader term than government. Though lacking a settled or agreed definition, governance refers, in its widest sense, to the various way through which social life is co-ordinated. Government can therefore be seen as one of the organizations involved in governance; it is possible, in other words, to have 'governance without government' (Rosenau and Czenpiel, 1992). The principal modes of governance are markets, hierarchies and networks. Markets co-ordinate social life through a price mechanism that is structured by the forces of supply and demand. Hierarchies, which include bureaucracy and thus traditional forms of government organization, operate through 'top-down' authority systems. Networks are 'flat' organizational forms characterized by informal relationships between essentially equal agents or social agencies.

Significance
Governance has become an increasingly popular, if imprecise, term since the 1980s. This reflects a series of changes that have taken place within government as well as

in wider society in general. These include the development of new forms of public management in which government is increasingly confined to 'steering' (that is, setting targets and strategic objectives) as opposed to 'rowing' (that is, administration or service delivery); the blurring of the distinction between government and markets through the growth of public/private partnerships and the introduction of 'internal markets'; the recognition of the importance to policy formulation of so-called policy networks; and the emergence of complex policy processes in which political authority is distributed at different levels of territorial aggregation, or what is called 'multi-level governance'. While the 'governance turn' in political analysis initially focused primarily on developments that were taking place at national or state level, growing attention has been paid since the 1990s to the phenomenon of global governance. The shift from a focus on government to a focus on governance has nevertheless not escaped ideological controversy, particularly as the latter is sometimes seen to convey a preference for a minimal state or 'less government'.

GOVERNMENT

To 'govern', in its broadest sense, is to rule or exercise control others. Government can therefore be taken to include any mechanism through which ordered rule is maintained, its central features being the ability to make collective decisions and the capacity to enforce them. A form of government can thus be identified in almost all social institutions: families, schools, businesses, trade unions and so on. However, 'government' is more commonly understood to refer to the formal and institutional processes that operate, usually at the national level, to maintain order and facilitate collective action. In that sense, government is the part of the state that guides and controls, using the instruments of law and policy. The core functions of government are thus to make law (legislation), implement law (execution) and interpret law (adjudication). In some cases, the political executive alone is referred to as 'the government', making it equivalent to 'the administration' in presidential systems. Governmental processes also operate at local, regional and international levels.

Significance

Government has traditionally been the principal object of political analysis. Some, indeed, identify politics with government, in treating political activity as the art of government, the exercise of control within society through the making and enforcement of collective decisions. This overriding concern with government has been evident in both political philosophy and political science. Political philosophers from Aristotle (384–22 BCE) onwards have evaluated forms of government on normative grounds in the hope of identifying the 'ideal' constitution. Similarly, social contract theorists focused political analysis on the nature of governmental authority and the basis of citizens' obligation to government. Political scientists who adopt the once dominant but still influential constitutional–institutional approach to the discipline also accord government central importance. This involves either analysing the legislative, executive and judicial processes of government and examining the relationships between and among different levels of government, or comparing systems of government with a view to developing a broader classification or highlighting the distinctive features of each system.

Some political thinkers have nevertheless questioned whether government is centrally important to politics. In the case of anarchism, government is rejected as being fundamentally evil and unnecessary, and political activity is focused on strategies for its abolition. Liberals, who accept that government is vital, place a heavy emphasis on the need to check or limit government in view of the potential tyranny it embodies. Marxists and feminists, for their part, tend to treat government as a secondary political formation derived from, or operating within, a wider system of, respectively, class politics or sexual politics. Academic political scientists have also in some ways looked beyond government. Systems theory, for example, examines not the mechanisms of government, but rather the structures and processes through which these interact with the larger society, while political sociology interprets the working of government in terms of wider social structures and power systems. As modern societies have become increasingly complex, political analysts have also been inclined to focus less on government as a set of institutional arrangements and more on the broader notion of 'governance'.

GREAT POWER

A great power is a state deemed to rank among the most powerful in a hierarchical state system. The criteria that define a great power are subject to dispute, but four are often identified:

- Great powers are in the first rank of military prowess, having the capacity to maintain their own security and, potentially, to influence other powers.
- They are economically powerful states, though (as Japan shows) this is a necessary but not a sufficient condition for great power status.
- They have global, and not merely regional, spheres of interests. Great powers thus differ from regional powers.
- They adopt a 'forward' foreign policy and have an actual, and not merely a potential, impact on international affairs (during its isolationist phase, the USA was thus not a 'great power').

Significance

The notion of a great power emerged as an orthodox diplomatic concept through the Concert system, which developed out of the Congress of Vienna of 1815. In the aftermath of the Napoleonic Wars, Austria, Britain, France, Prussia and Russia informally conferred the status of a great power on themselves as they assumed responsibility for managing the European state system. The concept was also acknowledged in the structure of the League of Nations in 1920 and the United Nations in 1945 – in the case of the League of Nations, through the permanent members of the Council (Britain, France and Italy, with Japan, Germany and the USSR becoming members later); and in the case of the United Nations, through the permanent 'veto powers' of the Security Council (Britain, China (originally Taiwan, but later replaced by the People's Republic), France, the USSR and the USA).

Within the field of international relations, the term great power is associated most clearly with realist analysis, where it helps to acknowledge that, despite the formal equality of states as sovereign entities, some states are significantly more powerful than others. Indeed, categorizing certain states as great powers introduces an element of order into the theoretically anarchic international system, as great powers are capable of intervening in the affairs of 'weak', and sometimes 'middling', powers. Realist theorists have therefore tended to analyse world politics in terms of the number of great powers at any point in time and the distribution of power among them, as indicated by the notion of polarity. However, the term great power has featured less prominently in academic and wider discourse since 1945, for a number of reasons. These include the belief that the Cold War had brought a new category of power into existence, in the form of the superpower; the recognition that deepening interdependence in world affairs means that no state, not even a great power, can any longer be viewed as an independent actor; and the broader shift away from state-centric approaches to world politics, with greater attention being paid to non-state actors of various kinds.

HARD/SOFT POWER

'Hard' power is the ability of one actor (usually but not necessarily a state) to influence another through the use of inducements ('carrots') or threats ('sticks'); it is sometimes called 'command power'. As such, hard power encompasses both military and economic power. 'Soft' power, by contrast, is the ability to influence other actors by persuading them to follow or agree to norms and aspirations that produce the desired behaviour. Soft power rests on the ability to shape the preferences of others by *attraction* rather than *coercion* (Nye, 2004). Whereas hard power draws on resources such as force, sanctions, payments and bribes, soft power operates largely through culture, political ideals and foreign policies (especially when these are seen to be attractive, legitimate or to possess moral authority). The use of soft power backed up by the possible use of hard power is often referred to a 'smart power' (see Figure 4).

Significance

Until the 1980s, the prevalent understanding about power in international relations was based on realist assumptions about the primacy of states and the importance of military might and economic strength in world affairs. This 'hard' conception of power nevertheless became less persuasive over time, because of a variety of developments. These included the collapse of the Cold War's bipolar threat system and an awareness of growing interdependence and interconnectedness, but of particular significance in highlighting the need for a revised understanding of power were the deep difficulties experienced by the USA after 9/11 in waging the 'war on terror'.

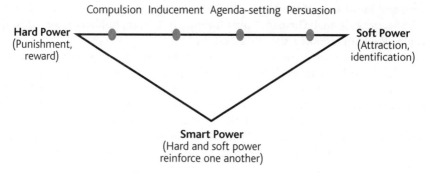

Figure 4 Hard, soft and smart power

The Bush administration's attempt to deal with the threat of terrorism primarily through military means was seen by some as counter-productive, in that it provoked increased anti-Americanism across the Arab and wider Muslim worlds, and possibly even fuelling support for terrorism. From 2009 onwards, the Obama administration placed a noticeably heavier emphasis on the use of soft-power strategies aimed at winning 'hearts and minds' across the region. This did not, however, mean that hard power was abandoned in favour of soft power; rather, the two forms of power have more commonly been used in tandem, with the balance between them fluctuating over time. There are nevertheless some cases in which soft power operates in the absence of hard power, examples sometimes cited including the Vatican, the Dalai Lama, and the governments of Canada and Norway.

HEGEMONY

Hegemony (from the Greek *hegemonia*, meaning 'leader') is, in its simplest sense, the ascendancy or domination of one element of the system over others. For example, a state that is predominant within a league, confederation or region can be said to enjoy hegemony. In Marxist theory the term is used in a more technical and specific sense. In the writings of Antonio Gramsci (1891–1937), hegemony refers to the ability of a dominant social class to exercise power by winning the consent of those it subjugates, as an alternative to the use of coercion. As a non-coercive form of class rule, hegemony is typically understood as a cultural or ideological process that operates through the dissemination of bourgeois values and beliefs throughout society. However, it also has a political and economic dimension: consent can be manipulated by pay increases, or by political or social reform.

Significance

The idea of ideological hegemony is used by Marxist theorists as an alternative to the more conventional notion of political culture. It is based on Karl Marx's (1818–83) concept of ideology, which acknowledges that the ruling class is not only the ruling material force in society, but also its ruling intellectual force. This implies both that ideas, values and beliefs are class-specific, in the sense that they reflect the distinctive social existence of each class, and that the ideas of the ruling class enjoy a decisive advantage over those of other classes, thereby becoming the 'ruling ideas of the age'. Capitalist societies are thus dominated by bourgeois ideology. Gramsci's *Prison Notebooks* (1929–35/1971) drew attention to the degree to which the class system is upheld, not simply by unequal economic and political power, but also the ruling class's spiritual and cultural supremacy, understood as hegemony. Bourgeois values and beliefs pervade civil society (the mass media, churches, youth movements, trade unions and so on), extending beyond formal learning and education and becoming the very common sense of the age. For socialism to be achieved, a 'battle of ideas' therefore has to be waged through which proletarian principles, values and theories displace, or at least challenge, bourgeois ones. The main criticisms of the idea of hegemony are that it overestimates the role of ideas in politics, amounting to a form of 'ideologism', and that it underestimates the cultural diversity of capitalist societies that have, over time, become increasingly complex and pluralistic.

HISTORICAL MATERIALISM

Historical materialism is the theory of history developed by Karl Marx (1818–83), described by his friend and collaborator Friedrich Engels (1820–95) as 'the materialist conception of history'. It highlights the importance of economic life and the conditions under which people produce and reproduce their means of subsistence. This is reflected, simplistically, in the belief that the economic 'base', consisting essentially of the 'mode of production', or economic system, conditions or determines the ideological and political 'superstructure', which encompasses all other institutions including politics, law, religion, art and so on. Another formulation of this is Marx's assertion that '[humankind's] social being determines consciousness'. Historical materialism therefore explains social, historical and cultural development in terms of material and class factors. Considerable debate has nevertheless surrounded the precise nature of the 'base/superstructure' relationship. Marx's early writings are dialectical in the sense that they acknowledge a two-way relationship between human beings and the material world, an idea that Engels attempted to acknowledge in describing economic factors as 'the *ultimately* determining element in history'. Historical materialism should be distinguished from 'dialectical materialism', which dominated intellectual life in the USSR and had an overtly mechanistic and determinist character.

Significance

Historical materialism has had considerable significance as the philosophical cornerstone of Marxism and therefore as the basis of social and political analysis for generations of Marxist thinkers. Its attraction as a means of enquiry has undoubtedly been that it promises to explain virtually all aspects of social and political existence, and uncovers the significance of processes that conventional theory ignores.

In particular, it establishes what V. I. Lenin (1870–1924) referred to as 'the primacy of economics' and allows all other aspects of life to be interpreted in material or class terms. However, historical materialism can be criticized in a number of ways. These include that it is based on questionable philosophical assumptions about the impact material production and social existence have on consciousness, and that there are technical difficulties regarding the precise meaning of and relationship between the 'base' and the 'superstructure'. Moreover, as neo-Marxists accept, it overstates the importance of economics and threatens to turn into a form of materialist reductionism. The final problem is that, if the 'base' *determines* the 'superstructure', then historical materialism is determinist, and if it does not, the theory has no predictive value.

HUMAN DEVELOPMENT

Human development is a standard of human well-being that takes into account of people's ability to develop their full potential and lead fulfilled and creative lives in accordance with their needs and interests. It is often simply defined in terms of enlarging people's choices. The idea of human development has been elaborated most fully through the Human Development Index (HDI), which is used to rank countries in the UN's *Human Development Reports*. The key HDIs are:

- Leading a long and healthy life (life expectancy and health profile)
- Acquiring knowledge (education and literacy)
- Access to resources needed for a decent standard of living (fuel, sanitation, shelter and so on)
- Preserving resources for future generations (demographic trends and sustainability)
- Ensuring human security (food, jobs, crime, the alleviation of personal distress)
- Achieving equality for all women and men (education, careers/jobs, political participation).

Significance

The notion of human development has been central to the UN's approach to poverty and development since 1990, when the first *Human Development Report* was published. It emerged as a result of growing dissatisfaction with a narrowly income-based definition of poverty (for example, using 1 US dollar a day as the marker for the international poverty line). This stemmed from a recognition that that poor people suffer from multiple deprivation involving a failure to meet their non-material needs as well as their material ones. Amartya Sen (1999) contributed to such thinking in pointing out that famines often arise not from a lack of food, but from a complex of social, economic and political factors such as rising food prices, poor food distribution systems and government inefficiency. Poverty is therefore as much about restricting opportunities and the absence of freedom, in particular positive freedom, as it is about lack of income and resources.

HUMAN NATURE

Human nature refers to the essential and immutable character of all human beings. It highlights what is innate and 'natural' about human life, as opposed to what human beings have gained from education or through social experience. This does not, however, mean that those who believe that human behaviour is shaped more by society than it is by unchanging and inborn characteristics have abandoned the idea of human nature. Rather, such a view makes clear assumptions about innate human qualities; in this case, the capacity to be shaped or moulded by external factors. Moreover, a concept of human nature does not reduce human life to a one-dimensional caricature. Most political thinkers are aware that human beings are complex, multifaceted creatures, made up of biological, physical, psychological, intellectual, social and perhaps spiritual elements. The concept of human nature does not conceal or overlook this complexity so much as attempt to impose order on it by designating certain features as natural or 'essential'. While this human 'core' will usually be manifest in human behaviour, this is not necessarily the case. Human beings may, for example, be encouraged to deny their 'true' natures through the influence of a corrupt society.

Significance

Almost all political doctrines and beliefs are based on some kind of theory of human nature, sometimes formulated explicitly but in many cases simply implied. Assumptions regarding the content of human nature structure political enquiry in a number of important ways. The most obvious of these is the so-called 'nurture/nature' debate, the question of whether the essential core of human nature is fixed or given, fashioned by 'nature', or whether it is moulded or structured through social experience or 'nurture'. An emphasis on nature, as adopted, for example, by most liberals and conservatives, suggests that the individual is the key to the understanding of society: social and political life ultimately reflect characteristics and behavioural patterns that are innate within each human being. This is evident in methodological individualism. On the other hand, nurture theorists, including most socialists, communists and anarchists, argue that as human nature is 'plastic', the human character and sensibilities can be developed through the reconstruction of society. In this case, society provides the key to the understanding of the individual.

Another important debate about human nature centres on the relative importance of competition and co-operation. Much of liberal ideology and many of the ideas of conventional social and political science reflect assumptions about self-seeking and egotistical human behaviour. If human beings are essentially greedy and competitive, a capitalist economic system is natural and inevitable. However, socialists have traditionally stressed that human beings are naturally sociable, co-operative and gregarious, motivated by altruism and a sense of social responsibility. From this perspective, capitalism merely serves to corrupt human nature by suppressing our inclination towards collective human endeavour and equality. Only a limited number of political thinkers have openly rejected the idea of human nature. Jean-

Paul Sartre (1905–80), however, argued that 'existence comes before essence', meaning that human beings enjoy the freedom to define themselves through their own actions and deeds. If this is so, the assertion of any concept of human nature is an affront to that freedom.

HUMAN RIGHTS

Human rights are rights to which people are entitled by virtue of being human; they are a modern and secular version of 'natural' rights, which were believed to be God-given. Human rights are therefore universal, fundamental and absolute. They are universal in the sense that they belong to all humans everywhere, regardless of nationality, ethnic or racial origin, social background and so on. They are fundamental in that they are inalienable: human rights can be denied or violated but a human being's entitlement to them cannot be removed. They are absolute in that, as the basic grounds for living a genuinely human life, they cannot be qualified (though some argue that all rights are relative as they conflict with one another, rights being a 'zero-sum' game). Human rights can be distinguished from civil rights, on the grounds that the former are moral principles that claim universal jurisdiction, while the latter depend on the freedoms and status accorded citizens in particular societies. However, the notions of civil rights and civil liberties often rest on an underlying belief in human rights, and are viewed as moral principles given legal expression in the form of citizenship.

Significance

In certain parts of the world, human rights have come to be accorded a near-religious significance. Supporters of human rights argue that they constitute the basic grounds for freedom, equality and justice, and embody the idea that all human lives are worthy of respect. In that sense, human rights can be said to give political expression to moral values found in all the world's major religions and these transcend conventional ideological divisions. As such they have been accepted as one of the cornerstones of international law, sometimes being viewed as superior to state sovereignty and thereby being used to justify humanitarian and even military intervention (as in cases such as Iraq and Serbia in the 1990s). The most authoritative definition of human rights is found in the United Nations Declaration of Human Rights (1948), though other documents, such as the European Convention on Human Rights and Fundamental Freedoms (1953), have also been influential.

However, the doctrine of human rights has also attracted criticism. A variety of philosophical difficulties have been raised. These include the arguments that human rights are merely moral assertions and lack any empirical justification; that it is difficult to view them as absolute because rights, such as the right to life and the right to self-defence, are often balanced against one another; and that it is not always clear when a person should be regarded as 'human' and therefore entitled to human rights (which is particularly controversial in relation to abortion). Political objections come from conservatives and communitarians, who point out that it is nonsense to suggest that individuals have rights that are separate from the traditions, cultures and societies to which they belong. Marxists, for their part, have argued traditionally that natural or human rights protect private property by giving all people the right to use their unequal social resources. Finally, it is often claimed that human rights are intrinsically linked to the ideas and assumptions of political liberalism. In this case, to portray them as being universally applicable is to indulge in a form of ideological imperialism, suggesting that Western liberal values are superior to all others.

HUMANITARIAN INTERVENTION

Humanitarian intervention refers to military intervention that is carried out in pursuit of humanitarian rather than strategic objectives. However, the term is contested and deeply controversial, not least because, by portraying an intervention as 'humanitarian', it is deemed to be legitimate and defensible. The use of the term is therefore necessarily evaluative and subjective. Nevertheless, some define humanitarian intervention in terms of intentions: an intervention is 'humanitarian' if it is motivated *primarily* by the desire to prevent harm to other people, accepting that there will always be mixed motives for intervention. Others define humanitarian intervention in terms of outcomes: an intervention is 'humanitarian' only if it results in a net improvement in conditions and a reduction in human suffering.

Significance

Key examples of humanitarian intervention (Northern Iraq, Haiti, Kosovo, East Timor and so on) occurred during the 1990s, which is often seen as the 'golden age' of humanitarian intervention. This happened for a number of reasons. First, the end of the Cold War appeared to have brought an end to an age of power politics. This allowed (albeit briefly) a 'liberal peace' to reign, founded on a common recognition of international norms and standards of morality. Second, in a world of '24/7' news and current affairs, and global television coverage and communications, governments often came under considerable public pressure to act in the event of humanitarian crises and emergencies. Third, emergence of the USA as the world's sole superpower created circumstance in which Russia and China were (temporarily) unwilling or unable to block the USA, the major driving force behind most interventions. However, the incidences of humanitarian intervention declined markedly after the advent of the 'war on terror', not least because of the difficulties the USA and its allies experienced in extricating themselves from military involvements in Afghanistan and Iraq (even though neither was an example of humanitarian intervention).

Humanitarian intervention nevertheless remains one of the most hotly disputed issues in world politics. Its proponents tend to argue that, in the light of the doctrine of human rights, moral responsibilities can no longer be confined merely to one's own people or state. There is therefore an obligation to 'save strangers', if the resources exist to do so and the cost is not disproportionate. Such thinking has led to the wider acceptance of the principle of the 'responsibility to protect' (R2P), under which intervention is justified in the event of an actual or apprehended large-scale loss of life or large-scale ethnic cleansing. Humanitarian intervention has also been defended on the grounds that it may help to prevent, for instance regional instability of major refugee crises. Critics, however, emphasize that humanitarian intervention is a flagrant breach of international law, which is grounded in the norm of state sovereignty and only authorizes intervention in the case of self-defence. Furthermore, however well intentioned interventions may be, there is a danger that they will do more harm than good, setting off chains of events that are difficult to predict and still more difficult to control.

IDEALISM

Idealism is understood in one of two senses, metaphysical and political. *Metaphysical idealism* is the belief that, in the final analysis, only ideas exist. The structure of reality is thus understood in terms of consciousness, as in the work of Plato (427–347 BCE), Immanuel Kant (1724–1804) and G. W. F. Hegel (1770–1831). Kant's 'transcendental idealism' holds that meaning is not inherent in the external world but is imposed by the knowing subject. Idealism in this sense contrasts with philosophical materialism (as opposed to historical materialism), the belief that nothing exists except matter, and empiricism, the theory that knowledge is derived from experience or observation of the external world. *Political idealism* refers to theories or practices characterized by an unbending commitment to stipulated ideals or principles (the term is sometimes used pejoratively to suggest a belief in an impossible goal). As a theoretical school of international politics, idealism views international relations from the perspective of values and norms, such as justice, peace and international law. It thus contrasts with realism in that it is concerned less with empirical analysis (with how international actors behave) than with normative judgements (with how they should behave). Political idealism may be seen as a species of utopianism.

Significance

Metaphysical idealism underpinned much of the political philosophy of the classical, medieval and early modern periods. Its strength was that, in holding that values such as justice, natural law and reason are implicit in the structure of reality itself, it gave thinkers a firm and universalist perspective from which to judge existing arrangements and engage in political advocacy. However, the status of metaphysical individualism was gradually eroded by the emergence of empirical and scientific approaches to political theorizing. Political idealism has been criticized on the grounds that it encourages political energies to be expended on goals that may be unrealistic or unachievable; that it fails to recognize the extent to which political action is determined by practical considerations such as the pursuit of power or the satisfaction of material interests; and that, in any case, political ideals may be contested and lack universal authority. For example, realist theorists in international politics have long ridiculed the idealist's faith in collective security and international harmony. Nevertheless, as examples such as Mahatma Gandhi (1869–1948) and Martin Luther King (1929–68) demonstrate, idealism has an undoubted and enduring capacity to inspire commitment and stimulate political activism. Similarly, to downgrade the importance of ideals and principles in political analysis may simply be to legitimize power-seeking and unprincipled behaviour. Thus, disenchantment with the amoral power politics of the superpower era has led in international politics to the emergence of neo-idealism, a perspective that emphasizes the practical value of morality and, in particular, of respect for human rights and national interdependence.

IDENTITY POLITICS

Identity politics is an orientation towards social theorizing and political practice, rather than a coherent body of ideas with a settled political character. Its central feature is that it seeks to challenge and overthrow oppression by reshaping a group's identity through what amounts to a process of politico-cultural self-assertion. Manifestations of identity politics are varied and diverse, ranging from second-wave feminism and the gay and lesbian movement to ethnic nationalism, multiculturalism and religious fundamentalism. Identity can therefore be reshaped around many principles – gender, sexuality, culture, ethnicity, religion and so on. All forms of identity politics nevertheless exhibit two characteristic beliefs. First, group marginalization is understood not merely as a legal, political or social phenomenon, but is, rather, a cultural phenomenon. Second, subordination can be challenged by reshaping identity to give the group concerned a sense of (usually publicly proclaimed) pride and self-respect – 'black is beautiful', 'gay pride' and so on.

Significance

While identity politics can be traced back to the emergence of the black consciousness movement in the early decades of the twentieth century, it has had its greatest impact since the 1970s. The upsurge in identity politics occurred in the light of growing attacks on liberal universalism, as greater emphasis was placed on the issues of difference and diversity, and the decline of socialism, which, until the 1970s, had been the dominant means through which the interests of subordinate groups had been expressed. The potency of identity politics derives from its capacity to expose and challenge the deeper processes through which group marginalization and subordination take place. As such, it goes beyond conventional approaches to social advancement, based on the politics of rights (liberalism) and the politics of redistribution (social democracy), and instead offers a politics of recognition, based on an assertion of group solidarity. Identity politics has nevertheless also attracted significant criticism. Among other things, detractors have argued that it 'miniaturizes' humanity, by seeing people only in terms of group belonging; that it fosters division, often because it embraces exclusive and quasi-absolutist notions of identity; and that it embodies tensions and contradictions (for example, between the women's liberation movement and patriarchal religious fundamentalists).

IDEOLOGY

Ideology is one of the most contested of political terms. It is now used most widely in a social-scientific sense to refer to a more or less coherent set of ideas that provide the basis for some kind of organized political action. In this sense all ideologies therefore, first, offer an account or critique of the existing order, usually in the form of a 'world view'; second, provide the model of a desired future, a vision of the 'good society'; and, third, outline how political change can and should be brought about (see Figure 5). Ideologies thus straddle the conventional boundaries between descriptive and normative thought, and between theory and practice. However, the term was coined by Destutt de Tracy (1754–1836) to describe a new 'science of ideas', literally an 'idea-ology'. Karl Marx (1818–83) used ideology to refer to ideas that serve the interests of the ruling class by concealing the contradictions of class society, thereby promoting false consciousness and political passivity among subordinate classes. In this view, a clear distinction can be drawn between ideology and science, representing falsehood and truth, respectively. Later Marxists adopted a neutral concept of ideology, regarding it as the distinctive ideas of any social class, including the working class. Some liberals, particularly during the Cold War period, have viewed ideology as an officially sanctioned belief system that claims a monopoly of truth, often through a spurious claim to be scientific. Conservative thinkers have sometimes followed Michael Oakeshott (1901–90) in treating ideologies as elaborate systems of thought that orientate politics towards abstract principles and goals and away from practical and historical circumstances.

Significance

The concept of ideology has had a controversial career. For much of its history, ideology has carried starkly pejorative implications, being used as a political weapon to criticize or condemn rival political stances. Indeed, its changing significance and use can be linked to shifting patterns of political antagonism. Marxists, for example, have variously interpreted liberalism, conservatism and fascism as forms of 'bourgeois ideology', committed to the mystification and subordination of the oppressed proletariat. Marxist interest in ideology, often linked to Antonio

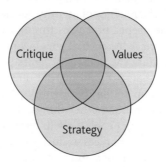

Figure 5 Political ideology

Gramsci's (1891–1937) theory of ideological hegemony, grew markedly during the twentieth century as Marxist thinkers sought to explain the failure of Marx's prediction of proletarian revolution. The deepening of the Cold War in the 1950s encouraged liberal theorists to identify similarities between fascism and communism, both being inherently repressive 'official' ideologies that suppressed opposition and demanded regimented obedience. However, the 1950s and 1960s also witnessed growing claims that ideology had become superfluous and redundant, most openly through the 'end of ideology' thesis advanced by Daniel Bell (1960). This view reflected not only the declining importance in the West of ideologies such as communism and fascism, but also that similarities between liberalism, conservatism and socialism had apparently become more prominent than their differences.

Nevertheless, the proclaimed demise of ideology has simply not materialized. Since the 1960s, ideology has been accorded a more important and secure place in political analysis, for a number of reasons. First, the wider use of the social-scientific definition of ideology means that the term no longer carries political baggage and can be applied to all 'isms' or action-orientated political philosophies. Second, a range of new ideological traditions have steadily emerged, including feminism and ecologism in the 1960s, the New Right in the 1970s and religious fundamentalism in the 1980s. Third, the decline of simplistically behavioural approaches to politics has led to growing interest in ideology both as a means of recognizing how far political action is structured by the beliefs and values of political actors, and as a way of acknowledging that political analysis always bears the imprint of values and assumptions that the analyst him- or herself brings to it.

IMPERIALISM

Imperialism is the policy of extending the power or rule of a state beyond its boundaries. In its earliest usage, imperialism was an ideology that supported military expansion and imperial acquisition, usually by drawing on nationalist or racialist doctrines. The term is now used more commonly used to describe the system of political domination or economic exploitation that the pursuit of such goals helps to establish. The key feature of imperialism is therefore the asymmetrical relationship between the imperial power and its client territory or peoples. A distinction is often drawn between imperialism and colonialism. Some treat colonialism as a distinctive form of imperialism, in that colonies are territorially ruled directly by the imperial power, whereas empires may allow client rulers to continue in power and enjoy significant discretion; others point out that imperial territories may be inhabited by members of the same ethnic group, whereas the inhabitants of colonies are typically ethnically distinct from their colonial rulers; and others emphasize that colonies have been settled or 'colonized' and have not merely been subject to imperial conquest. What is called *neo-imperialism* or 'neo-colonialism' refers to the process through which industrially developed powers control foreign territory by economic or cultural domination while respecting the territory's formal political independence.

Significance

The phenomenon of imperialism has been ever-present in politics. Empires have, in fact, been the most common supranational bodies, ranging from the ancient empires of Egypt, China, Persia and Rome to the modern European empires of Britain, France, Portugal and the Netherlands. Although colonies continue to exist – for example, Tibet's subordination to China – the collapse of the USSR in 1991 brought to an end the last of the major empires, the Russian empire. Modern imperialism therefore usually takes the form of neo-colonialism and operates through structures of economic and cultural domination rather than overt political control. Debates about the merits of imperialism have also largely been abandoned. Nineteenth-century justifications for imperialism, in terms of the capacity of European colonizers to bring about moral and social development in Africa and Asia in particular, are now exposed as crass self-justifications. Quite simply, the acceptance of modern ideas such as democracy and national sovereignty means that imperialism is universally condemned as a form of oppression or exploitation.

The major debates about imperialism centre on its causes and the forms it takes. In the Marxist tradition, imperialism is seen as an economic phenomenon that typically results from the pressure to export capital. V. I. Lenin (1870–1924) was the principal exponent of this view, arguing that imperialism is the 'highest' (that is, the final) stage of capitalism. However, rival views suggest that imperialism is often fuelled by political rather than economic factors and is more commonly linked to popular nationalism than to the desire for profit; that imperialism is not confined to capitalist states but has been practised by pre-capitalist as well as socialist ones; and that imperialism may prove to be an economic burden to imperial powers and not a boon, most commonly in the form of 'imperial overreach' (the tendency of expansionism to impose increases in military expenditure that outstrip the growth of the domestic economy). Debates about modern imperialism are dominated by the neo-Marxist emphasis on the structure of global capitalism and the growing power of transnational corporations. In this view, the global structure of production and exchange has divided the world into 'core' and 'peripheral' areas. Core areas in the industrialized North are technologically advanced and better integrated into the global economy, while peripheral areas, such as the less developed South, provide a source of cheap labour and are characterized by underdevelopment and a simple product mix.

INDIVIDUALISM

Individualism is a belief in the primacy, or supreme importance, of the individual over any social group or collective body. It is usually viewed as the opposite of collectivism. Individualism, however, may be either a descriptive or a normative concept. As a descriptive concept, in the form of *methodological individualism*, it suggests that the individual is central to any political theory or social explanation – all statements about society should be made in terms of the individuals who compose it. As Margaret Thatcher put it, 'there is no such thing as society, only individuals and their families'. As a normative concept, in the form of ethical individualism, it implies that society should be constructed so as to benefit the individual, giving priority to the individual's rights, needs or interests.

What ethical individualism means in practice nevertheless depends on one's view of the individual or theory of human nature. In its most familiar form, *egoistical individualism* (also called 'market', 'possessive' or 'atomistic' individualism), it stresses human self-interestedness and self-reliance. The individual is the exclusive possessor of his or her own talents, owing nothing to society and being owed nothing in return (this form of individualism overlaps most clearly with methodological individualism). On the other hand, what may be called *developmental individualism* emphasizes personal growth and human flourishing, and is expressed in the idea of individuality. As this form of individualism allows for social responsibility and even altruism, it blurs the distinction between individualism and collectivism.

Significance

The doctrine of individualism emerged in the seventeenth and eighteenth centuries as a result of the development of market or capitalist societies, in which individuals were expected to make a wider range of economic and social choices and to take personal responsibility for their own lives. It constitutes the basic principle of liberalism and, as such, has come to be one of the major components of Western political culture. Methodological individualism has a long and impressive history, having been employed by social contract theorists such as Thomas Hobbes (1588–1679) and John Locke (1632–1704), by utilitarians such as Jeremy Bentham (1748–1832), by economic theorists from Adam Smith (1723–90) onwards, and by modern rational choice theorists. Its attraction as a mode of analysis is that it enables theories to be constructed on the basis of seemingly empirical, and even scientific, observations about human behaviour. In short, understand the individual, and social and political institutions and mechanisms become explicable. However, the drawback of any form of methodological individualism is that it is both asocial and ahistorical. By building political theories on the basis of a pre-established model of human nature, individualists ignore the fact that human behaviour varies from society to society, and from one historical period to the next. If experience and the social environment shape human nature, the individual should be seen as the product of society, not the reverse.

As an ethical or political principle, however, individualism has usually had strongly anti-statist implications. For classical liberals, the New Right and individualist anarchists, the central thrust of individualism is to expand the realm of civil society and the 'private' sphere at the expense of political authority. Individualism thus implies negative freedom, the expansion of individual choice and responsibilities. However, this egoistical individualism has been rejected by socialists, traditional conservatives and modern communitarians. In the view of socialists, individualism promotes greed and competition, weakening the bonds of community; in the view of conservatives, it produces insecurity and rootlessness and undermines traditional values; and in the view of communitarians, it robs society of its capacity to establish moral order and encourage collective endeavour.

INSTITUTIONALISM

An institution is an enduring and stable set of arrangements that regulates individual and/or group behaviour on the basis of established rules and procedures. Political institutions have a formal and often legal character, employ explicit and usually enforceable rules and decision-making procedures, and are typically part of the machinery of the state. For this reason, political institutions have been defined as 'the rules of the game'. Examples of political institutions include constitutions, elections, parliaments, bureaucracies, judiciaries, party systems and so on. Institutionalism, as an approach to political analysis, is the attempt to make sense of political realities by studying the causes and consequences of political institutions. It thus views institutions as political actors in their own right, independent of and capable of influencing wider social, economic and cultural forces.

Traditional institutionalism took political institutions to be the key political actors in that it encouraged reflection on politics to focus on descriptions of institutional behaviour, the analysis of formal or legal rules, or a comparative or historical examination of institutional structures. The idea of *new institutionalism* or neo-institutionalism has been increasingly fashionable since the 1980s. While it does not have a clear or developed meaning, it tends to be characterized by a recognition of the importance of informal as well as formal institutions, and looks beyond traditional institutionalism by accepting that formal–legal approaches to political understanding have only a limited value. As such, it reflects a shift in perspective away from government and towards governance. The principal forms that new institutionalism has taken are historical institutionalism, rational-choice institutionalism and sociological institutionalism.

Significance

Institutionalism was the dominant tradition of political analysis until the 1950s. In a sense it can be traced back to the classical political theory of Plato (427–347 BCE) and Aristotle (384–322 BCE), and was developed by Niccolò Machiavelli (1469–1527), Thomas Hobbes (1588–1679), John Locke (1632–1704) and Jean-Jacques Rousseau (1712–78), in that such thinkers not only grappled with political ideals such as justice, order and freedom, but also examined the political institutions most likely to secure these political goods. In the nineteenth and early twentieth centuries, this developed into a constitutional-institutional approach to political analysis that emphasized, for example, differences between codified and uncodified constitutions, parliamentary and presidential systems, and federal and unitary systems. However, the institutional approach became distinctively less fashionable in the 1950s and 1960s in the light of the rise of behaviouralism, systems theory and subsequently a growing interest in Marxism.

The main criticisms of institutionalism are that it is guilty of the sin of what David Easton (1981) called 'hyperfactualism', a reverence for facts and a disregard for theory; that it ignores non-institutional influences on policy and the distribution of power; and that it is an entirely state-centred approach to politics that ignores the degree to which the state is linked to and shaped by society. Nevertheless, institutionalism continued to be a significant school of political analysis and, since the 1970s, has been revived through a growing interest in constitutional reform, public administration and policy analysis. While an exclusive focus on institutions may reduce political analysis to dull legalism, to neglect political institutions on the grounds that they may be merely a reflection of, for example, the utility-maximizing behaviour of their members (as rational choice theory suggests), the distribution of power among groups (pluralism or elitism), or the basic economic structure of society (Marxism), is to ignore the fact that state structures and the organization of government matter.

INTERDEPENDENCE

Interdependence refers to a relationship between two or more parties in which each is affected by decisions that are taken by the others. Interdependent relationships are thus characterized by reciprocal causation, or mutual conditioning. Thus, if A, B and C are interdependent, any change in B will result in a change in A and C; any change in A will result in changes in B and C; and any change in C will result in changes in A and B. Interdependence makes it difficult to think in terms of linear, causal relationships; meaning that events may have an unpredictable and seemingly arbitrary character (as highlighted by chaos theory). More radically, it makes it difficult to think in terms of 'A-ness', 'B-ness' and so on, or, indeed, in terms of 'thing-ness' in any sense.

Significance

The concept of interdependence plays a major role in ecologism and liberalism in particular. A belief in interdependence suffuses ecological thought, its central principle, ecology, reflecting the idea that all organisms are sustained by self-regulating natural systems – ecosystems – composed of living and non-living elements. Such thinking is taken furthest in what is called 'deep' ecology, the green ideological perspective that totally rejects anthropocentrism (human-centredness) and gives priority instead to the maintenance of nature. It is often claimed that that this implies a paradigm shift, as the mechanistic thinking that is associated with conventional science (which views the world as a 'Newtonian world machine') is overthrown and replaced by a new paradigm that stresses organicism or holism. Holism is particularly important in this respect, as it advances the belief that the whole is more important than its component parts, implying that nature is ultimately an indivisible whole. This image is one of radical interdependence.

While interdependence is by no means as philosophically integral to liberalism as it is to ecologism (indeed, individualism, the core principle of liberalism, emphasizes separation and independence rather than connectedness and interdependence), certain liberal theories rely heavily on assumptions about interdependence. This certainly applies in the case of economic liberalism, which justifies laissez-faire principles on the grounds that the complex interactions within a market economy – between employers and employees, buyers and sellers and so on – tend naturally towards equilibrium. Markets are therefore self-regulating. Similar thinking has been applied to liberal theorizing about international affairs. For example, nineteenth-century 'commercial' liberals extolled the virtues of free trade in promoting general prosperity and reducing the incidence of war, based on economic interdependence. In the modern period, neoliberal institutionalists such as Keohane and Nye (1977) have highlighted the growth of 'complex interdependence, reflecting the extent to which peoples and governments in the contemporary world are affected by what happens elsewhere, a development associated with globalization but also factors ranging from climate change to human rights.

INTERGOVERNMENTALISM

Intergovernmentalism is any form of interaction between states which takes place on the basis of sovereign independence. Intergovernmentalism is therefore usually distinguished from supranationalism, in which there is an authority that is 'higher' than that of the nation-state. The most common form of intergovernmentalism is treaties or alliances, the simplest of which involve bilateral agreements between states. The intergovernmental aspect of treaties is embodied in the fact that they are voluntary agreements based on the consent of all relevant parties. The other main forms of intergovernmentalism are leagues or confederations, such as the League of Nations, the Organization of Petroleum Exporting Countries (OPEC), the Organisation for Economic Co-operation and Development (OECD), and the Commonwealth of Nations. These are transnational or international organizations of states, in which sovereignty is preserved through a process of unanimous decision-making that gives each state a veto, at least over matters of vital national importance.

Significance

Intergovernmentalism has been the most common form of international co-operation between states. Its growing significance from the twentieth century onwards reflects both a recognition of the greater independence of states, which has spread from strategic and economic matters into political, social and cultural spheres of life, and the fact that intergovernmental bodies are relatively easy to form. Treaties, alliances, leagues and confederations have the virtue that they allow states to work together and perhaps undertake concerted action but without sacrificing national independence. In cases such as OPEC's ability to regulate oil prices, particularly in the 1970s and 1980s, co-ordinated action through intergovernmental co-operation has been very effective.

However, the preservation of state sovereignty is also the central weakness of intergovernmentalism. In short, it restricts the scope of international co-operation to those areas where mutual trust exists, and where national interests clearly coincide. International treaties, for example, may be broken with impunity and, in cases such as arms control, they are very difficult to negotiate. Similarly, as member states retain their independence and are very reluctant to be bound by majority decisions, confederations have rarely been able to undertake united and effective action, sometimes being reduced to mere talking shops. This is why some confederations, such as the Confederation of Independent States (CIS), formed in 1991 by the former Soviet republics, have become entirely irrelevant, while others, such as the European Economic Community (EEC), later transformed into the European Union (EU), have gradually given way to supranational co-operation based on the principle of federalism.

INTERNATIONAL AID

International aid (sometimes called 'foreign' aid or 'overseas' aid) refers to the transfer of goods or services from one country to another, motivated, at least in part, by the desire to benefit the recipient country or its people. Aid may take the form of the provision of funds, resources and equipment, or of staff and expertise. While *bilateral aid* is direct country-to-country aid, *multilateral aid* is provided by or through an international organization. *Humanitarian aid* (or emergency relief) differs from *development aid*, in that the former addresses immediate and basic needs, whereas the latter is concerned with longer-term projects. The term 'international aid' is controversial because it assigns an altruistic motive to actions that may essentially be self-serving, as aid is not always clearly humanitarian (loans are often treated as aid, for example).

Significance

International aid is the principal way in which countries discharge their development responsibilities and help to promote socio-economic development in another countries. Nevertheless, considerable controversy surrounds the issue of whether international aid works The key argument in favour of aid is that it serves to counter structural disparities within the global economy that favour rich countries at the expense of poor ones, not least to do with the impact of free trade. The idea that self-reliance and global market forces will 'raise all boats' is therefore fundamentally wrong. In this view, the solution to global poverty is not only for rich countries to boost their levels of international aid, but also to ensure that, aside from humanitarian relief, aid is targeted on long-term development projects and orientated around capacity-building for the future. Some argue further that there is a moral duty to provide international aid, as the wealth and prosperity of the global North has been, in substantial part, built on the mistreatment of the global South.

The idea that international aid promotes development has not gone unchallenged, however. Economic liberals have even gone as far as to argue that aid is a 'poverty trap', helping to entrench deprivation and perpetuate global disparities. From this perspective, international aid tends to promote dependency, sap initiative and undermine the operation of free markets. A major factor accounting for this gloomy picture has been the growth in corruption. Government-to-government aid to authoritarian or dictatorial regimes is therefore often siphoned off for the benefit of elite groups and contributes little to the alleviation of poverty or deprivation. Moreover, aid is rarely donated disinterestedly. Realist theorists argue that aid, if it is provided at all, invariably reflects donor-state national interests. It comes with 'strings attached', often related to trade agreements. Similarly, food aid that appears to be designed to relieve hunger commonly takes the form of 'food dumping', which undercuts local farmers, who cannot compete and may be driven out of jobs and into poverty.

INTERNATIONAL LAW

International law is the law that governs states and other international actors. As defined by the Statute of the International Court of Justice (ICJ), there are four sources of international law: treaties and international conventions, international custom, the general principles of law, and legal scholarship. There are two branches of international law: private and public. Private international law refers to the regulation of international activities carried out by individuals, companies and other non-state actors. As such, it relates to the overlapping jurisdictions of domestic legal systems, and so is sometimes called a 'conflict of laws'. Public international law applies to states, which are viewed as legal 'persons'. As such, it deals with government-to-government relations as well as those between states and international organizations or other actors. International law nevertheless differs from domestic law in that it operates in the absence of an international legislative body and system of enforcement.

Significance

International law is an unusual phenomenon. As traditionally understood, law consists of a set of compulsory and enforceable rules, reflecting the will of a sovereign power. And yet no central authority exists in international politics that is capable of enforcing rules, legal or otherwise. International law is therefore 'soft' rather than 'hard' law. Some, as a result, dismiss the idea of international law as nothing more than a collection of moral principles and ideals. Nevertheless, international law has greater substance and significance than first appearances might suggest. In particular, more often than not, international law is obeyed and respected, meaning that it provides an important – and, indeed, an increasingly important – framework within which states and other international actors interact. The main reasons why states comply with international law include self-interest (it establishes a framework of reciprocal relationships that make inter-state relations more orderly and predicable) and the reputational damage that breaching international law may cause.

The scope and purpose of international law have become a matter of increasing dispute in recent decades, however. In its traditional or 'classical' tradition, international law has been firmly state-centric. This is the sense in which it is properly called 'international' law: it is a form of law that governs states and determines relations among states, and its founding principle is state sovereignty. The ICJ, the principal judicial organ of the United Nations, operates on the basis of this conception of international law, which means that its scope is strictly confined to arbitration in relation to disputes between states. A rival conception, which can be traced back probably to the impact of World War I on Western consciousness, but which has gained particular prominence since the 1990s, is concerned more with justice than with order. International law has been transformed into what is sometimes called 'supranational' or 'world' law by the growing recognition of individuals, corporations, NGOs and other non-state bodies as legal 'persons'. This has allowed ad hoc international criminal tribunals and the International Criminal Court (ICC), founded in 2002, to take action over a wide range of human rights and humanitarian issues. However, it also creates confusion, as the disputed legality of humanitarian intervention highlights.

INTERNATIONAL ORGANIZATION

An international organization (sometimes called an international governmental organization, or IGO) is an institution with formal procedures and a membership comprising three or more states. International organizations are characterized by rules that seek to regulate relations among member states and by a formal structure that implements and enforces these rules. Nevertheless, international organizations may be viewed as instruments, arenas or actors (Ritterberger et al., 2012). As *instruments*, they are mechanisms through which states pursue their own interests. As *arenas*, they facilitate debate and information exchange, serving as permanent institutions of conference diplomacy. As *actors*, they enable states to take concerted action, which requires some measure of 'pooled' sovereignty.

Significance

The number and membership of international organizations gradually increased during the nineteenth and early twentieth centuries, with major surges coming after both World War I and World War II. This process reflected not only an awareness of growing interdependencies among states, linked to concerns over power politics, economic crises, human rights violations, developmental disparities and environmental degradation, but also the emerging hegemonic role of the USA, which saw the pursuit of US national interests and the promotion of international co-operation as being mutually sustaining goals. By the mid-1980s, the number of international organizations had reached 378, with the average membership per organization standing at over 40 (compared with 18.6 in 1945). Despite their number subsequently declining, largely because of the dissolution of Soviet bloc organizations at the end of the Cold War, this masks a substantial growth in international agencies and other institutions, as the number of bodies spawned by international organizations themselves has continued to grow.

Nevertheless, there is significant debate about the nature and role of international organizations. From the liberal institutionalist perspective, for example, states co-operate through the auspices of international bodies because it is in their collective interests to do so. This does not imply that state interests are always harmoniously in agreement, but only that there are important, and growing, areas of mutual interest where co-operation among states is rational and sensible. International organizations are therefore a reflection of the extent of interdependence in the global system, an acknowledgement by states that they can often achieve more by working together than by working separately. Realists, on the other hand, tend to be more sceptical about international organizations. In their view, as world politics continue to be shaped by the struggle for power among states rather than a harmony of interests, there is little scope for the levels of co-operation and trust that would allow international organizations to develop into meaningful and significant bodies. Moreover, in so far as they exert influence, realists tend to view international organizations as mechanisms for pursuing the interests of major states – in particular those of hegemonic powers.

INTERNATIONAL RELATIONS

The term 'international relations' was coined by Jeremy Bentham (1748–1832), and used in his *Principles of Morals and Legislation* ([1789] 1948). Bentham's use of the term acknowledged a significant shift: that, by the late eighteenth century, territorially-based political units were beginning to have a more clearly national character, making relations between them appear genuinely 'inter-national'. However, while most states are, or aspire to be, nation-states, it is the possession of statehood rather than nationhood that allows them to act effectively on the world stage. 'International' politics should thus, more properly, be described as 'inter-state' relations.

The academic discipline of international relations (frequently shortened to IR) emerged in the aftermath of World War I, and was largely shaped by the desire to uncover the conditions for enduring peace (a concern with policy relevance that has never applied in the same way to political science). The central focus of the discipline has been on the relations of states, and those relations have traditionally been understood in diplomatic, military and strategic terms. However, the nature and focus of the discipline has changed significantly over time, not least through a series of so-called 'great debates':

- The first 'great debate' took place between the 1930s and the 1950s, and was between liberal internationalists, who emphasized the possibility of peaceful co-operation, and realists, who believed in inescapable power politics. By the 1950s, realism had gained ascendancy within the discipline.
- The second took place during the 1960s and was between behaviouralists and traditionalists over whether it is possible to develop objective laws of international relations.
- The third, sometimes called the 'inter-paradigm debate', was between realists and liberals, on the one hand, and Marxists on the other, who interpreted international relations in economic terms.

- The fourth began in the late 1980s, and was between positivists and so-called post-positivists over the relationship between theory and practice. This reflected the growing influence within IR of a range of critical perspectives, including constructivism, critical theory, post-colonialism and feminism.

Significance

World affairs have traditionally been understood on the basis of an international paradigm. In this view, states are taken to be the essential building blocks of world politics, meaning that world affairs boil down, most simply, to relations between states. This suggests that once one is aware of the factors that influence the way that states interact, one understands how the world works. However, since the 1980s, an alternative globalization paradigm has become fashionable. This reflects the belief that world affairs have been transformed in recent decades by the growth of global interconnectedness and interdependence. In this view, the world no longer operates as a disaggregated collection of states, or 'units', but rather as an integrated whole, as 'one world'. However, it is difficult to see how either of these paradigms can, on its own, adequately explain the complexities of the contemporary world. For example, it is equally absurd to dismiss states and national government as irrelevant in world affairs as it is to deny that, over a significant range of issues, states now operate in a context of global interdependence.

The changes that have taken place in world affairs in recent decades have also encouraged some to question the relevance of the disciplinary fault line between political science and IR (Hay, 2002). This fault line is based on the distinction between domestic politics, which is concerned with the state's role in maintaining order within its own borders, and international politics, which is concerned with relations between and among states. This domestic/international divide separates what have conventionally been seen as two quite different spheres of political inter-action. While political science has tended to view states as macro-level actors within the political world, IR has typically treated them as micro-level actors within the larger international arena. However, the disciplinary fault line has become increasingly difficult to sustain because of the advent of the interdependent world, in which what happens within the state, and what goes on between states, influence each other to a greater degree than perhaps ever before. Globalization, climate change, terrorism, crime and disease are only a few examples of the issues that breach the domestic/international divide, and their number is escalating.

INTERNATIONAL SOCIETY

The term international society suggests that relations between and among states are conditioned by the existence of norms and rules that establish the regular patterns of interaction that characterize a 'society'. This view modifies the realist emphasis on power politics by suggesting the existence of a 'society of states' rather than simply a 'system of states', implying both that international relations are rule-governed and that these rules help to maintain international order. The chief institutions that generate cultural cohesion and social integration are inter-national law, diplomacy and the activities of international organizations. Hedley Bull (2012) thus advanced the notion of an 'anarchical society', in place of the conventional idea of international anarchy. A distinction is often drawn between the 'solidarist', or 'Grotian' (after Hugo Grotius – 1583–1645), conception of inter-national society and the 'pluralist' one. In the former, states subscribe to a clear and common set of values and priorities, especially regarding the welfare of the individual and the importance of enforcing international law, while in the latter states with quite different political arrangements and cultural identities can co-exist in international society.

Significance

The notion of international society has been crucial to the 'English school' of interna-tional relations, which holds that international politics is best explained in the light of both liberal and realist insights, recognizing the counterbalancing forces of conflict and co-operation. As such, it amounts to a form of liberal realism. The strength of the concept of international society is thus that it draws on thinking associated with each of the two key mainstream theories of international relations, without being constrained by either. In this way, it can help us to generate insights into issues related to both power and justice. The notion has its critics, however. Realists, for their part, argue that international society over-emphasizes the degree to which states are able to set aside considerations of narrow self-interest for the wider benefits this may bring. In this view, international society may simply be a bogus idea. A postcolonial critique of international society has also been developed. From this perspective, international society is invariably constructed on the basis of Eurocentric norms and values, and so implies that certain, usually Western, states can (acting, supposedly, as the 'interna-tional community') claim the authority to 'sort out' less favoured parts of the world, not least though humanitarian intervention.

INTERNATIONALISM

Internationalism is the theory or practice of politics based on transnational or global co-operation. As a political ideal it is based on the belief that political nationalism should be transcended, because the ties that bind the peoples of the world are stronger than those that separate them. The goal of internation-alism is thus to construct political structures that can command the allegiance of all the peoples of the world, regardless of religious, racial, social and national differences. The major internationalist traditions are drawn from liberalism and socialism. Liberal internationalism is based on individualism. This is reflected, for example, in the belief that universal human rights ultimately have a 'higher' status than the sovereign authority of the nation. Socialist internationalism is grounded in a belief in international class solidarity (proletarian internationalism), under-pinned by assumptions about a common humanity. Feminism, racialism and reli-gious fundamentalism may be seen to support weak forms of internationalism, in that they highlight, respectively, gender, racial and religious cleavages that cut across national boundaries.

Significance

The radical edge of internationalism is associated with its condemnation of nationalism as both unnecessary and wrong. Internationalists deny the basic nationalist assertion that the nation is the sole legitimate unit of political rule, often arguing that nations are political constructs manufactured by rulers and elite groups to maintain social cohesion and political passivity. The moral force of internationalism is evident in its association with the ideas of global peace and co-operation. Such 'one-worldism' has, for example, provided the basis for the idealist tradition in international relations, which is characterized by a belief in universal morality. Immanuel Kant (1724–1804) is often seen as the father of this tradition, having envisaged a kind of 'league of nations' based on the assertion that reason and morality combine to dictate that 'There should be no war'.

The weakness of internationalism is that it has generally underestimated the potency of nationalism and failed to establish international structures that can rival the nation's capacity to stimulate political allegiance. The dominant tradition in international relations has thus not been idealism but realism, which highlights the role of power politics and the nation-state. Liberal internationalism has drawn particular criticism from conservatives and developing-world nationalists. The former allege that the idea of universal human rights simply fails to take into account of distinctive national traditions and cultures, while the latter go further and argue that, as human rights are essentially a manifestation of Western liberalism, their spread amounts to a covert form of imperialism. Socialist internationalism has been criticisized on two grounds. The first is that the various Internationals that socialists have set up have either been mere talking shops or, in the case of the Communist International, or Comintern, have been tools of Soviet imperialism. The second is that socialists have often overestimated the appeal of the internationalist ideal and have so missed the opportunity to link socialist goals and principles to national symbols and national culture.

ISLAMISM

Islamism (also called 'political Islam', 'radical Islam' or 'militant Islam') is a controversial term with a variety of definitions. It is usually used to describe a politico-religious ideology, as opposed to simply a belief in Islam (though Islamists themselves reject this distinction, on the grounds that Islam is a holistic moral system that applies to 'public' affairs as well as 'private' affairs). While Islamist ideology has no single creed nor political manifestation, certain common beliefs can be identified. These include:

- Society should be reconstructed in line with the religious principles and ideals of Islam, and particularly the *Sharia* (divine Islamic law).

- The modern secular state is rejected in favour of an 'Islamic state', or *Caliphate*, meaning that religious principles and authority have primacy over political principles and authority.
- The West and Western values are viewed as being corrupt and corrupting, justifying, for some, the notion of a *jihad* against them.

The two most influential forms of Islamism stem from Salafism and Shia Islam. Salafism (or Wahhabism) emerged within Sunni Islam and is the official version of Islam in Saudi Arabia. Salafis seek to restore Islam by purging it of heresies and modern inventions; among other things, they ban pictures, photographs, musical instruments, singing, television and celebrations of Mohammad's birthday. Salafi ideas and beliefs have influenced the Muslim Brotherhood as well as groups such as al-Qaeda, the Taliban and the Islamic State of Iraq and al-Sham (ISIS), also known as the Islamic State (IS). Shia Islamism derives from the quite different temper and doctrinal character of the Shia sect as opposed to the Sunni sect. Shias believe that divine guidance is about to re-emerge into the world with the return of the 'hidden imam', or the arrival of the Mahdi, a leader directly guided by God. Such ideas have given the Shia sect a distinctly messianic and emotional quality. Shia Islamism inspired Iran's 'Islamic Revolution' and is reflected in the beliefs of groups such as Hezbollah and Hamas.

Significance

While modern Islamism can be traced back to the founding of the Muslim Brotherhood in Egypt in 1928, its most significant developments have come since the establishment of an 'Islamic Republic' in Iran in 1979. The Soviet war in Afghanistan, 1979–89, led to the growth of the Mujahideen, a loose collection of religiously-inspired resistance groups, out of which emerged the Taliban, who ruled Afghanistan from 1996 to 2001, and a range of *jihadi* movements including al-Qaeda. These aimed both to overthrow 'corrupt' or 'unIslamic' Muslim rules and to remove Western, and especially US, influence from the Islamic world. However, the nature and significance of Islamism has been the subject of considerable debate, with at least three interpretations being advanced.

First, the source of Islamist militancy has been seen to lie within Islam itself. Such a view is in line with the 'conflict of civilizations' thesis, in that it implies a basic incompatibility between Islamic values and those of the liberal-democratic West. This suggests that the rivalry between Islam and the West will continue until one or other of them is finally defeated. Second, resurgent Islamism has been portrayed as a specific response to particular historical circumstances. Bernard Lewis (2005), for example, argued that the Muslim world is in crisis largely because of the decline and stagnation of the Middle East and the sense of humiliation that has therefore gripped the Islamic, and more specifically Arab, world, not least linked to the protracted Arab–Israeli conflict. Third, Islamism has been interpreted as a manifestation of a much broader, and arguably deeper, ideological tendency: anti-Westernism. In the light of this, political Islam has much in common with fascism and communism, in that each of them promises to rid society of corruption and immorality and to make society anew as a 'single, blocklike structure, solid and eternal' (Berman, 2003).

JIHAD

Jihad literally means to 'struggle' or 'strive'; it is used to refer to the religious duty of Muslims. However, the term has been used in at least two contrasting ways. In the form of the 'greater' *jihad*, it is understood as an inner or spiritual quest to overcome one's sinful nature. In the form of the 'lesser' *jihad*, struggle is understood more as an outer or physical struggle against the enemies of Islam. This is the sense in which *jihad* is translated (often unhelpfully) as 'holy war'. Bernard Lewis (2005) argued that *jihad* has a military meaning in the large majority of cases, though some scholars maintain it also refers to non-violent ways to struggle against the enemies of Islam.

Significance

The notion of military *jihad* has gained particular prominence since the 1970s, through the emergence of militant Islamist groups and movements. Religiously inspired guerrillas fighting the Russian occupation of Afghanistan in the 1980s thus portrayed themselves as the Mujahideen, denoting that they were engaged in *jihad*. In this context, *jihad* came to refer to an armed conflict aimed at 'purifying' the Islamic world through the removal of Western influence and by the overthrow of 'corrupt' or 'tyrannical' Muslim rulers. *Jihad*, in this sense, is part of a global struggle for supremacy, and places an obligation on Muslims everywhere to advance the cause of Islam, with, for militant Salafi Muslims in particular, an emphasis being placed on '*jihad* by the sword' (*jihad bis saif*). However, such issues are a matter of significant debate within Islam. Many authorities, for example, argue that if Muslims live in a society ruled by non-Muslims but are under no threat and can perform their religious duties, then *jihad* is not obligatory. It is also perfectly permissible, in this view, for Islamic states to have harmonious relations with non-Muslim powers. In any event, it is wrong to use *jihad* to suggest that Islam is more bellicose than other world religions, as this is not supported by the historical record.

JUDICIARY

The judiciary is the branch of government empowered to decide legal disputes. The central function of judges is therefore to adjudicate the meaning of law, in the sense that they interpret or 'construct' law. Despite the role of the judiciary varying from state to state and from system to system, the judiciary is often accorded unusual respect and regarded as being distinct from other political institutions. This is because of the supposed link between law and justice, reflected in the capacity of judges to decide disputes in a fair and balanced fashion. Judiciaries and court systems are invariably structured in a hierarchical fashion, reflecting the different types and levels of law, allowing for an appeals process and ensuring consistency of interpretation through the overriding authority of a supreme or high court. Increasingly, however, national judiciaries are subject to the authority of supranational courts, such as the European Court of Justice, the European Court of Human Rights, and the World Court.

Significance

The two chief issues concerning the judiciary are whether judges are political, and whether they are policy-makers. Certain political systems make no pretence of judicial neutrality or impartiality. For example, in orthodox communist regimes, the principle of 'socialist legality' dictated that judges interpret law in accordance with Marxism-Leninism, subject to the ideological authority of the state's communist party. Judges thus became mere functionaries who carried out the political and ideological objectives of the regime itself, as was demonstrated by the 'show trials' of the 1930s in the USSR. The German courts during the Nazi period were used in a similar way as instruments of ideological repression and political persecution.

Liberal-democratic states, however, have emphasized the principles of judicial independence and neutrality. Judicial independence is the principle that there should be a strict separation between the judiciary and other branches of government, and is thus an application of the separation of powers. Judicial neutrality is the principle that judges should interpret law in a way that is uncontaminated by social, political and other biases. Taken together, these principles are intended to establish a strict separation between law and politics, and to guarantee that the rule of law is upheld. The devices used to ensure judicial objectivity range from security of tenure and the independence of the legal profession (as in the USA and the UK) to specialized professional training (as widely adopted in continental Europe). However, the image of judicial objectivity is always misleading. The judiciary is best thought of as a political, not merely a legal, institution. The main ways in which political influences intrude into judicial decision-making are through breaches in independence, often linked to the appointment system or the wider use of judges in state roles, and to the threat to neutrality posed by the fact that judges everywhere are socially and educationally unrepresentative of society at large.

The image of judges as simple appliers of law has also always been a myth. Judges cannot apply the so-called 'letter of the law', because no law, legal term or principle has a single, self-evident meaning. In practice, judges impose meaning on law through a process of 'construction' that forces them to choose among a number of possible meanings or interpretations. In this sense, all law is judge-made law. However, two major factors affect the degree to which judges make policy. The first is the clarity and detail with which law is specified. Generally, broadly framed laws or constitutional principles allow greater scope for judicial interpretation. The second factor is the existence of a codified or 'written' constitution. The existence of such a document enhances the status of the judiciary significantly, investing it with the power of judicial review – the ability of the judiciary to consider and possibly invalidate laws, decrees and the actions of other branches of government if they are incompatible with the constitution. In its classical sense this implies that the judiciary is the supreme constitutional arbiter. A more modest form of judicial review, found in uncodified constitutional systems, is restricted to the review of executive actions in the light of ordinary law, using the principle of *ultra vires* (beyond the powers).

JUST WAR

A just war is a war that, in its purpose and conduct, meets certain ethical standards, and so is (allegedly) morally justified. Just war theory, which was first addressed systematically by figures such as Augustine (354–430) and Aquinas (1225–74), addresses two separate but related issues: *jus ad bellum* (just recourse to war), reflected in principles that restrict the legitimate use of force, and *jus in bello* (just conduct of war), reflected in principles that stipulate how wars should be fought.

The principles of *jus ad bellum* are:

- *Last resort*. All non-violent options must have been exhausted before force can be justified.
- *Just cause*. The purpose of war is to redress a wrong that has been suffered. This is usually associated with self-defence in response to military attack.
- *Legitimate authority*. This is usually interpreted as implying the lawfully consti- tuted government of a sovereign state, rather than a private individual or group.
- *Right intention*. War must be prosecuted on the basis of aims that are morally acceptable, rather than revenge or the desire to inflict harm.
- *Reasonable prospect of success*. War should not be fought in a 'hopeless cause', in which life is expended for no purpose or benefit.
- *Proportional means*. War should result in more good than evil, in that any response to an attack should be measured and proportionate.

The principles of *jus in bello* are:

- *Discrimination*. Force must be directed at military targets only, on the grounds that civilians or non-combatants are 'innocent'.
- *Proportionality*. This holds that the force used must only be sufficient to ensure military success and be no greater than the provoking cause.
- *Humanity*. Force must not be directed against enemy personnel if they are captured or wounded.

Significance

Those who subscribe to the just war tradition base their thinking on two assump- tions. First, human nature is composed of an unchangeable mixture of good and evil components, implying that war is inevitable. Second, the suffering that war leads to can be ameliorated by subjecting warfare to moral constraints. As politi- cians, the armed forces and civilian populations become sensitized to the principles of a just war, the hope is that fewer wars will occur and the harm done by warfare will be reduced. Just war theory has nevertheless been subject to criticism from various directions. In the first place, however desirable they might be, the elements that make up a just war may set standards for states with which it is impossible to comply. It is questionable whether there has ever been a war in which one side at least has followed fully the rules of a just war. Second, attempts to apply just war principles may result in the 'wrong' outcome. This could happen as the require-ments of *jus in bello* may contradict those of *jus ad bellum*, in the sense that a party with a just cause risks defeat because it is fighting with its 'hands tied behind its back'. Surely, once a war has started, military tactics should be determined by practical considerations, aimed at ensuring a swift and certain victory, rather than moral considerations? Third, just war thinking may be applicable only in circum-stances in which the parties to a dispute share the same or similar cultural and moral beliefs. Only then can one party be deemed to be just, while the other is unjust.

JUSTICE

Justice is the idea of a morally justifiable distribution of rewards or punishments. Justice, in short, is about giving each person what he or she is 'due', often seen as his or her 'just deserts'. In this sense justice can be applied to the distribution of any 'goods' in society: freedom, rights, power, wealth, leisure and so on. However, as the grounds for just distribution may vary enormously, justice can perhaps be seen as the archetypal 'essentially contested' concept. A distinction can nevertheless be made between procedural and substantive notions of justice. *Procedural justice*, or 'formal' justice, refers to the manner in which outcomes are arrived at, and thus to the rules that govern human conduct and interaction. For example, any outcome of a sporting competition is considered, so long as it results from the application of fair rules independently adjudicated – in short, there should be a 'level playing field'. *Substantive justice*, or 'concrete' justice, on the other hand, is concerned with the substance of the outcomes themselves; that is, with the nature of the end-point. This can be seen in the idea that the punishment should 'fit' the crime; in other words, that penalties should be appropriate and justifiable in themselves.

The two most common applications of the concept of justice are legal justice and social justice. *Legal justice* refers to the apportionment of punishments and rewards as a result of wrongdoing and, in particular, law-breaking. The judicial system is sometimes therefore described as the administration of justice. However, law should not be equated with justice: laws may be just or unjust, as may be the court system through which they are administered. *Social justice* refers to a morally justi-fiable distribution of material or social rewards, notably wealth, income and social status. Many take social justice to imply equality, even viewing it as a specifically socialist principle. However, concepts of social justice may be inegalitarian as well as egalitarian, and even when socialists use the term it tends to imply a weak form of equality: a narrowing of material inequalities, often justified in terms of equality of opportunity.

Significance

Justice has been portrayed as the master concept of political thought. Since the time of Plato (427–347 BCE) and Aristotle (384–322 BCE), political thinkers have seen the 'good' society as a 'just' society. Much of political theory therefore consists of a debate about 'who should get what?' In relation to legal justice, this issue has largely been resolved through the development of widely accepted procedural rules regarding, for example, access to legal advice and representation, judicial neutrality, rules of evidence, and the use of juries, though there may be important substantive differences between the laws that operate in liberal-democratic societies and, say, *Sharia* law found in Islamic states.

However, controversies over social justice have been deep and recurrent. Some, including supporters of the New Right, dismiss the very idea of social justice on the grounds that it is inappropriate to apply moral principles such as justice to the distribution of wealth and income, because these are strictly economic matters and can be judged only by criteria such as efficiency and growth. From this perspective, to portray the poor as 'victims' of injustice is simply absurd. Socialists and modern liberals, in contrast, have been attracted to the idea of social justice precisely because they are unwilling to divorce economics from ethics, and because they are unwilling to leave issues related to wealth and poverty to the vagaries of the market. Sympathy for social justice therefore usually goes hand-in-hand with support for government intervention in economic and social life. However, there are quite different liberal and socialist models of social justice. The liberal model is rooted in individualism and based on a commitment to meritocracy, while the socialist model is rooted in collectivism and exhibits greater support for social equality and community.

LAISSEZ-FAIRE

Laissez-faire (in French, meaning literally 'leave to do') is the principle of non-intervention of government in economic affairs. It is the heart of the doctrine that the economy works best when not interfered with by government. The central assumption of laissez-faire is that an unregulated market economy tends naturally towards equilibrium. This is usually explained by the theory of 'perfect competition', based on the working of a hypothetical market in which there are an unlimited number of producers creating a homogenous product, and an unlimited number of consumers, each enjoying perfect knowledge of the marketplace.

Significance

The principal of laissez-faire was taken up by classical economists such as Adam Smith (1723–90), David Ricardo (1772–1823) and John Stuart Mill (1806–73), and became economic orthodoxy in the nineteenth and early twentieth centuries, in the UK and the USA in particular. Though it became profoundly unfashionable after World War II because of the rise of Keynesian demand management, laissez-faire thinking (though not the term itself) has experienced a revival since the 1970s, in association with neoliberalism. Proponents of laissez-faire argue that unregulated market competition is the only reliable means of generating wealth and delivering general prosperity, in which case any government intervention that hampers market forces can only have a negative effect. Critics, on the other hand, point out that the image of 'pure' capitalism, on which 'perfect competition' is based, is, and has always been, a myth. Not only do all market economies contain flaws and imperfections (monopolies, price fixing and so on), but markets may suffer from structural faults, such a tendency towards inequality and an inability to revive growth in times of depression, (the problem highlighted by J. M. Keynes (1883–1946). Economic debate has therefore come to focus not so much on whether governments should or should not intervene in the economy but, rather, on the nature and extent of that intervention.

LAW

Law is a set of public and enforceable rules that apply throughout a political community. Law can be distinguished from other social rules on four grounds. First, as law is made by the government and thus reflects the 'will of the state', and it takes precedence over all other norms and social rules. Second, law is compulsory; citizens are not allowed to choose which laws to obey and which to ignore, because law is backed up by a system of coercion and punishment. Third, law consists of published and recognized rules that have been enacted through a formal, usually public, legislative process. Fourth, law is generally recognized as binding on those to whom it applies; law thus embodies moral claims, implying that legal rules should be obeyed.

Natural law is usually distinguished from positive law. *Natural law* is law that conforms to higher moral or religious principles, meaning that it is a vehicle through which justice is expressed or guaranteed. Natural law theories can be traced back to Plato (427–347 BCE) and Aristotle (384–22 BCE), and to the idea of God-given 'natural rights' in the early modern period. They became fashionable again in the twentieth century in association with the ideas of civil liberty and human rights. *Positive law* is defined by the fact that it is established and enforced. The law is the law because it is obeyed. The 'science of positive law' therefore frees the understanding of law from moral, religious and mystical assumptions, a position developed by John Austin (1790–1859) into the theory of 'legal positivism'. H. L. A. Hart (1961) refined legal positivism by distinguishing between a primary and secondary level of law. The role of primary rules is to regulate social behaviour; these are thought of as the 'content' of the legal system (for example, criminal law). Secondary rules, on the other hand, are rules that confer powers on the institutions of government; they lay down how primary rules are made, enforced and adjudicated, and so determine their validity. Another distinction is between public and private law. Public law lays down the powers and duties of governmental bodies and establishes the legal relationship between the state and its citizens. It therefore includes constitutional and administrative law, and taxation and welfare law, and is usually also considered to encompass criminal law. Private law apportions rights and responsibilities among private citizens and bodies, and thus establishes the legal relationships within civil society. It includes the law of contract and property law.

Significance

Law is found in all modern societies, and is usually regarded as the bedrock of civilized existence. Nevertheless, questions about the actual and desirable relationship between law and politics – reflecting on the nature of law, and its function and proper extent – have provoked deep controversy. Liberal theorists portray law as an essential guarantee of stability and order. The role of law is to protect each member of society from his or her fellow members, thereby preventing individual rights from being encroached on; as John Locke (1632–1704) put it, 'without law there is no liberty'. Law should therefore be 'above' politics, in the sense that it applies equally to all citizens and is administered impartially by the judiciary. This is reflected in the principle of the rule of law, the idea that law 'rules' in the sense that it establishes a framework to which all conduct and behaviour conform, no distinction being drawn between government officials and private citizens, the rich and the poor, men and women, and so on. However, in believing that law's central purpose is to protect liberty, liberals have always insisted that the proper sphere of law must be limited. The classical interpretation of this position was developed in J. S. Mill's (1806–73) 'harm principle': the idea that the only legitimate use of law is to prevent 'harm to others'.

Conservative theorists, in contrast, link law more closely to order, even to the extent that 'law and order' becomes a single, fused concept. This position draws on a more pessimistic, even Hobbesian, view of human nature, and on the belief that social stability depends on the existence of shared values and a common culture. Patrick Devlin (1968) thus argued that society has the right to enforce 'public morality' through the instrument of law. This position goes clearly beyond Mill's libertarianism in implying, for example, that society has the right to protect itself against 'non-consensus' practices, such as homosexuality and drug taking. In the 1980s and 1990s the New Right took up a very similar position in extolling the virtues of 'traditional morality' and 'family values', believing also that these should be upheld through the authority of law. Alternative and more critical views of law have been advanced by Marxists, feminists and anarchists. Marxists have traditionally argued that class biases operate within the legal system that uphold the interests of property and capitalism. Feminists have linked law to patriarchy and argued that it is one of the principal devices through which women's silence and subordination is maintained. Anarchists, for their part, portray law as being unnecessary and intrinsically oppressive, and look towards the construction of a lawless society regulated by reason and human sympathy alone.

LEADERSHIP

Leadership can be understood as a pattern of behaviour, as a personal quality and as a political value. As a pattern of behaviour, leadership is the influence exerted by an individual or group over a larger body to organize or direct its efforts towards the achievement of desired goals. As a personal attribute, leadership refers to the character traits that enable the leader to exert influence over others. Leadership in this sense is equated effectively with charisma, charm or personal power. As a political value, leadership refers to guidance and inspiration, the capacity to mobilize others through moral authority or ideological insight.

Significance

In some respects the subject of political leadership appears to be outdated. The division of society into leaders and followers is rooted in a pre-democratic culture of deference and respect in which leaders 'knew best' and the public needed to be led, mobilized or guided. Democratic pressures may not have removed the need for leaders, but they have certainly placed powerful constraints on leadership, notably by making leaders publicly accountable and establishing institutional mechanisms through which they can be removed. In other respects, however, the politics of leadership has become increasingly significant. For example, to some extent democracy itself has enhanced the importance of personality by forcing political leaders, in effect, to 'project themselves' in the hope of gaining electoral support. This tendency has undoubtedly been strengthened by modern means of mass communication (especially television), which tend to emphasize personality rather than policies, and provide leaders with powerful weapons with which to manipulate their public images. Furthermore, as society becomes more complex and fragmented, people may look increasingly to the personal vision of an individual leader to give coherence and meaning to the world in which they live.

The question of political leadership is nevertheless surrounded by deep ideological controversy. Its principal supporters have been on the political right, influenced by a general belief in natural inequality and a broadly pessimistic view of the masses. In its extreme form this was reflected in the fascist 'leader principle', which holds that there is a single, supreme leader who alone is capable of leading the masses to their destiny, a theory derived from Friedrich Nietzsche's (1844–1900) notion of the *Übermensch* ('superman'). Among the supposed virtues of leadership are that it:

- Mobilizes and inspires people who would otherwise be inert and directionless
- Promotes unity and encourages members of a group to pull in the same direction
- Strengthens organizations by establishing a hierarchy of responsibilities and roles.

Liberals and socialists, on the other hand, have usually warned that leaders should not be trusted, and treated leadership as a basic threat to equality and justice. Nevertheless, this has not prevented socialist regimes from employing leadership systems, and, in the case of V. I. Lenin's (1870–1924) theory of the vanguard party, they have sometimes stressed the need for political leadership.

The alleged dangers of leadership include that it:

- Concentrates power, and can thus lead to corruption and tyranny, hence the democratic demand that leadership should be checked by accountability
- Engenders subservience and deference, thereby discouraging people from taking responsibility for their own lives
- Narrows debate and argument, because of its emphasis on ideas flowing down from the top, rather than up from the bottom.

LEFT/RIGHT

Left and right are terms used as a shorthand method for describing political ideas and beliefs, summarizing the ideological positions of politicians, political parties and movements. They are usually understood as the poles of a political spectrum, enabling people to talk about the 'centre-left', 'far right' and so on. The most common application of the left/right distinction is in the form of a linear political spectrum that travels from left wing to right wing, as shown in Figure 6.

Communism   Socialism   Liberalism   Conservatism   Fascism

Figure 6   Linear spectrum

However, the terms left and right do not have exact meanings. In a narrow sense, the political spectrum summarizes different attitudes towards the economy and the role of the state: left-wing views support intervention and collectivism; and right-wing ones favour the market and individualism. However, this distinction supposedly reflects deeper, if imperfectly defined, ideological or value differences. Ideas such as freedom, equality, fraternity, rights, progress, reform and internationalism are generally seen to have a left-wing character, while notions such as authority, hierarchy, order, duty, tradition, reaction and nationalism are generally seen as having a right-wing character. In some cases 'the Left' and 'the Right' are used to refer to collections of people, groups and parties that are bound together by broadly similar ideological stances.

Significance

The origin of the terms left and right dates back to the French Revolution and the seating arrangements adopted by aristocrats and radicals at the first meeting of the Estates General in 1789. The left/right divide was therefore originally a stark choice between revolution and reaction. The wider use of the terms demonstrates their general value in locating political and ideological positions, However, the terms are simplistic and generalized, and must always be used with caution. Problems with the conventional left/right divide include the fact that it appears to offer no place for anarchism, which may be both ultra left-wing and ultra right-wing; that it ignores that communism and fascism to some extent resemble one another by virtue of a shared tendency towards totalitarianism; and that it attempts to reduce politics to

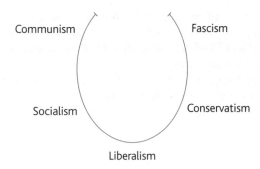

Figure 7 Horseshoe spectrum

a single dimension – the market–state divide – and thereby ignores other political distinctions such as the libertarian–authoritarian divide and the autocratic–democratic divide. For these reasons, various horseshoe-shaped and two-dimensional spectrums have been developed to offer a more complete picture of ideological positions (see Figures 7 and 8). Finally, some argue that the emergence of new political issues such as feminism, ecologism and animal rights, which simply do not fit in to the conventional spectrum, and the development of 'third way' politics have rendered the ideas of left and right largely redundant.

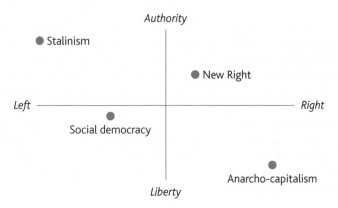

Figure 8 Two-dimensional spectrum

LEGITIMACY

Legitimacy (from the Latin *legitimare*, meaning 'to declare lawful') broadly means rightfulness. Legitimacy confers on an order or command an authoritative or binding character, thus transforming power into authority. It differs from legality in that the latter does not necessarily guarantee that government is respected, or that citizens acknowledge a duty of obedience. However, the term legitimacy is used differently in political philosophy and political science.

Political philosophers generally treat legitimacy as a moral or rational principle, as the grounds on which governments may demand obedience from their citizens. The *claim* to legitimacy is thus more important than the *fact* of obedience. Political scientists, on the other hand, usually view legitimacy in sociological terms; that is, as a willingness to comply with a system of rule regardless of how this is achieved. Following Max Weber (1864–1920), this position takes legitimacy to mean a *belief* in legitimacy; in other words, a belief in the 'right to rule'.

Significance

The issue of legitimacy is linked to the oldest and one of the most fundamental of political debates: the problem of political obligation. In examining whether citizens have a duty to respect the state and obey its laws, social contract theorists such as Thomas Hobbes (1588–1679) and John Locke (1632–1704) were considering the question of when, and on what basis, may government exercise legitimate authority over society? In modern political debate, however, legitimacy addresses not the question of why people *should* obey the state, in an abstract sense, but rather the question of why they do obey a particular state or system of rule. The classic contribution to the understanding of legitimacy as a sociological phenomenon was provided by Weber, who identified three types of political legitimacy based, respectively, on history and customs (traditional authority), the power of personality (charismatic authority) and a framework of formal, legal rules (legal-rational authority). In Weber's view, modern societies are characterized increasingly by the exercise of legal-rational authority and a form of legitimacy that arises from respect for formal and usually legal rules.

An alternative to the Weberian approach to legitimacy has been developed by neo-Marxist theorists, who focus on the mechanisms through which capitalist societies constrain class antagonisms; that is, by manufacturing consent via the extension of democracy and social reform. Legitimacy is thus linked to the maintenance of ideological hegemony. In this light, neo-Marxists such as Jürgen Habermas (1973) have identified 'legitimation crises' in capitalist societies that make it difficult for them to maintain political stability through consent alone. At the heart of these 'crisis tendencies' lies the alleged contradiction between the logic of capitalist accumulation on the one hand, and the popular pressures which democratic politics unleashes on the other.

LIBERAL DEMOCRACY

Liberal democracy is a form of democratic rule that balances the principle of limited government against the ideal of popular consent. Its 'liberal' features are reflected in a network of internal and external checks on government designed to guarantee liberty and afford citizens protection against the state. Its 'democratic' character is based on a system of regular and competitive elections, conducted on the basis of universal suffrage and political equality. While it may be used to describe a political principle, the term liberal democracy more commonly describes a particular type of regime.

The core features of a liberal-democratic regime are:

- Constitutional government based on formal, usually legal, rules
- Guaranteed civil liberties and individual rights
- Institutional fragmentation and a system of checks and balances
- Regular elections respecting the principles of universal suffrage and 'one person, one vote'
- Political pluralism in the form of electoral choice and party competition
- A healthy civil society in which organized groups and interests enjoy independence from government
- A capitalist or private enterprise economy organized along market lines.

Significance

Liberal democracy is the dominant political force found in the developed world, and increasingly in the developing world. Indeed, the collapse of communism and the advance of 'democratization' (usually understood to imply liberal-democratic reforms; that is, electoral democracy and economic liberalization) in Asia, Latin America and Africa, especially during the 1980s, led 'end of history' theorists such as Francis Fukuyama (1989) to proclaim the worldwide triumph of Western liberal democracy. In Fukuyama's view, liberal democracy is 'the final form of human government'. The remarkable success of liberal democracy stems from two chief factors. First, liberal democratic systems are highly responsive, in that they establish a number of channels of communication between government and the governed. Second, because liberal democracy invariably goes hand-in-hand with capitalism, it is associated with widespread consumer prosperity. Liberal-democratic theorists point out that it is the only political system capable of delivering both political freedom and economic opportunity, and that liberal-democratic processes are sufficiently responsive and robust to articulate the concerns of all significant sections of society. Among the strongest advocates of liberal democracy have been pluralist theorists, who praise its capacity to ensure a wide distribution of political power among competing groups.

Nevertheless, liberal democracy does not command universal approval or respect. Its principal critics have been elitists, Marxists, radical democrats and feminists. Elitists have drawn attention to the capacity of electoral democracy to replace one elite with another, but not challenge the fact of elite rule. From this perspective, the principle of political equality and the process of electoral competition on which liberal democracy is founded are nothing more than a sham. The traditional Marxist critique of liberal democracy has focused on the inherent contradiction between democracy and capitalism. The egalitarianism of political democracy merely masks a reality of unequal class power; the dominant economic class 'rules' democratic governments through its control of wealth and other resources. Radical democrats object to the limited and non-participatory character of liberal democracy, pointing out that the act of voting every few years is a poor manifestation of popular rule and no means of securing genuine accountability. Feminists, for their part, have drawn attention to the patriarchal character of liberal-democratic systems that apply democracy only to traditionally male realms such as government and the state, while ignoring the structures of male power that traditionally operate through the family and domestic life.

LIBERALISM

Liberalism is a political ideology whose central theme is a commitment to the individual and to the construction of a society in which individuals can satisfy their interests or achieve fulfilment. The core values of liberalism are individualism, rationalism, freedom, justice and toleration. The liberal belief that human beings are, first and foremost, individuals, endowed with reason, implies that each individual should enjoy the maximum possible freedom consistent with a like freedom for all. However, while individuals are 'born equal' in the sense that they are of equal moral worth and should enjoy formal equality and equal opportunities, liberals generally stress that they should be rewarded according to their differing levels of talent or willingness to work, and therefore favour the principle of meritocracy. A liberal society is characterized by diversity and pluralism and organized politically around the twin values of consent and constitutionalism, combined to form the structures of liberal democracy.

Significant differences nevertheless exist between classical and modern liberalism. *Classical liberalism* is distinguished by a belief in a 'minimal' state, whose function is limited to the maintenance of domestic order and personal security. Classical liberals emphasize that human beings are essentially self-interested and largely self-sufficient; as far as possible, people should be responsible for their own lives and circumstances. As an economic doctrine, classical liberalism extols the merits of a self-regulating market in which government intervention is seen as both unnecessary and damaging. Classical liberal ideas are expressed in certain natural rights theories and utilitarianism, and provide one of the cornerstones of libertarianism. *Modern liberalism* (sometimes portrayed as social or welfare liberalism) exhibits a more sympathetic attitude towards the state, born out of the belief that unregulated capitalism merely produces new forms of injustice. State intervention can therefore enlarge liberty by safeguarding individuals from the social evils that blight their existence. Whereas classical liberals understand freedom in 'negative' terms, as the absence of constraints on the individual, modern liberals link freedom to personal development and self-realisation. This creates clear overlaps between modern liberalism and social democracy.

Liberal ideas and theories have also had a major impact on the discipline of international relations, and constitute the principal mainstream alternative to realism. Liberal international theory is based on the assumption that the belief in balance or harmony that runs throughout liberalism can also be applied to the relations between states. This disposes liberals to believe in internationalism, and to hold that realists underestimate substantially the scope for co-operation and integration within the state system. However, in the liberal view, international co-operation does not arise spontaneously; instead, it is a consequence of economic, political or institutional structures. So-called commercial liberals have drawn attention to the capacity of free trade to generate peace and prosperity. Republican liberals highlight the pacific tendencies inherent in democratic governance, in line with the democratic peace thesis. And liberal institutionalists argue that stability and order can be introduced into state systems by the construction of international organizations.

Significance

Liberalism has undoubtedly been the most powerful ideological force shaping the Western political tradition. Indeed, some portray liberalism as the ideology of the industrialized West, and identify it with Western civilization in general. Liberalism was the product of the breakdown of feudalism, and the growth, in its place, of a market or capitalist society. Early liberalism certainly reflected the aspirations of a rising industrial middle class, and liberalism and capitalism have been closely linked (some have argued intrinsically linked) ever since. In its earliest form, liberalism was a political doctrine. It attacked absolutism and feudal privilege, instead advocating constitutional and, later, representative government. In the nineteenth century, classical liberalism, in the form of economic liberalism, extolled the virtues of *laissez-faire* capitalism and condemned all forms of government intervention. From the late nineteenth century onwards, however, a form of social liberalism emerged, characteristic of modern liberalism, which looked more favourably on welfare reform and economic intervention. So-called 'end of ideology' theorists such as Francis Fukuyama (1992) argued that the history of ideas had culminated with the final, worldwide triumph of liberalism. This supposedly reflected the collapse of all viable alternatives to market capitalism as the basis of economic organization, and to liberal democracy as the basis of political organisation.

The attraction of liberalism is its unrelenting commitment to individual freedom, reasoned debate and to balance within diversity. Indeed, it has become fashionable to portray liberalism not simply as an ideology but as a 'meta-ideology', that is, as a body of rules that specifies the grounds on which political and ideological debate can take place. This reflects the belief that liberalism gives priority to 'the right' over 'the good'. In other words, liberalism strives to establish conditions in which people and groups can pursue 'the good life' as each defines it, but it does not prescribe or try to promote any particular notion of what is good. Criticisms of liberalism nevertheless come from various directions. Marxists have argued that, in defending capitalism, liberalism attempts to legitimize unequal class power and so constitutes a form of bourgeois ideology. Radical feminists point to the linkage between liberalism and patriarchy, which is rooted in the tendency to construe the individual on the basis of an essentially male model of self-sufficiency, thereby encouraging women to be 'like men'. Communitarians condemn liberalism for failing to provide a moral basis for social order and collective endeavour, arguing that the liberal society is a recipe for unrestrained egoism and greed, and so is ultimately self-defeating.

LIBERTARIANISM

Libertarianism is an ideological stance that gives strict priority to liberty or freedom (specifically 'negative' freedom) over other values, such as authority, tradition and equality. Libertarians thus seek to maximize the realm of individual freedom and minimize the scope of public authority, typically seeing the state as the principal threat to liberty. This anti-statism differs from classical anarchist doctrines in that it is based on an uncompromising individualism that places little or no emphasis on human sociability or co-operation. The two best-known libertarian traditions are rooted in, respectively, the idea of individual rights and laissez-faire (literally 'leave to do', meaning unconstrained by government) economic doctrines. Libertarian theories of rights generally stress that the individual is the owner of his or her person and thus that people have an absolute entitlement to the property that their labour produces. Libertarian economic theories emphasize the self-regulating nature of the market mechanism and portray government intervention as always being unnecessary and counter-productive. Despite all libertarians rejecting government's attempts to redistribute wealth and deliver social justice, a division can nevertheless be drawn between those libertarians who subscribe to anarcho-capitalism and view the state as an unnecessary evil, and those who recognize the need for a minimal state, sometimes styling themselves 'minarchists'.

Significance

Libertarianism has influenced a number of ideological forms. It clearly overlaps with classical liberalism (though the latter refuses to give priority to liberty over order); it constitutes one of the major traditions on which the New Right draws; and, in the form of socialist libertarianism, it has encouraged a preference for self-management rather than state control. In embodying an extreme faith in the individual and in freedom, libertarianism provides a constant reminder of the oppressive potential that resides within all actions of government. However, criticisms of libertarianism fall into two general categories. One sees the rejection of any form of welfare or redistribution as an example of capitalist ideology, linked to the interests of business and private wealth. The other highlights the imbalance in libertarian philosophy that allows it to stress rights but ignore responsibilities, and which values individual effort and ability but fails to take into account the extent to which these are a product of the social environment.

LOCAL GOVERNMENT

Local government, in its simplest sense, is government that is specific to a particular locality, for example a village, district, town, city or county. More particularly, it is a form of government that has no share in sovereignty, and is thus entirely subordinate to central authority or, in a federal system, to state or regional authority. Although While the functions of, and services provided by, local authorities or councils vary from state to state and over time, they usually include some responsibility for education, planning, refuse collection, local trade and perhaps transport, leisure and recreation, and personal social services. The term local government is sometimes used to refer to all political institutions whose authority or jurisdiction is confined to a territorial portion of a state. In this case, three levels of local government can be identified: a basic level (district councils in England and Wales, municipalities or towns in the USA, and communes in France); an intermediate level (counties in England and Wales and in the USA, and *départements* in France); a state or regional level (states in the USA, *Länder* in Germany, and *régions* in France).

Significance

It would be a mistake to assume that the constitutional subordination of local government means that it is politically irrelevant. In the first place, all political systems feature some form of local government. This reflects the fact that it is both administratively necessary – centralization ultimately involves unacceptable diseconomies of scale – and, because it is 'close' to the people, it is easily intelligible. Central–local relationships are usually conducted through some form of bargaining and negotiation rather than by diktat from above. The balance between central government and local government is affected by a number of factors. These include the following:

- Whether local politicians are appointed or elected; the latter possess an independent power base and exercise a measure of democratic legitimacy
- The range and importance of locally provided services and the discretion available to local authorities
- The number and size of local authorities and the structure of authority within them
- Local government's tax-raising powers and its degree of fiscal autonomy
- The extent to which local politics is 'politicized', in the sense that national parties operate in and through local politics.

The defence of local government goes well beyond its capacity to provide a convenient, and perhaps indispensable, method of delivering public services. Following J. S. Mill (1806–73), local government has been praised both as a means of guaranteeing liberty by checking the exercise of central power, and as a mechanism through which popular participation, and thus political education, can be broadened. This is to defend local government in terms of its capacity to deliver local democracy, a principle that combines the idea of local autonomy with the goal of popular responsiveness. From a more radical perspective, anarchists and council communists have favoured communes as a model of local self-government, on the grounds that they constitute 'human-scale' communities which allow people to manage their own affairs through face-to-face interaction, rather than through depersonalized and bureaucratic processes. On the other hand, local government has been criticized for entrenching a concern with parochial issues and local interests rather than matters of broader public importance; for promoting disunity and divisions within states; and for challenging the democratic legitimacy of national politicians.

MANDATE

A mandate is an instruction or command from a higher body that demands compliance. Policy mandates can be distinguished from governing mandates. A *policy mandate* arises from the claim on behalf of a winning party in an election that its manifesto promises have been endorsed, giving it authority to translate these into a programme of government. This is sometimes portrayed as a 'popular' mandate or 'democratic' mandate. A *governing mandate* is, in effect, a mandate to govern. It is more flexible in that it attaches to an individual leader (in the case of a 'personal' mandate) or to a political party or government, rather than a set of policies. Whereas policy mandates bind politicians and parties, and limit their freedom of manoeuvre, it is difficult to see how governing mandates in any way restrict politicians once they are in power.

Significance

The doctrine of the mandate is an important model of representation. It holds that politicians serve their constituents not by thinking for themselves or acting as a channel to convey their own views, but by remaining loyal to their party and its policies. The strength of the mandate doctrine is that it takes into account the undoubted practical importance of party labels and policies. Moreover, it provides a means of imposing some kind of meaning on election results, as well as a way of ensuring politicians keep their word. The doctrine of the mandate thus guarantees responsible party government, in that the party in power can only act within the mandate it has received from the electorate. Nevertheless, the doctrine has also stimulated fierce criticism. First, it is based on a highly questionable model of voting behaviour, in so far as it suggests that voters select parties on the grounds of policies and issues, rather than on the basis of 'irrational' factors such as the personality of leaders, the image of parties, habitual allegiances and social conditioning. Second, the doctrine imposes a straitjacket on government, in that it leaves no scope for policies to be adjusted in the light of changing circumstances. What guidance do mandates offer in the event of, say, international or economic crises? Third, the doctrine of the mandate can be applied only in the case of majoritarian electoral systems in which a single party wins power, and its use even there may appear absurd if the winning party fails to gain 50 per cent of the vote. Fourth, policy mandates are always in danger of being translated into governing mandates, which are open to clear abuse and have only a tenuous link to representation.

MARKET

A market is a system of commercial exchange that brings buyers wishing to acquire goods or services into contact with sellers offering the same for purchase. In all but the simplest markets, money is used rather than barter as a convenient means of exchange. Markets are impersonal mechanisms in that they are regulated by price fluctuations that reflect the balance of supply and demand – so-called market forces. The terms market economy and capitalism are often used interchangeably, but market forms may also develop in other social systems (as the idea of market socialism demonstrates), and capitalist systems themselves subject markets to a greater or lesser degree of regulation.

Significance

The market is the central organizing principle within a capitalist economy. It has been applied to the organization of some socialist societies, as well as to public services such as education and health (using the idea of 'internal markets'). Market forms and market structures have become increasingly prominent in modern society given the failure of alternative planning arrangements, most spectacularly in the collapse of communism in the revolutions of 1989–91, and because globalization has gone hand-in-hand with marketization. This has occurred through the market's capacity to regulate highly complex interactions among human beings in a way that balances dynamism against equilibrium, a capacity that appears to outstrip that of rational human agents, however well-informed and technologically advanced they might be.

Nevertheless, while support, sometimes grudging, for the market now extends to many socialists, the market continues to stimulate deep political and ideological controversy. Supporters of the market argue that its advantages include the following:

- It promotes efficiency through the discipline of the profit motive.
- It encourages innovation in the form of new products and better production processes.
- It allows producers and consumers to pursue their own interests and enjoy freedom of choice.
- It tends towards equilibrium through the co-ordination of an almost infinite number of individual preferences and decisions.

Critics nevertheless point out that the market has serious disadvantages, including the following:

- It generates insecurity because people's lives are shaped by forces they cannot control and do not understand.
- It widens material inequality and generates poverty.
- It increases the level of greed and selfishness, and ignores the broader needs of society.
- It promotes instability through periodic booms and slumps.

MARXISM

Marxism is an ideological system within socialism that developed out of, and drew inspiration from, the writings of Karl Marx (1818–83). However, Marxism as a codified body of thought came into existence only after Marx's death. It was the product of the attempt, notably by Friedrich Engels (1820–95), Karl Kautsky (1854–1938) and Georgi Plekhanov (1856–1918), to condense Marx's ideas and theories into a systematic and comprehensive world view that suited the needs of the growing socialist movement. The core of Marxism is a philosophy of history that outlines why capitalism is doomed, and why socialism and eventually communism are destined to replace it. This philosophy is based on historical materialism, the belief that economic factors are the ultimately determining force in human history, developed into what Marx and Engels classified as 'scientific socialism'. In Marx's view, history is driven forward through a dialectical process in which internal contradictions within each mode of production, or economic system, are reflected in class antagonism. Capitalism, then, is only the most technologically advanced of class societies, and is itself destined to be overthrown in a proletarian revolution that will culminate in the establishment of a classless communist society.

However, there are a number of rival versions of Marxism, the most obvious ones being classical Marxism, orthodox Marxism and modern Marxism. *Classical Marxism* is the Marxism of Marx and Engels (though Engels' *Anti-Dühring*, written in 1876, is sometimes seen as the first work of Marxist orthodoxy, since it emphasizes the need for adherence to an authoritative interpretation of Marx's work). *Orthodox Marxism* is often portrayed as 'dialectical materialism' (a term coined by Plekhanov and not used by Marx), and later formed the basis of Soviet communism. This 'vulgar' Marxism placed a heavier stress on mechanistic theories and historical inevitability than did Marx's own writings. However, further complications stem from the breadth and complexity of Marx's own writings and the difficulty of establishing the 'Marxism of Marx'. Some see Marx as a humanist socialist, while others proclaim him to be an economic determinist. Moreover, distinctions have also been drawn between his early and later writings, sometimes presented as a distinction between the 'young' Marx and the 'mature' Marx. The 'young' Marx developed a form of socialist humanism that stressed the link between communism and human fulfilment through unalienated labour, while the 'mature' Marx paid much greater attention to economic analysis and appeared to subscribe to a belief in historical inevitably. *Modern Marxism* (sometimes called Western or neo-Marxism) has tried to provide an alternative to the mechanistic and determinist ideas of orthodox Marxism by looking to Hegelian philosophy (see dialectic), anarchism, liberalism, feminism and even rational choice theory, and has been concerned to explain the failure of Marx's predictions, looking, in particular, at the analysis of ideology and the state.

Significance

Marxism's political impact has been related largely to its ability to inspire and guide the twentieth-century communist movement. The intellectual attraction of Marxism has been that it embodies a remarkable breadth of vision, offering to understand and explain virtually all aspects of social and political existence, and uncovering the significance of processes that conventional theories ignore. Politically, it has attacked exploitation and oppression, and had a particularly strong appeal to disadvantaged groups and peoples. However, Marxism's star has dimmed markedly since the late twentieth century. To some extent this occurred as the tyrannical and dictatorial features of communist regimes themselves were traced back to Marx's ideas and assumptions. Marxist theories were, for example, seen as implicitly monistic in that rival belief systems are dismissed as ideological. The crisis of Marxism, however, intensified as a result of the collapse of communism in the Eastern European Revolutions of 1989–91. This suggested that, if the social and political forms that Marxism had inspired (however unfaithful they might have been to Marx's original ideas) no longer exist, Marxism as a world-historical force is dead. The alternative interpretation is that the collapse of communism provides an opportunity for Marxism, now divorced from Leninism and Stalinism, to be rediscovered as a form of humanist socialism, particularly associated with the ideas of the 'young' Marx.

MASS MEDIA

The media comprises those societal institutions that are concerned with the production and distribution of all forms of knowledge, information and entertainment. The 'mass' character of the mass media is derived from the fact that the media channel communication towards a large and undifferentiated audience using relatively advanced technology. Grammatically and politically, the mass media are plural. The *broadcast media*, including television, radio and, increasingly, 'new' media (electronic communications made possible through digital or computer technology, such as mobile phones and the internet), can be distinguished from the *print media*, which encompass newspapers, magazines and publishing generally. Similarly, different messages may be put out by, for example, public and private television channels, and by tabloid and broadsheet newspapers. The growth of 'new' media, particularly since the 1990s, has subverted the notion of mass media by dramatically increasing audience fragmentation.

Significance

Interest in the political impact of the mass media burgeoned during the twentieth century, initially through the growth of the popular press, but subsequently because of the growing penetration of television in particular throughout modern society. There can be no doubt that most political information is now disseminated by the mass media. When communication systems are subject to formal political control – as in state socialist, fascist or authoritarian regimes – the media become little more than a propaganda machine. However, there is considerable debate about its impact in liberal-democratic regimes. Some view the media's influence as being broadly positive. Pluralist theorists, for example, tend to argue that, so long as the media are independent from the state, they serve to promote democracy and protect freedom by providing a forum that allows a variety of political views to be debated and discussed. Moreover, as most forms of media are privately owned and so are sensitive to market demand, the media do not impose their own views but merely reflect those of their audience, listeners or readers.

Nevertheless, both left-wing and right-wing critics have complained about media bias, stemming from the fact that all forms of communication involve the selection, prioritization and interpretation of information. The most common version of this view, advanced especially by Marxists, regards the mass media as perhaps the key means of propagating bourgeois ideas and maintaining capitalist hegemony. Such ideas generally highlight the political power that flows from media ownership. An alternative version of the media bias argument holds that the mass media articulate the values of groups that are disproportionally represented among its senior professionals, be they left-leaning intellectuals, middle-class conservatives, or men. A more subtle, but nevertheless important form of media influence is summed up in Marshall McLuhan's famous aphorism – 'the medium is the message'. For example, the political impact of television may be less related to its content and more to its tendency to privatize leisure time and reduce achievement levels in children, thereby creating a 'post-civic' generation.

MERITOCRACY

Meritocracy literally means rules by the able or talented, merit being talent plus hard work. The term, however, is most commonly used as a principle of social justice, implying that social position and material rewards should reflect the distribution of ability and effort in society at large. Different implications can nevertheless be drawn from meritocracy, depending on whether emphasis is placed on talent or hard work. Meritocratic systems that focus primarily on talent are designed to encourage people, and particularly the talented, to realize their natural ability to its fullest potential. Those who primarily emphasize hard work regard effort only as morally laudable, on the grounds that to reward talent is to create a 'natural lottery' (Rawls, 1971). Meritocracy differs from hierarchy in that it allows for social mobility and a flexible pattern of inequalities, as opposed to fixed and structural gradations in social position and wealth.

Significance

Meritocracy is a key liberal social principle and can be seen as one of the basic values of liberal capitalism. Its defenders argue that it has both economic and moral virtues, including the following:

- It guarantees incentives by encouraging people to realize their talents and by rewarding hard work.
- It ensures that society is guided by wise and talented people who are better able to judge the interests of others.
- It is just in that distribution according to merit gives each person what he or she is 'due' and respects the principle of equality of opportunity.

However, the principle of meritocracy is by no means universally accepted. Its principal critics have been socialists, but traditional conservatives have also objected to it. Among their criticisms are:

- It threatens community and social cohesion by encouraging competition and self-striving; R. H. Tawney (1880–1962) called it a 'tadpole philosophy'.
- It is unjust because it implies that inequalities reflect unequal personal endowment when, in reality, they usually reflect unequal social treatment.
- It is contradictory because, on the one hand, it justifies social inequality, and on the other it can be achieved only through the redistribution of wealth to create a 'level playing field'.

MILITARISM

The term militarism can be used in two ways. First, it refers to the achievement of ends by the use of military force. Any attempt to solve problems by military means can be described as militarism in this sense. Second, and more commonly, militarism is a cultural and ideological phenomenon in which military priorities, ideals and values come to pervade the larger society. This typically includes the glorification of the armed forces; a heightened sense of national patriotism; the recognition of war as a legitimate instrument of policy; and an atavistic belief in heroism and self-sacrifice. In some cases, but not all, militarism is characterized by the abuse by the military of its legitimate functions, and its usurpation of responsibilities normally ascribed to civilian politicians.

Significance

Militarism, in it cultural or ideological sense, is a common feature of military regimes and totalitarian dictatorships. The defining feature of military rule is that members of the armed forces displace civilian politicians, meaning that the leading posts of government are filled on the basis of the person's position within the military chain of command. However, military rule may take a variety of forms, including collective military government, classically in the form of a military junta (from the Spanish *junta*, meaning 'council' or 'board'), a military dictatorship dominated by a single individual (for example, Colonel Papadopoulos in Greece, 1967–74, General Pinochet in Chile, 1973–90, and General Abacha in Nigeria, 1993–8), and situations in which the armed forces 'pull the strings' behind the scenes while allowing civilian political leaders to retain formal positions of power.

In such circumstances, militarism is a direct means of legitimizing the military's control of political life. In the case of totalitarian dictatorships, charismatic leaders such as Mussolini, Hitler and Saddam Hussein have used militarism in more subtle ways to consolidate power. By wearing military uniforms, associating themselves with the armed forces and using martial and militaristic rhetoric, they have attempted to imbue their regimes and societies with military values such as discipline, obedience, and a heightened sense of collective purpose, usually linked to chauvinist nationalism. However, militarism as a mechanism of regime consolidation is likely to be effective only in a context of war or intensifying international conflict, as is demonstrated by the fact that militarism is invariably accompanied by terroristic policing and widespread repression. Marxists have sometimes highlighted a link between militarism, in the limited sense of a disposition towards war and the use of military means, and capitalism, on the grounds that only high levels of defence spending, justified by the regular use of the military, ensure that domestic demand is buoyant and that profit levels remain high.

MINORITY RIGHTS

Minority rights are rights that are specific to the groups to which they belong, and not shared by the larger society. They are sometimes, on that basis, thought of as 'special' rights. Though minority rights have been claimed on behalf of people with disabilities and women (for whom the term draws attention to their minority status in positions of power, not in the general population), they are most commonly claimed on the basis of cultural difference, linked to factors such as ethnicity, religion and language. In this sense, they have been referred to as 'multicultural' rights. Will Kymlicka (1995) identified three kinds of minority rights:

* *Polyethnic rights* – rights and immunities that help to preserve a group's distinctive values and way of life
* *Representation rights* – rights that aim to redress a group's under-representation in education and positions of power
* *Self-government rights* – rights that afford a group (usually a national minority) political autonomy, but which stop short of sovereign independence.

Significance

The issue of minority rights have provoked particular controversy in relation to multiculturalism. A number of arguments have been advance in favour of minority rights. First, they have been viewed as a guarantee of individual freedom and personal autonomy. This is based on the assumption that people derive an important sense of who they are from the cultural groups to which they belong, suggesting that individual rights are intrinsically tied up with minority rights. Second, minority rights are seen as a way of countering oppression. In this view, groups are marginalized and disempowered through pressure to conform to the dominant culture, leading to a lack of recognition of their values and distinctive way of life. Third, minority rights are supported on the grounds that they redress social injustice. Minority rights, from this perspective, are a compensation for present or past disadvantages and unfair treatment, usually addressed through a programme of 'positive' discrimination, or 'affirmative action'.

The criticisms that have been made of minority rights include that, in addressing the distinctive needs of particular groups, minority rights may block the integration of the related group into the larger society. This may both harm the group itself and damage social cohesion. In addition, advancing the interests of minority groups through 'positive' discrimination has been condemned as demeaning and possibly counter-productive (because it implies that such groups cannot gain advancement through their own efforts). Finally, there is inevitable tension between minority rights and individual rights, in that cultural belonging is usually a product of family and social background, rather than personal choice. As most people do not 'join' a cultural group, it is difficult to see how or why they should be defined in terms of its beliefs and practices.

MONARCHY

A monarchy is a system of rule dominated by a single individual (it literally means 'rule by one person'). In general usage, however, it is the institution through which the post of head of state is filled through inheritance or dynastic succession. *Absolute monarchies* nevertheless differ from constitutional monarchies. Absolute monarchies are ones in which the monarch claims a monopoly of political power; the monarch is thus literally a sovereign. The classical basis of monarchical absolutism is the doctrine of divine right, the belief that the monarch has been chosen by God and so rules with God's authority on earth. *Constitutional monarchies* are ones in which sovereignty is vested elsewhere, and the monarch fulfils an essentially ceremonial role largely devoid of direct political significance. In some cases, constitutional monarchs may carry out residual political functions, such as selecting the prime minister, while in other cases they serve as nothing more than formal heads of state.

Significance

Absolute monarchy was the dominant form of government from the sixteenth to the nineteenth centuries, but now only exists in a handful of states, with examples including Brunei, Qatar, Saudi Arabia and Vatican City. The dynamics of monarchical absolutism are complex, however. While the monarch is, in theory, absolute, in practice power is usually shared between the monarch, economic elites (generally the landed aristocracy), and the established church, the formal source of the monarch's authority. Absolute monarchy was nevertheless unable to withstand the pressures generated by the modernization process, meaning that where monarchy has survived in developed states such as the UK, the Netherlands and Spain, it has done so in a strictly constitutional form. In the UK, while the royal prerogative is now exercised by the prime minister and other ministers accountable to Parliament, the monarch retains potentially significant political influence in her or his ability to choose a prime minister and dissolve Parliament in the event of a 'hung' Parliament (when no party has majority control of the House of Commons). The advantages associated with the constitutional monarchy include the following:

- It provides a solution to the need for a non-partisan head of state who is 'above' party politics.
- The monarch embodies traditional authority, and so serves as a symbol of patriotic loyalty and national unity.
- The monarch constitutes a repository of experience and wisdom, especially in relation to constitutional matters, available to elected governments.

The disadvantages of a constitutional monarchy include the following:

- It violates democratic principles in that political authority is not based on popular consent and is no way publicly accountable.
- The monarch symbolizes (and possibly supports) conservative values such as hierarchy, deference and respect for inherited wealth and social position.
- The monarchy binds nations to outmoded ways and symbols of the past, thus impeding modernization and progress.

MULTICULTURALISM

Multiculturalism reflects, most basically, a positive endorsement of communal diversity, usually arising from racial, ethnic and language differences. As such, multiculturalism is more a distinctive political stance than a coherent and programmic political doctrine. One key source of multicultural thinking stems from the attempt to refashion liberal beliefs to take into account the importance of communal belonging. In this view, individuals are seen as being culturally embedded creatures who derive their understanding of the world and their framework of moral beliefs and sense of personal identity largely from the culture in which they live and develop. Distinctive cultures therefore deserve to be protected or strengthened, particularly when they belong to minority or vulnerable groups. This leads to an emphasis on the politics of recognition and support for minority rights, which, in the case of national minorities, or 'First Nations', may extend to the right to self-determination. However, a more radical strain within multicultural thinking endorses a form of value pluralism which holds that, as people are bound to disagree about the ultimate ends of life, liberal and non-liberal, or even illiberal, beliefs and practices are equally legitimate. From this pluralist or 'post-liberal' perspective, liberalism 'absolutizes' values such as toleration and personal autonomy, so provides an inadequate basis for diversity. A further strain within multicultural theory attempts to reconcile multiculturalism with cosmopolitanism, placing a particular emphasis on hybridity and cultural mixing.

Significance

Multiculturalism first emerged as a theoretical stance through the activities of the black consciousness movement of the 1960s, primarily in the USA. During this phase it was largely concerned with establishing black pride, often through reconstructing a distinctive African identity, and overlapped in many ways with postcolonialism. It has also been shaped by the growing political assertiveness, sometimes expressed through ethnocultural nationalism, of established cultural groups in various parts of the world, and by the increasing cultural and ethnic diversity of many Western societies.

The attraction of multiculturalism is that it seeks to offer solutions to challenges of cultural diversity that cannot be addressed in any other way. Only enforced assimilation or the expulsion of ethnic or cultural minorities will re-establish monocultural nation-states. Indeed, in some respects, multiculturalism has advanced hand in hand with the seemingly irresistible forces of globalization. However, multiculturalism is by no means universally accepted. Its critics argue that, since it regards values and practices as acceptable so long as they generate a sense of group identity, non-liberal forms of multiculturalism may endorse reactionary and oppressive practices, particularly ones that subordinate women. Moreover, multiculturalism's model of group identity pays insufficient attention to diversity within cultural or religious groups and risks defining people on the basis of group membership alone. The most common criticism of multiculturalism is nevertheless that it is the enemy of social cohesion. In this view, shared values and a common culture are a necessary precondition for a stable and successful society.

MULTILATERALISM

Multilateralism is a process that co-ordinates behaviour among three or more states on the basis of generalized principles of conduct (Ruggie, 1993). For a process to be genuinely multilateral, it must conform to three principles. These are non-discrimination (all participating countries must be treated alike); indivisibility (participating countries must behave as if they were a single entity); and diffuse reciprocity (obligations among countries must have a general and enduring character, rather than being examples of episodic or 'single-shot' co-operation). Multilateralism may be formal, reflecting the acceptance of common norms and rules by three or more countries, or formal, and therefore institutional.

Significance

The concept of multilateralism has been widely used to draw attention to the stability of state relations in the West after World War II, by contrast with the inter-war period. This can be seen in particular in the construction of a liberal world economic order through the Bretton Woods agreement of 1944. To prevent a return to the so-called 'beggar-my-neighbour' policies of the 1930s (protectionism, competitive currency devaluations and so on), the 'Bretton Woods system' (comprising the IMF, the World Bank and the GATT, later replaced by the WTO) was set up to facilitate economic co-operation in key areas, notably a system of fixed exchange rates and free trade. The principle of non-discrimination was, for example, evident in the requirement of the GATT/WTO that all states must extend 'most favoured nation' status to all other members (meaning that each state is entitled to all and any favourable trading terms that apply to other states). However, it would be a mistake to portray Bretton Woods simply in terms of multilateralism and the recognition of mutual interests. This would be to ignore the crucial role played in the process by the USA, motivated, its critics have alleged, by the quest for global hegemony.

Interest in multilateralism was renewed in the early post-Cold War period, especially as the advance of globalization was associated with deepening economic interdependence. The founding of the WTO in 1995 thus marked a strengthened commitment to establishing a liberal trading system, and led to a proliferation of regional trade agreements as well as generally more effective regulation of the trade agreements already in existence. The emergence of the USA as the world's sole superpower nevertheless weakened multilateralism in the area of military and strategic affairs, as demonstrated by the USA's strongly unilateralist response to the

9/11 terrorist attacks. Debate about the prospects for multilateralism in the twenty-first century is commonly linked to the implications of rising multipolarity and, in particular, to whether a greater diffusion of global power will stimulate co-operation or spark conflict and rivalry.

MULTI-LEVEL GOVERNANCE

Multi-level governance (see Figure 9) is a governance system in which political authority is distributed at different levels of territorial aggregation. The 'vertical' conception of multi-level governance takes into account the interdependence of actors in the policy process at sub-national, national and transnational levels. Policy-making responsibility has therefore been both 'sucked up' from the national level and 'drawn down', creating a fluid process of negotiation. Much of the complexity of multi-level governance nevertheless derives from 'horizontal' developments such as the growth of relationships between states and non-state actors, and the emergence of new forms of public–private partnership.

Significance

Interest in the notion of multi-level governance has grown since the 1980s, reflecting an awareness that it is increasingly difficult to portray government as a specifically national activity that takes place within discrete societies. This traditional approach to government has been thrown into doubt by two developments. The first was a strengthening of centrifugal pressures within the state, which has taken place since the 1960s and has often been linked to the rise of ethnic and cultural nationalism. The second was the advent, from the 1980s onwards, of globalization. By intensifying interdependence and interconnectedness, this both fuelled the growth of regional and global governance and, by diminishing the nation-state, further strengthened centrifugal tendencies. The policy-making process was thus reconfigured, as bodies and related interests both 'above' and 'below' national government exerted a greater

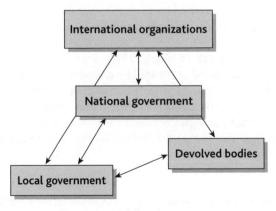

Figure 9 Multilevel governance

influence, and more time was spent on vertical relationships. However, the notion of multi-level governance is sometimes criticized for over-stating the extent to which national governments at large have lost policy-making authority. For example, multi-level governance may only be meaningful within the context of the European Union (the EU being the sole example of a regional body that exerts supranational authority), and then only when member states have a decentralized constitutional system, based on devolution or federalism.

NATION

Nations (from the Latin *nascinatio*, meaning 'to be born') are complex phenomena that are shaped by a collection of cultural, political and psychological factors. Culturally, a nation is a group of people bound together by a common language, religion, history and traditions. There is, however, no objective blueprint for the nation, because all nations exhibit some degree of cultural heterogeneity. Politically, a nation is a group of people who regard themselves as a natural political community. Although this is expressed classically in the form of a desire to establish or maintain statehood, it also takes the form of civic consciousness. Psychologically, a nation is a group of people distinguished by a shared loyalty or affection in the form of patriotism. Nevertheless, such an attachment is not a necessary condition for membership of a nation; even those who lack national pride may still recognize that they 'belong' to the nation.

However, such complexity has allowed quite different models of the nation to develop. Historians have sometimes distinguished between cultural nations and political nations. A *cultural nation* (such as the Greeks, the Germans, the Russians, the English and the Irish) has a national identity that is rooted in a common cultural heritage and language that may long pre-date the achievement of statehood or even the quest for national independence. A *political nation* (such as the British, the Americans and the South Africans) is bound together primarily by shared citizenship and may encompass significant cultural and ethnic divisions. Similarly, political thinkers may advance rival civic and organic views of the nation. The 'civic' concept of nationhood, supported, for example, by liberals and socialists, is inclusive in the sense that it places heavier emphasis on political allegiance than on cultural unity, and stresses that the nation is forged by shared values and expectations. The 'organic' concept of nationhood (advanced by conservatives and, more radically, by fascists) is exclusive in that it gives priority to a common ethnic identity and, above all, a shared history. Inclusive concepts of the nation tend to blur the distinction between the nation and the state, between nationality and citizenship. Exclusive concepts of the nation tend to blur the distinction between the nation and the race, between nationality and ethnicity.

Significance

For over 200 years the nation has been regarded as the most appropriate (and perhaps the only proper) unit of political rule. Indeed, international law is largely based on the assumption that nations, like individuals, have inviolable rights, notably the right to political independence and self-determination. The importance of the nation to politics is demonstrated most dramatically demonstrated by the enduring potency of nationalism and by the fact that the world is largely divided into nation-states. However, there is considerable disagreement about as to whether the nation plays a necessary or desirable role in political life. Supporters of the national principle portray nations as organic communities. In this light, humankind is naturally divided into a collection of nations, each possessing a distinctive character and separate identity. This, nationalists argue, is why a 'higher' loyalty and deeper political significance attaches to the nation than to any other social group or collective body. National ties and loyalties are thus found in all societies, they endure over time, and they operate at an instinctual, even primordial, level. On the other hand, critics of the national principle argue that nations are political constructs, 'imagined' or 'invented' communities whose purpose is to prop up the established order in the interests of rulers and elite groups. In this view, nationalism creates nations, not the other way round. Those who adopt this view have typically looked beyond the nation and supported forms of internationalism.

NATION-STATE

The nation-state is both a form of political organization and a political ideal. In the first case it is an autonomous political community bound together by the overlapping bonds of citizenship and nationality. It is thus an alternative to multinational empires and city-states. In the latter case the nation-state is a principle, reflected in Giuseppe Mazzini's (1805–72) goal: 'Every nation a state, only one state for the entire nation.' In practice, however, the nation-state is an ideal type and has probably never existed in perfect form anywhere in the world. No state is culturally homogeneous; all contain some kind of cultural or ethnic mix. There are two contrasting views of the nation-state. For liberals, and most socialists, the nation-state is largely fashioned out of civic loyalties and allegiances, while for conservatives and nationalists it is based on ethnic or organic unity.

Significance

The nation-state is widely considered to be the only viable unit of political rule and is generally accepted to be the basic element in international politics. The vast majority of modern states are, or claim to be, nation-states. The great strength of the nation-state is that it offers the prospect of both cultural cohesion and political unity. When a people who share a common cultural or ethnic identity gain the right to self-government, community and citizenship coincide. This is why nationalists believe that the forces that have created a world of independent nation-states are natural and irresistible, and that no other social group could constitute a meaningful political community. This view also implies that supranational bodies such as the European Union (EU) will never be able to rival the capacity of national governments to establish legitimacy and command popular allegiance. Clear limits should therefore be placed on, in this case, the process of European integration, because people with different languages, cultures and histories will never come to think of themselves as members of a united political community.

Nevertheless, powerful forces have emerged that threaten to make the nation-state redundant, and there are those who argue that the nation-state ideal has always been a regressive one. A combination of internal pressures and external threats has produced what is commonly referred to as a 'crisis of the nation-state'. Internally, nation-states have been subject to centrifugal pressures, generated by an upsurge in ethnic and regional politics. This has meant that ethnicity or religion have sometimes displaced nationality as the central organizing principle of political life. Externally, nation-states have arguably been rendered redundant by the advent of globalization. This has meant that major decisions in the economic, cultural and diplomatic spheres are increasingly made by supranational bodies and transnational corporations, which nation-states have only a limited capacity to influence. Those who criticize the nation-state ideal point out either that a 'true' nation-state can be achieved only through a process of 'ethnic cleansing' – as Hitler and the Nazis recognized – or that nation-states are always primarily concerned primarily with their own strategic and economic interests, and are therefore an inevitable source of conflict or tension in international affairs.

NATIONALISM

Nationalism can broadly be defined broadly as the belief that the nation is the central principle of political organization. As such, it is based on two core assumptions: first, humankind is naturally divided into distinct nations, and second, the nation is a political community in the sense that it is the most appropriate, and perhaps the only legitimate, unit of political rule. There is, nevertheless, disagreement about as to whether nationalism is a doctrine or an ideology. The doctrine of nationalism, or what is seen as 'classical' political nationalism, is the belief that all nations are entitled to independent statehood, suggesting that the world should consist of a collection of nation-states. This doctrine may, in turn, be reworked or reinterpreted when it is absorbed into one of a number of political ideologies. However, if nationalism is regarded as an ideology in its own right, it is seen to encompass a diverse range of forms:, political, cultural and ethnic. *Political nationalism* includes any attempt to use the nation ideal to further specifically political ends, which may be highly diverse, as explained below. *Cultural nationalism* emphasizes the regeneration of the nation as a distinctive civilization, and thus stresses the need to defend or strengthen a national language, religion, or way of life rather than achieve overt political ends. *Ethnic nationalism* overlaps with cultural nationalism, but as ethnic groups are seen, correctly or otherwise, to have descended from common ancestors, it implies a stronger and perhaps more intense sense of distinctiveness and exclusivity.

Political nationalism is a complex and diverse phenomenon. Its major forms are liberal nationalism, conservative nationalism, expansionist nationalism, and anti-colonial nationalism. *Liberal nationalism* assigns to the nation a moral status to the nation similar to that of the individual, meaning that nations have rights, in particular the right to self-determination. As liberal nationalism holds that all nations are equal, it proclaims that the nation-state ideal is universally applicable. *Conservative nationalism* is concerned less with the principled nationalism of self-determination and more with the promise of social cohesion and public order embodied in the sentiment of national patriotism. From this perspective patriotic loyalty and a consciousness of nationhood is largely rooted in the idea of a shared past, turning nationalism into a defence of traditional values and institutions that have been endorsed by history. *Expansionist nationalism* is an aggressive and militaristic form of nationalism that is invariably associated with chauvinistic beliefs and doctrines, which tends to blur the distinction between nationalism and racialism. In its extreme form, sometimes referred to as 'integral' nationalism, it arises from a sentiment of intense, even hysterical, nationalist enthusiasm. Anti-colonial nationalism linked the struggle for 'national liberation' in Africa, Asia and Latin America to the desire for social development, and was typically expressed through socialist doctrines, most commonly through the vehicle of revolutionary Marxism. However, developing-world nationalism has since the 1970s assumed a postcolonial character, which has been expressed most clearly through religious fundamentalism.

Significance

It would be difficult to overestimate the significance of nationalism to modern politics. For over 200 years nationalism has helped to shape and re-shape history in all parts of the world, making it perhaps the most successful of political creeds. The rising tide of nationalism re-drew the map of Europe in the nineteenth century as autocratic and multinational empires crumbled in the face of liberal and nationalist pressures. This process was continued in the twentieth century through the Treaty of Versailles (1919) and culminated in 1991 with the collapse of the political successor to the Russian empire, the USSR. Both World Wars I and II were arguably the result of an upsurge in aggressive nationalism, and most regional and international conflicts are to some extent fuelled by nationalism. The political face of the developing world has been transformed since 1945 by the rise of anti-colonialism and a subsequent postcolonial process of 'nation building', both of which are essentially manifestations of nationalism. On the other hand, there have been claims since the late twentieth century that nationalism has become an anachronism. These claims are based variously based on the fact that nationalism has achieved its aim in that the world is now mainly composed mainly of nation-states; that nation-states are themselves losing authority as a result of globalization and the growth of supranationalism; and that ethnic and regional political identities are displacing national ones.

The normative character of nationalism is notoriously difficult to judge. This is because nationalism has a two-sided political character. At different times, nationalism has been progressive and reactionary, democratic and authoritarian, rational and irrational, and left-wing and right-wing. Nationalists argue that a 'higher' loyalty and deeper political significance attaches to the nation than to any other social group or collective body, because nations are natural political communities. Nationalism is merely the recognition of this fact given ideological form. Supporters of nationalism, moreover, view nationalism as a means of enlarging freedom and defending democracy, since it is grounded in the idea of self-government. Such a defence of nationalism is developed most easily developed in relation to liberal nationalism and anti-colonial nationalism. However, opponents of nationalism argue that it is implicitly, and sometimes explicitly, oppressive, and that it is invariably linked to intolerance, suspicion and conflict. Nationalism is oppressive, both in the sense that it submerges individual identity and conscience within that of the national whole, and because of the potential it gives political leaders and elites to manipulate and control the masses. The argument that nationalism is inherently divisive stems from the fact that it highlights difference among humankind and legitimizes an identification with, and a preference for, one's own people or nation; in short, it breeds tribalism. This may be implicit in conservative nationalism and explicit in expansionist nationalism, but all forms of nationalism may harbour a darker face that is essentially chauvinistic and potentially aggressive.

NAZISM

Nazism, or national socialism, is an ideological tradition within fascism that is fashioned from a combination of racial nationalism, anti-Semitism and social Darwinism. The core of Nazi ideology is a set of racial theories, encouraging some to define Nazism as 'fascism plus racialism'. German Nazism, the original and archetypal form of Nazism, portrayed the German people as supremely gifted and organically unified, and with their creativity resting on the purity of their blood. For the Nazis, this was reflected in Aryanism – the belief that the Aryans or Germans are a 'master race' ultimately destined for world domination. The Jews, in contrast, were seen as being fundamentally evil and destructive; in *Mein Kampf* (1925/1969), Hitler portrayed the Jews as a universal scapegoat for all Germany's misfortunes. Nazism thus portrayed the world in pseudo-religious and pseudo-scientific terms as a struggle for dominance between the Germans and the Jews, representing, respectively, the forces of 'good' and 'evil'. The logic of Hitler's world view was that this racial struggle could only end either in the final victory of the Jews and the destruction of Germany, or in Aryan world conquest and the elimination of the Jewish race. Forms of Nazism that have sprung up outside Germany since 1945, sometimes termed neo-Nazism, have retained the cult of Hitler but have often reassigned Hitler's racial categories. The Aryans are defined more broadly as the Nordic peoples – pale-skinned people of north European stock – or simply as the 'whites'. Their enemies are not only the Jews but any convenient racial minority, but most commonly the 'blacks'.

Significance

Nazism had profound and tragic consequences for world history in the twentieth century. The Hitler regime, established in 1933, embarked on a programme of remilitarization and expansionism that resulted in World War II, and in 1941 the Nazis instigated what they called the 'final solution' – the attempt to exterminate European Jewry in an unparalleled process of mass murder. This resulted in the death of some six million people. Historians have nevertheless debated how far such events can be explained in terms of the ideological goals of Nazism. One school of thought insists that the entire regime was geared to the fulfilment of Hitler's world view as outlined in *Mein Kampf*, while another suggests that genocidal slaughter and world war, while consistent with Hitler's goals, were in fact the outcome of tactical blunders and the institutional chaos of a Nazi regime that was structured by bureaucratic rivalries and Hitler's laziness. Germany's susceptibility to Nazism in the 1930s is usually linked to a combination of frustrated nationalism, defeat in World War I and the terms of the Treaty of Versailles, and to the deep instabilities of the Weimar republic, exacerbated by the world economic crisis. If Nazism is a specifically German phenomenon, it is associated with chauvinist and anti-Semitic currents that ran through traditional German nationalism and flourished in the peculiar historical circumstances of the inter-war period. However, as a general ideology of racial hatred, Nazism (or neo-Nazism) may remain a constant threat as a means of articulating the anger and resentment of socially insecure groups that have become disengaged from conventional politics.

NEOLIBERALISM

Neoliberalism (sometimes called neoclassical liberalism) is an updated version of classical liberalism and particularly classical political economy. Its central theme is market fundamentalism, an absolute faith in the market, reflected in the belief that the market mechanism offers solutions to all economic and social problems. Neoliberals thus argue that, while unregulated market capitalism delivers efficiency, growth and widespread prosperity, the 'dead hand' of the state saps initiative and discourages enterprise. In short, the neoliberal philosophy is: 'market good; state bad'. Key neoliberal policies include privatization, low public spending, deregulation, tax cuts (particularly corporate and direct taxes) and reduced welfare provision.

Significance

The rise of neoliberalism can be seen in the broad shift since the 1970s from inter-ventionist economic strategies to market-based strategies, though the 'neoliberal revolution' has affected some countries and regions much more than others. The earliest experiment in neoliberalism occurred in Chile, following the CIA-backed military coup that overthrew Salvador Allende in 1973, its influence subse-quently spreading to Brazil, Argentina and elsewhere in South America. During the 1980s, neoliberalism was extended to the USA and the UK, in the forms of 'Reaganism' (after President Reagan, 1981–98) and 'Thatcherism' (after Prime Minister Thatcher, 1979–91), with other countries such as Canada, Australia and New Zealand quickly following suit. The wider, and seemingly irresistible, advance of neoliberalism occurred during the 1990s, through the influence of the institutions of global economic governance and the growing impact of globaliza-tion. During the 1980s, the World Bank and the IMF were converted to the idea of what later became known as the 'Washington consensus', which was aligned to the economic agendas of Reagan and Thatcher, and focused on policies such as free trade, the liberalization of capital markets, flexible exchange rates, balanced budgets and so on.

Deep controversy nevertheless surrounds neoliberalism. For neoliberals and their supporters, the clearest argument in favour of market reforms and economic liberalization is that they have worked. The advance of neoliberalism coincided not only with three decades of growth in the USA and its renewed economic ascendancy, but also three decades of growth in the world economy. In this light, neoliberalism was based on a new growth model that has clearly demonstrated its superiority over the Keynesian–welfarist orthodoxy of old. On the other hand, critics have argued that, in rolling back welfare provision and promoting an ethic of material self-interest ('greed is good'), neoliberalism struggles to maintain popular legitimacy as an economic doctrine because of its association with widening inequality and social breakdown. The economic credentials of neoliberalism have, furthermore, been brought into question by the failure of 'shock therapy' market reforms in countries ranging from Chile and Argentina to Russia, and more significantly by the global financial crisis of 2007–09, which exposed the dangers inherent in under-regulated banking and financial markets.

NEUTRALITY

Neutrality is the absence of any form of partisanship or commitment; it consists of a refusal to 'take sides'. In international relations, neutrality is a legal condition through which a state declares non-involvement in a conflict or war, and indicates its intention to refrain from supporting or aiding either side. As a principle of indi-vidual conduct, applied to the likes of judges, civil servants, the military and other public officials, it implies, strictly speaking, the absence of political sympathies and ideological leanings. Neutral actors are thus political eunuchs. In practice, the less exacting requirement of impartiality is usually applied. This allows that political sympathies may be held as long as these do not intrude into a person's professional or public responsibilities.

Significance

The principle of neutrality is crucial to the theory and practice of liberal-democratic government. At its core is a belief in state neutrality, the idea that the state harbours no economic, social or other biases and therefore treats all individuals and groups alike. This is reflected in the constitutional principle of neutrality as it applies to state bodies and officials, notably the judiciary, the civil service, the police and the military. Neutrality thus guarantees that the state is kept separate from the govern-ment, in the sense that public officials are not contaminated by the political and ideological enthusiasms of professional politicians. From this perspective, political neutrality has two key benefits. It ensures fairness in the sense that all people are treated equally regardless of social background, race, religion, gender and so on, and it fosters objectivity in allowing decisions to be made on the basis of reason and evidence, rather than irrational prejudice. However, neutrality has been criticized on three grounds. First, Marxists, feminists and others have portrayed it as a façade designed to mask the degree to which the state, often via the structure and composition of state institutions, articulates the interests of powerful or propertied groups in society. Second, some dismiss neutrality as simply a myth, arguing that no one is capable of suppressing values and beliefs that are formed through one's social background and group membership. Third, neutrality may be considered undesirable by those who believe that it engenders indifference or allows public officials to resist the will of democratically elected governments.

NON-GOVERNMENTAL ORGANIZATION

A non-governmental organization (NGO) is a private, non-commercial group or body which seeks to achieve its ends through non-violent means. The World Bank defines NGOs as 'private organizations that pursue activities to relieve suffering, promote the interests of the poor, protect the environment, provide basic social services, or undertake community development'. A distinction is often drawn between operational NGOs and advocacy NGOs, although many NGOs combine both roles. *Operational NGOs* are ones whose primary purpose is the design and implementation of development-related projects; they may be either relief-orientated or development-orientated, and may be community-based, national or international. *Advocacy NGOs* exist to promote or defend a particular cause; they are sometimes called promotional pressure groups or public interest groups.

Significance

During the 1990s, the steady growth in the number of NGOs became a veritable explosion. By 2000, over 1,000 groups had been granted consultative status by the UN (although this includes business organizations and faith groups, as well as NGOs), with estimates of the total number of international NGOs usually exceeding 30,000. The major international NGOs have developed into huge organizations. For example, Care International, dedicated to the worldwide reduction of poverty, controls a budget worth more than US$100m, Greenpeace has a membership of 2.5 million and a staff of over 1,200, and Amnesty International is better resourced than the human rights arm of the UN. There can be little doubt that major international NGOs and the NGO sector as a whole are now significant actors on the world stage. Though lacking the economic leverage that transnational corporations (TNCs) can exert, advocacy NGOs have proved highly adept at mobilizing 'soft' power and popular pressure. Operational NGOs, for their part, have come to deliver about 15 per cent of international aid, often demonstrating a greater speed of response and level of operational effectiveness than governmental bodies, national or international, can muster.

Nevertheless, the rise of the NGO has provoked considerable political controversy. Supporters of NGOs argue that they benefit and enrich world politics. They counterbalance corporate power, challenging the influence of TNCs; democratize global politics by articulating the interests of people and groups who have been disempowered by the globalization process; and act as a moral force, widening peoples' sense of civic responsibility and even promoting global citizenship. In these respect, they are a vital component of an emergent global civil society. Critics, however, argue that NGOs are self-appointed groups that have no genuine democratic credentials, often articulating the views of a small group of senior professionals. In an attempt to gain a high media profile and attract support and funding, NGOs have been accused of making exaggerated claims, thereby distorting public perceptions and the policy agenda. Finally, to preserve their 'insider' status, NGOs tend to compromise their principles and 'go mainstream', becoming, in effect, de-radicalized social movements.

OBLIGATION

An obligation is a requirement or duty to act in a particular way. Legal obligations are nevertheless different from moral obligations. *Legal obligations*, such as the requirement to pay taxes and observe other laws, are enforceable through the courts and backed up by a system of penalties. 'Being obliged' to do something implies an element of coercion; legal obligations may thus be upheld on grounds of simple prudence: whether laws are right or wrong, they are obeyed out of a fear of punishment. *Moral obligations*, on the other hand, are fulfilled not because it is sensible to do so, but because such conduct is thought to be rightful or morally correct. 'Having an obligation' to do something suggests only a moral duty. To give a promise, for example, is to be under a moral obligation to carry it out, regardless of the consequences that breaking the promise will entail. The most important form of moral obligation is 'political obligation' – the duty of the citizen to acknowledge the authority of the state and obey its laws. Obligation can therefore be thought of as one of the key components of citizenship, the rights and obligations of the citizen being reverse sides of the same coin.

Significance

The issue of political obligation has been one of the central themes in political theory. This is because the question of obligation addresses the moral basis of political rule. The classic explanation of political obligation is found in the idea of a 'social contract', an agreement made among citizens, or between citizens and the state, through which they accept the authority of the state in return for benefits that only a sovereign power can provide. For Plato (427–347 BCE), the obligation to obey the state is based on an implicit promise made by the fact that citizens choose to remain within its borders; for Thomas Hobbes (1588–1679) and John Locke (1632–1704), it was based on the state's ability to deliver order and stability; and for Jean-Jacques Rousseau (1712–78), it followed from the state's capacity to articulate the 'general will' or collective good.

However, conservatives and communitarians have gone further and suggested that obligation is not merely contractual but is an intrinsic feature of any stable society. From this perspective, obligation is a form of natural duty, reflecting the fact that our values and identities are largely derived from the societies in which we live. The only theorists who reject the idea of political obligation are philosophical anarchists, who insist on absolute respect for personal autonomy.

OPPOSITION

Opposition, in its everyday sense, means hostility or antagonism. However, in its political sense, opposition usually refers to antagonism that has a formal character and operates within a constitutional framework. This is seen most clearly in relation to parliamentary systems of government, in which the political parties outside of government are generally viewed as being opposition parties, the largest of them sometimes being designated as 'the opposition'. In two-party systems, parliamentary procedures often take into account formal rivalry between the two major parties, acting as government and opposition, respectively, with the opposition sometimes replicating the structure of government by forming a 'shadow' cabinet and operating as a 'government in waiting'.

The notion of opposition is usually developed less formally in multi-party systems and in presidential systems of government. In multi-party systems the government-versus-opposition dynamic is weakened by the fact that government, being a coalition, is not a cohesive force but contains internal sources of rivalry, and that there is rarely a single opposition party that has the potential to form a government on its own. In presidential systems the opposition party is technically the party that does not hold the presidency; however, this party may nevertheless be the majority party in the legislature and thus be able to wield considerable policy-making influence. Opposition may, on the other hand, have an extra-parliamentary and anti-constitutional character. In such cases it refers to political groupings, movements or parties that reject established political procedures and challenge, sometimes through revolution, the principles on which the political system is based.

Significance

Opposition is a vital feature of liberal-democratic government. It serves three major functions. First, it helps to ensure limited government and so protect freedom by serving as a formal check on the government of the day. Second, it guarantees scrutiny and oversight, improving the quality of public policy and making government accountable for its blunders. Third, it strengthens democratic accountability by creating a more informed electorate and offering a choice between meaningful parties of government. In addition, especially in two-party systems, parliamentary opposition ensures a smooth and immediate transfer of power because an alternative government is always available. There are, nevertheless, concerns about the effectiveness and value of constitutional opposition. Some argue that parliamentary opposition is merely tokenistic, in that, behind a façade of debate and antagonism, both government and opposition support the existing constitutional arrangements and, as long as power alternates, both benefit from them. Much opposition is therefore a parliamentary ritual that has little impact on the content of public policy. An alternative concern is that opposition, particularly in a two-party context, may result in adversary politics, a style of politics that turns political life into an ongoing battle between major parties aimed at winning electoral support. When oppositions oppose for the sake of opposing, political debate is reduced to what has sometimes been called 'yah-boo politics'.

ORDER

Order, in everyday language, refers to regular and tidy patterns, as when work is set out in an 'orderly' manner or the universe is described as being 'ordered'. In social life, order describes regular, stable and predictable forms of behaviour, for which reason social order suggests continuity, even permanence. Social disorder, by contrast, implies chaotic, random and violent behaviour that is by its very nature unstable and continually changing. As a political principle, therefore, order is associated with personal security: physical security, freedom from intimidation and violence and the fear of such; and psychological security, the comfort and stability that only regular and familiar circumstances engender. However, order may be conceived of as being either a political or a natural phenomenon. *Political order* stands for social control, imposed 'from above' through a system of law and government. Order in this sense is linked to the ideas of discipline, regulation and authority. *Natural order*, on the other hand, arises 'from below' through the voluntary and spontaneous actions of individuals and groups. In this sense, order is linked to ideas such as social harmony and equilibrium.

Significance

A fear of disorder and social instability has been one of the most fundamental and abiding concerns of Western political philosophy. Order has, moreover, attracted almost unqualified approval from political theorists, at least in so far as none of them is prepared to defend disorder. However, there are deep differences regarding the most appropriate solutions to the problem of order. The public/natural order divide has profound implications for government and reflects differing views of human nature. At one extreme, Thomas Hobbes (1588–1679) argued that absolute government is the only means of maintaining order because the principal human inclination is a 'perpetual and restless desire for power, that ceaseth only in death'. At the other extreme, Pyotr Kropotkin (1842–1921) supported anarchism on the grounds that order can be established by 'liberty and fraternal care', and that crime is merely the result of 'idleness, law and authority'.

In modern politics, the conservative view of order links it closely to law, often viewing 'law and order' as a single, fused concept. Domestic order is therefore best maintained through a fear of punishment, based on the strict enforcement of law and stiff penalties, and on respect for traditional values, seen as the moral bedrock of society. Modern liberals and socialists, in contrast, have argued traditionally that a reliance on fear and respect is inadequate, because disorder is largely a consequence of poverty and social deprivation. From this perspective, order is best maintained through social reform, designed, for example, to improve housing conditions, reduce unemployment and counter urban decay.

PACIFISM

Pacifism is the belief that all war is morally wrong. Such a stance is based on two lines of thought. The first is that war is wrong because killing is wrong. This principled rejection of war and killing in all circumstances is based on underpinning assumptions about the sanctity or oneness of life, often (but not always) rooted in religious conviction. Strains of pacifism have been found within Christianity, particularly associated with the Quakers and the Plymouth Brethren, within Hinduism – especially with Gandhi's ethic of non-violence, and within Buddhism and Jainism. The second line of argument, sometimes called 'contingent pacifism', places greatest stress on the wider and often longer-term benefits of non-violence for human well-being. From this perspective, violence is never a solution because it breeds more violence through developing a psychology of hatred, bitterness and revenge. This has been reflected in the use of pacifism or non-violence as a political tactic, which derives its force from it being morally uncontaminated, as in most cases of civil disobedience.

Significance

Pacifism has served as an important force in international politics in two main ways. First, in the form of 'legal pacifism', it has provided support for the establishment of intergovernmental bodies, such as the League of Nations and the United Nations, which aim to ensure the peaceful resolution of international disputes by upholding a system of international law. Second, pacifism has helped to fuel the emergence of a growing, if disparate, 'peace' movement. Peace activism first emerged as a response to the advent of the nuclear era, reflecting the belief that the invention of nuclear weapons had fundamentally altered calculations about the human cost, and therefore the moral implications, of warfare.

However, pacifism has been associated with deep moral and philosophical difficulties. First, it has been regarded as incoherent in that it is based on the right to life, but this can only be defended, in certain circumstances, through a willingness to use force to protect oneself or others. In this view, the right not to be attacked must include the right to defend oneself with, if necessary, killing force when attacked. The second difficulty concerns the implications of according overriding importance to the avoidance of killing, a position that treats other considerations, such as those about freedom, justice, recognition and respect, as being of secondary importance. However, the value of life is closely, and inevitably, linked to the conditions in which people live, which implies a necessary trade-off between the avoidance of killing and the protection of other values. It is precisely such a trade-off that has been used to justify humanitarian intervention.

PARADIGM

A paradigm is, in a general sense, a pattern or model that highlights relevant features of a particular phenomenon. As defined by Thomas Kuhn (1962), a paradigm is 'the entire constellation of beliefs, values, techniques and so on shared by members of a given community'. Any intellectual framework, comprising interrelated values, theories and assumptions within which the search for knowledge is conducted can therefore be termed a paradigm, in the Kuhnian sense. Though Kuhn developed the concept of paradigm specifically in relation to the natural sciences, it has come to be widely applied to the social sciences, including politics and international relations.

Significance

The value of paradigms is that they help us to make sense of what would otherwise be an impenetrably complex reality. They define what is important to study, and highlight significant trends, patterns and processes. In so doing, they draw attention to relevant questions and lines of enquiry, as well as indicate how the results of intellectual enquiry should be interpreted. What is more, as the limitations of an established paradigm are more widely recognized, not least through a growing recognition of anomalies that it is unable to explain, the search for knowledge can be reinvigorated dramatically by a 'paradigm shift', as the established paradigm breaks down and a new one is constructed in its place. This, for example, occurred in physics in the early twentieth century, through the transition from Newtonian mechanics to the ideas of quantum mechanics, made possible by the development of Einstein's theory of relativity. In economics, a similar process occurred during the 1970s and 1980s, as Keynesianism was displaced by monetarism.

However, paradigms may also foster tunnel vision and hinder intellectual progress. Paradigms may limit our perceptual field, meaning that we 'see' only what our favoured paradigm shows us, and, perhaps, are confined to the insights of but one discipline. Moreover, paradigms tend to generate conformity among students and scholars alike, unable – or unwilling – to think outside the currently dominant (or fashionable) paradigm. An example of this came with the end of the Cold War, which, while it was the most significant event in world politics since 1945, appeared to take international relations scholars as much by surprise as it did other commentators. Such concerns have encouraged some to advocate thinking either across paradigms or beyond them, something which, arguably, demands interdisciplinarity (Sil and Katzenstein, 2010).

PARLIAMENT

The terms parliament, assembly and legislature are often used interchangeably, but they have, to some extent, different implications. An assembly, in its simplest sense, is a collection or gathering of people, as in, for example, a school assembly. As a political term, assembly has come to be associated with representative and popular government, an assembly being viewed as a surrogate for the people. For this reason the term is sometimes reserved for the lower, popularly elected chamber in a bicameral system, or for the single chamber in a unicameral system. A legislature is a law-making body; however, even when assemblies are invested with formal and possibly supreme legislative authority, they never monopolize lawmaking power and rarely in practice control the legislative process. Parliament (from the French *parler*, meaning 'to speak') implies consultation and deliberation, and thus suggests that the primary role of an assembly is to act as a debating chamber in which policies and political issues can be openly discussed and scrutinized. Parliaments are generally categorized according to their capacity to influence policy. Policy-making parliaments enjoy significant autonomy and have an active impact on policy. Policy-influencing parliaments can transform policy but only by reacting to executive initiatives. Executive-dominated parliaments exert marginal influence or merely 'rubber-stamp' executive decisions.

Significance

Parliaments occupy a key position in the machinery of government. Traditionally they have been treated with special respect and status as the public, even democratic, face of government. Parliaments are respected because they are composed of lay politicians who claim to represent the people rather than being made up of trained or expert government officials. As such, parliaments provide a link between government and the people; that is, they are a channel of communication that can both support government and uphold the regime, and force government to respond to popular demands. The chief functions of a parliament are to enact legislation, act as a representative body, oversee and scrutinize the executive, recruit and train politicians, and assist in maintaining the political system's legitimacy.

However, parliaments are often subordinate bodies in modern political systems. Examples of policy-making assemblies are rare (the US Congress and the Italian Senate are exceptions). Most can be classified as either policy-influencing or executive-dominated parliaments. The amount of power a parliament has is determined by a variety of state-specific factors. These include the extent of the parliament's constitutional authority, its degree of political independence from the executive (notably, whether it operates within a parliamentary or a presidential system), the nature of the party system, and the parliament's level of organizational coherence (particularly the strength of its committee system).

Most commentators agree that parliaments have generally lost power since the late nineteenth century. This decline has occurred because of the executive's greater capacity to formulate policy and provide leadership; because of the growth in the role of government and the consequent increase in the size and status of bureaucracies; because of the emergence of disciplined political parties; and because of the increased strength of pressure groups, and the rise of the mass media as an alternative forum for political debate and discussion. There is, nevertheless, also evidence of a revival in parliamentary power, through, for example, the strengthening of specialist committees and a trend towards professionalization. This reflects the recognition of a link between the legitimacy and stability of a political system and the effectiveness of its parliament.

PARLIAMENTARY GOVERNMENT

A parliamentary system of government (see Figure 10) is one in which the government governs in and through the parliament or assembly, thereby 'fusing' the legislative and executive branches. While they are formally distinct, the parliament and the executive (usually seen as the government) are bound together in a way that violates the doctrine of the separation of powers, setting parliamentary systems of government clearly apart from presidential government.

The chief features of a parliamentary system are:

- Governments are formed as a result of parliamentary elections, based on the strength of party representation – there is no separately elected executive.
- The personnel of government are drawn from the parliament, usually from the leaders of the party or parties that have majority control.
- The government is responsible to the parliament, in the sense that it rests on the parliament's confidence and can be removed (generally by the lower chamber) if it loses that confidence.
- The government can, in most cases, 'dissolve' the parliament by calling a general election, meaning that electoral terms are usually flexible within a maximum limit.
- Parliamentary executives are generally collective in that they accept at least the formal principle of cabinet government.
- The posts of head of government (usually a prime minister) and head of state are separate, the latter being either a constitutional monarch or a non-executive president.

Significance

Most liberal democracies have adopted some form of parliamentary government. These are often seen as 'Westminster model' systems of government, in that they are based on the example of the UK Parliament, sometimes portrayed as the 'mother of parliaments'. However, the full 'Westminster model' also relies on features such as a two-party system, parliamentary sovereignty and collective responsibility that may be absent in other parliamentary systems, such as those in Germany, Sweden, India,

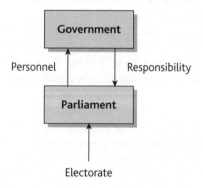

Figure 10 Parliamentary government

Japan, New Zealand and Australia. The chief strength of parliamentary government is that it supposedly delivers strong but responsible government. Government is strong in that it rests on the confidence of the parliament and so can, in most cases, ensure that its legislative programme is passed. In short, governments can get things done. However, responsible government is maintained because the government can govern only as long as it retains the confidence of the parliament. In theory, the parliament has the upper hand because it has a power it does not possess in a presidential system: the ability to remove the government or executive. Moreover, parliamentary government is often seen to promote democracy, parliamentary democracy being a form of responsible and representative government in which the parliament plays a vital deliberative role as a forum for national debate, constituting a popular check on government.

However, the workings of parliamentary government depend on a number of other factors, notably the nature of the party system and the political culture. Parliamentary government can, for example, become a form of party government. This occurs when the government is formed from a single, ideologically and organizationally cohesive party, which operates on the basis of a direct mandate from the electorate, rather than on the basis of parliamentary authority. Parliamentary government is also often associated with the problem of executive domination, what Lord Hailsham (1976), in the case of the UK system, referred to as 'elective dictatorship'. If governments have majority control and can maintain party discipline (easier in the case of single-party government) the parliament can be reduced to little more than a 'talking shop' and its members may become mere 'lobby fodder'. Finally, parliamentary systems have also been linked with weak government and political instability. This usually occurs when the party system is fractured, and is often associated with highly proportional electoral systems. In the French Fourth Republic (1946–58), for example, 25 governments came and went in just over 12 years, and Italy had no fewer than 63 governments between 1945 and 2014. Parliamentary government can thus, ironically, result in either excessive executive power or excessive legislative power.

PATRIARCHY

Patriarchy literally means rule by the *pater* (Latin) or father, and refers to the domination of the husband/father within the family, and the subordination of his wife and his children. However, the term is commonly used in the more general sense of 'rule by men', drawing attention to the totality of oppression and exploitation to which women are subject. The use of the patriarchy thus implies that the system of male power in society at large both reflects and stems from the domination of the father in the family. This is reflected in the radical feminist slogan: 'the personal is the political'. Kate Millett (1970) argued that patriarchy contains two principles: 'male shall dominate female, elder male shall dominate younger male', suggesting that a patriarchal society is characterized by interlocking systems of sexual and generational oppression.

Significance

The concept of patriarchy was introduced into wider political discourse through the emergence of so-called second-wave feminism in the 1960s. Its value is that it draws attention to the political significance of gender and to the political relationship between women and men. Whereas conventional political theory treats gender relations as natural, feminist theorists, through the notion of patriarchy, view them as part of the political institution of male power. However, patriarchy is interpreted differently by different schools of feminism. For radical feminists, patriarchy is a key concept, in that it emphasizes that gender inequality is systematic, institutionalized and pervasive; many radical feminists argue that patriarchy is evident in all social institutions and in every society, both contemporary and historical. Patriarchy thus expresses the belief that gender divisions are deeper and more politically significant than divisions based, say, on nationality, social class, race or ethnicity. Socialist feminists, in contrast, highlight links between gender inequality and social inequality, seeing patriarchy and capitalism as interdependent systems of domination. Liberal feminists, on the other hand, are sometimes reluctant to use the term patriarchy, on the grounds that they are less likely to prioritize gender divisions over other forms of inequality, and because they understand it in terms of the unequal distribution of rights and entitlements, rather than systematic and institutionalized oppression. Post-feminist theorists have also argued that the advances women have made, in developed societies at least, mean that patriarchy is no longer a useful or appropriate term, patriarchal institutions and practices having been substantially reformed.

PATRIOTISM

Patriotism (from the Latin *patria*, meaning 'fatherland') is a sentiment, a psychological attachment to one's nation, literally a 'love of one's country'. The terms patriotism and nationalism are often confused. Nationalism has a doctrinal character and embodies the belief that the nation is in some way the central principle of political organization. Patriotism provides the affective basis for that belief, and thus underpins all forms of nationalism. It is difficult to conceive of a national group demanding, say, political independence without possessing at least a measure of patriotic loyalty and national consciousness. In that sense, patriotism is sometimes considered to be a weak form of nationalism. However, not all patriots are nationalists. Not all of those who identify with or even love their nation see it as a means through which political demands can be articulated. For example, to support one's national team in sporting events does not necessarily imply support for national self-determination.

Significance

Patriotism is widely considered to be natural and healthy. It is natural, as socio-biologists have argued, for people to seek security through group membership and to identify with others who share similar characteristics to with themselves. It is desirable both because it is a means of generating national unity and solidarity and because it builds in individuals a sense of rootedness and belonging in individuals. Conservatives, and in a more extreme sense, fascists, have therefore seen patriotic loyalty as the basis of national identity, and linked patriotism to citizenship. However, patriotism has by no means been universally accepted. Opponents of patriotism, who tend to espouse forms of liberalism and socialism, view it as an irrational herd instinct that harbours chauvinism and breeds bigotry. In this light, patriotism operates through a distinction between 'them' and 'us': there has to be a 'them' to fear or hate in order to give 'us' a stronger sense of loyalty and identity.

PEACE-BUILDING

Peace-building is a long-term process of creating the necessary conditions for sustainable peace by addressing the deep-rooted, structural causes of violent conflict in a comprehensive manner. Strictly speaking, peace-building is a phase in the peace process that occurs after peacemaking and peacekeeping have been completed. However, these activities invariably overlap to a greater or lesser degree, meaning that peace-building resembles what is often called multidimensional peacekeeping. Peace-building as long-term conflict resolution involves a wide range of strategies – economic, political and social as well as military. These include: economic reconstruction; repairing or improving the economic and social infrastructure; de-mining; the demobilization and retraining of former combatants; the reintegration of displaced peoples; and establishing community organizations.

Significance

The notion of peace-building has attracted increasing attention since the end of the Cold War, as the limitations of classical or 'first generation' UN peacekeeping, aimed essentially at monitoring and observing the peace process in post-conflict situations, have been recognized. Ever since the 1992 UN report, *An Agenda for Peace*, there has been an acknowledgement that 'peacekeeping alone' is not enough to ensure lasting peace. The growing emphasis on peace-building reflects a desire to identify and support structures that will tend to strengthen and solidify peace in order to avoid a relapse into conflict, thus helping to establish 'positive' peace. Though the military remain the backbone of most peacekeeping operations, the many faces of peace-building now include administrators and economists, police officers and legal experts, mine-clearance personnel, and electoral observers, human rights monitors and specialists in civil affairs and governance. However, the record of peace-building operations, carried out under the auspices of the UN and other bodies, has been patchy at best, not least because of the deep complexities of so many conflict situations in the post-Cold War era, and the scope and scale of the transformations that may be needed to establish sustainable peace. It might therefore not be possible to distinguish between peace-building and 'state-building' or 'nation-building'. Not only do these amount to daunting challenges, but some argue that, by their nature, they are challenges that cannot be met primarily though external intervention.

PLURALISM

Pluralism can be defined broadly as a belief in, or a commitment to, diversity or multiplicity – the existence of many things. The term, however, is complex, because it can be used in both a normative and a descriptive sense (and sometimes combines descriptive observations with normative endorsements), and because it has a variety of applications. As a normative term it implies that diversity is healthy and desirable in itself, usually because it safeguards individual freedom and promotes debate, argument and understanding. As a descriptive term it can assume a variety of forms. *Political pluralism* denotes the existence of electoral choice and a competitive party system. *Moral pluralism* refers to a multiplicity of ethical values. *Cultural pluralism* suggests a diversity of lifestyles and cultural norms.

Pluralism, however, is used more narrowly as a theory of the distribution of political power. *Classical pluralism* holds that power is widely and evenly dispersed in society, rather than concentrated in the hands of an elite or a ruling class. In this form, pluralism is usually seen as a theory of group politics, in which individuals are largely represented through their membership of organized groups, and all such groups have access to the policy process.

The main assumptions of the pluralist perspective are:

- All citizens belong to groups and many will have multiple group membership.
- There is rough equality among groups, in that each group has access to government and no group enjoys a dominant position.
- There is a high level of internal responsiveness within groups, leaders being accountable to members.
- The state is neutral among groups and the governmental machine is sufficiently fragmented to offer groups a number of access points.
- Despite groups having competing interests, there is a wider consensus among groups on the nature of the political system and the values of openness and competition.

Reformed pluralism, or neo-pluralism, has revised classical pluralism in that it acknowledges that the distribution of power in modern societies is imperfect, elite and privileged interests persisting within a broader context of group competition. Western democracies are thus viewed as 'deformed polyarchies', in which major corporations in particular exert a disproportionate influence.

Significance

Pluralist ideas can be traced back to early liberal political philosophy, and notably to the ideas of John Locke (1632–1704) and C.-L. Montesquieu (1689–1775). Their first systematic development, however, was in the contributions of James Madison (1751–1836) to *The Federalist Papers* (1787–89), in which he advocated a system of divided government based on the separation of powers, bicameralism and federalism in order to resist majoritarianism and to provide minority interests with a guaranteed political voice. The link between pluralism and democracy has been emphasized by modern pluralist theorists such as Robert Dahl (2006). Political pluralism is widely regarded as the key feature of liberal democracy, in that it both allows electors to express independent views and gives them a mechanism through which they can remove unpopular governments. Nevertheless, pluralist thinkers generally emphasize that democracy in modern societies operates less through formal or electoral machinery and more through a constant interplay between government and organized groups or interests. In this sense, pluralist democracy can be seen as an alternative to parliamentary democracy and to any form of major-itarianism. Pluralist ideas and values have in many ways been revived by the emer-gence of postmodernism, which rejects all monolithic theories of society and extols the virtues of debate and discourse.

Pluralism has also been subject to a variety of criticisms, however. As a theory of the distribution of power, pluralism has been attacked by elitists, Marxists and the New Right. Elitists point out that many interests in society, such as the unem-ployed, the homeless or consumers, have no meaningful political voice because they are either poorly organized, or completely unorganized, and business groups that control employment and investment decisions in society are invariably dominant. Marxists, for their part, highlight the structural inequalities that flow from the system of ownership within capitalism, and argue that the state is invariably biased in favour of business interests. The New Right's critique of pluralism draws atten-tion to the problem of 'pluralistic stagnation', the growth of rival group pressures on government resulting in 'overload', and a spiralling increase in public spending and state intervention. In many ways, neo-pluralism has emerged as a response to such criticisms.While the spread of liberal-democratic values means that political pluralism attracts near-universal approval, the same may not be said of moral and cultural pluralism. While liberals believe that diversity in moral and cultural life is an essential expression of toleration, traditional conservatives have argued that it may weaken the foundations of a society which relies for its stability on shared values and a common culture. Religious fundamentalists have developed a similar attack on Western pluralism, believing that it fosters moral relativism and is unable to provide individuals with ethical guidance.

POLARITY

Polarity draws attention, in general terms, to the existence within a definable system of a number of 'poles', or significant actors. It implies that this is key to the key factor in explaining how the system itself works. While the concept of polarity has been applied in a number of contexts, including the study of government coalitions, it features most commonly as an analytical tool within international relations, where it is used to highlight the number of great powers within the international system. In this context, three forms of polarity are often identified:

- *Bipolarity* – an international system that revolves around two great powers (or major power blocs)

- *Multipolarity* – an international system in which there are three or more power centres
- *Unipolarity* – an international system in which there one power centre.

Significance

Polarity is one of the key analytical tools of neorealist theory, and is most commonly used to explain why bipolar international systems are more likely to deliver stability and peace than those that are either multipolar or unipolar. From the neorealist perspective, bipolarity, typified by the superpower rivalry of the Cold War period, has at least four key advantages. First, the existence of only two great powers encourages each to maintain the bipolar system as, in the process, they are maintaining themselves. Second, fewer great powers means that the possibility of great-power war is reduced. Third, the existence of only two great powers reduces the chances of miscalculation and makes it easier to operate a system of deterrence. By contrast, unipolarity, typified by US hegemony in the early post-Cold War period, tends to promote megalomania on the part of the dominant actor, as well as fear, hostility and resentment among others. For its part, multipolarity, typified by trends in the twenty-first century to date, creates a bias in favour of fluidity and uncertainty, which can lead only to instability and an increased likelihood of war.

Doubts about the value of polarity come from various directions, however. One concern arises from the difficulty of deciding when a state achieves great power status and so constitutes a 'pole', in view the highly complex nature of global power. Another suggests that the trend towards independence and interconnectedness makes it impossible to think any longer of the international system in terms of distinct 'poles', however many of these there may be. Liberals, for their part, have long argued that the external behaviour of major powers is determined more by their political and constitutional make-up than it is by the structural dynamics of the international system. Similarly, constructivists reject the assumption that great powers interact on the basis of interests and identities that are fixed and unchanging, instead holding, in effect, that 'polarity is what states make of it'.

POLICY

A policy, in a general sense, is a plan of action adopted by, for example, an individual, group, business or government. To designate something as a policy implies that a formal decision has been made, giving official sanction to a particular course of action. Public policy can therefore be seen as the formal or stated decisions of government bodies. However, policy is better understood as the linkage between intentions, actions and results. At the level of intentions, policy is reflected in the stance of government – what government says that it will do. At the level of actions, policy is reflected in the behaviour of government – what government actually does. At the level of results, policy is reflected in the consequences of government action – the impact of government on the larger society.

Significance

In a sense, policy is the aspect of government that concerns most people. As the 'outputs' of the political process, it reflects the impact government has on society; that is, its ability to make things better or make them worse. During the 1960s and 1970s, policy analysis emerged as a distinct area of study. It set out to examine both how policy is made (the 'how' of policy-making), and the impact of policy for the larger society (the 'what' of policy-making). Policy is usually seen to be 'made' though four distinct stages: initiation, formulation, implementation and evaluation. Policy initiation sets the political agenda by defining certain problems as 'issues', as matters that engage the interest of government, usually because they are the subject of public debate or disagreement. Policy formulation is often seen as the crucial stage in the policy process, because it develops a political issue into a firm policy proposal through a process of debate, analysis and review. Policy implementation comprises the actions though which policy is put into effect, sometimes in ways that differ from the original intentions of policy-makers. Policy evaluation is a review of the impact of public policy, which produces a policy feedback process by stimu- lating further policy initiation and shaping the formulation process.

Another aspect of policy analysis focuses on how decisions are made. Rational choice theorists, influenced by utilitarianism, assume that political actors are ration- ally self-interested creatures, who select whatever means are most likely to secure their desired ends. This emphasis on rationality has, however, been criticized by supporters of 'bounded rationality', who acknowledge that decision-making is essentially an act of compromising between differently valued and imprecisely calculated outcomes (Simon, 1983). The principal alternative to rational decision-making, incrementalism, has been described as the 'science of muddling through' (Lindblom, 1959). It views policy-making as a continuous, exploratory process; lacking overriding goals and clear-cut ends, policy-makers tend to operate within the existing pattern or frame- work, adjusting their position in the light of feedback in the form of information about the impact of earlier decisions. Bureaucratic organization models of decision-making shift attention away from the motives of political actors to the impact that the struc- ture of the policy-making process has on the resulting decisions. This either draws attention to the impact on decisions of the values, assumptions and regular patterns of behaviour that are found in any large organization, or the impact on decisions of bargaining between personnel and agencies, with each pursuing different perceived interests. Finally, there are decision-making models that place emphasis on the role of beliefs and ideology. These recognize that beliefs are the 'glue' of politics, binding together people on the basis of shared values and preferences. In the hands of Marxists and feminists, such ideas have led to the conclusion that the policy process is biased, respectively, in favour of capitalism, or in favour of men.

POLITICAL CULTURE

Culture, in its broadest sense, is the way of life of a people. Sociologists and anthro- pologists tend to distinguish between 'culture' and 'nature', the former encompassing what is passed on from one generation to the next by learning, the latter referring to what is acquired through biological inheritance. Political scientists use the term in a narrower sense to refer to a people's psychological orientation, political culture being the general 'pattern of orientations' to political objects such as parties, **government** and the **constitution**, expressed in beliefs, symbols and values. Political culture differs from public opinion in that it is fashioned from long-term values rather than simply from people's reactions to specific issues and problems.

Significance

Interest among political scientists in the idea of political culture emerged in the 1950s and 1960s as new techniques of behavioural analysis displaced more traditional, institutional approaches to the subject. The classic work in this respect was Almond and Verba's *The Civic Culture* (1963) – subsequently updated as *The Civic Culture Revisited* (1980), which used opinion surveys to analyse political attitudes in democracy in five countries: the USA, the UK, West Germany, Italy and Mexico. The civic culture model identified three general types of political culture: participant culture, subject culture and parochial culture. A 'participant' political culture is one in which citizens pay close attention to politics and regard popular participation as being both desirable and effective. A 'subject' political culture is characterized by more passivity among citizens, and the recognition that they have only a very limited capacity to influence government. A 'parochial' political culture is marked by the absence of a sense of **citizenship**, as people identify with their locality rather than the region, and having neither the desire nor the ability to participate in politics. Almond and Verba argued that the 'civic culture' is a blend of all three in that it reconciles the participation of citizens in the political process with the vital necessity for government to govern. Though interest in political culture faded in the 1970s and 1980s with the declining influence of **behaviouralism**, the debate was revitalized in the 1990s. This occurred both as a result of efforts by post-communist states to foster democratic values and expectations, and because of growing anxiety in mature democracies, such as the USA, about the apparent decline of social capital and civic engagement.

However, the civic culture approach to the study of political attitudes and values has been widely criticized. In the first place, Almond and Verba's 'sleeping dogs' theory of democratic culture, which emphasizes the importance of passivity and deference, has been rejected by those who argue that political participation is the very stuff of **democracy**. Low electoral turnouts, for example, may reflect widespread alienation and ingrained disadvantage, rather than political contentment. Second, a civic culture may be more a consequence of democracy rather than its cause. In other words, the assumption that political attitudes and values shape behaviour, and not the reverse, is unproven. Third, this approach tends to treat political culture as being homogeneous; that is, as little more than a cipher for national culture or national character. In so doing, it pays little attention to political sub-cultures and tends to disguise fragmentation and social conflict. Finally, the civic culture model has been condemned as politically conservative. Marxists in particular reject the 'bottom-up' implications of Almond and Verba's work, and adopt instead a dominant ideology model of political culture, which highlights the role of ideological hegemony and draws attention to the link between unequal class power and cultural and ideological bias.

POLITICAL ECONOMY

Political economy, in its most general sense, is the study of the interaction of politics and economics. The term may nevertheless refer to either a topic or a method. As a topic, political economy focuses on the relationship between states and markets. Although political economy, in this sense, encompasses a variety of perspectives and approaches, the term has sometimes been associated specifically with Marxism, born out of the tendency within Marxist analysis to link power to the ownership of wealth and to view politics as a reflection of the class system. As a method, political economy refers to the use of theories and approaches developed within economics to analyse politics, and includes rational-choice theory, public-choice theory, social-choice theory and game theory. What is called the 'new political economy' regards economic ideas and behaviour not as frameworks for analysis but as beliefs and actions that must themselves be explained (Mair, 1987).

Significance

The term political economy implies that the disciplinary separation of politics from economics is ultimately unsustainable. Political factors are crucial in determining economic outcomes, and economic factors are crucial in determining political outcomes. In short, there is no escaping political economy. While this lesson has been underlined by growing contemporary interest in political economy, not least in the emergence of the 'new political economy', it is one that has a long and respectable history dating back to Adam Smith (1723–90), David Ricardo (1772–1823) and Karl Marx (1818—83).

However, political economy encompasses a variety of perspectives, the main ones being state-centric political economy, classical/neo-classical political economy, and Marxist political economy. State-centric political economy developed out of mercantilism, which was most influential in Europe from the fifteenth to the late seventeenth centuries. This amounted to a form of economic nationalism that saw the state as a key to building national power, particularly through the use of protectionism. Classical political economy is based in liberal assumptions about human nature. Its central belief is that an unregulated market economy tends towards long-run equilibrium, in that the price mechanism – the 'invisible hand' of the market, as Smith put it – brings supply and demand into line with one another. This implies a policy of laissez-faire. Neo-classical political economy developed from the late nineteenth century onwards, drawing classical ideas and assumptions into more developed theories. Marxist political economy portrays capitalism as a system of class exploitation and treats social classes as the key economic actors. From the Marxist perspective, the relationship between the bourgeoisie (the ownership of productive wealth) and the proletariat (non-owners, who subsist through selling their labour power) is one of irreconcilable conflict, a flaw that dooms capitalism to inevitable collapse. However, political economy has been undermined in recent decades by the increasingly inward-looking character of economics as a discipline, and by its growing focus on technical matters.

POLITICAL PARTY

A political party is a group of people organized for the purpose of winning government power, by electoral or other means. Parties are often confused with pressure groups or social movements. Four characteristics usually distinguish parties from other groups. First, parties aim to exercise government power by winning office (though small parties may use elections more to gain a platform than to win power). Second, parties are organized bodies with a formal 'card-carrying' membership. This distinguishes them from broader and more diffuse social movements. Third, parties typically adopt a broad issue focus, addressing each of the major issues of government policy (small parties, however, may have a single-issue focus, thus resembling pressure groups). Fourth, to varying degrees, parties are united by shared political preferences and a general ideological identity.

However, political parties may be classified as mass and cadre parties, as representative and integrative parties, and as constitutional and revolutionary parties. A *mass party* places a heavy emphasis on broadening membership and constructing a wide electoral base, the earliest examples being European socialist parties, which aimed to mobilize working-class support, such as the UK Labour Party and the German Social Democratic Party (SPD). Such parties typically place heavier stress on recruitment and organization than on ideology and political conviction. Kirchheimer (1966) classified most modern parties as 'catch-all parties', emphasizing that they have reduced their ideological baggage dramatically to appeal to the largest number of voters. A *cadre party*, on the other hand, is dominated by trained and professional party members who are expected to exhibit a high level of political commitment and doctrinal discipline, as in the case of communist and fascist parties.

Neumann (1956) offered the alternative distinction between *representative parties*, which adopt a catch-all strategy and place pragmatism before principle, and *integrative parties*, which are proactive rather than reactive, and attempt to mobilize, educate and inspire the masses, instead of merely responding to their concerns. Occasionally, mass parties may exhibit mobilizing or integrative tendencies, as in the case of the UK Conservatives under Margaret Thatcher in the 1980s. Finally, parties can be classified as *constitutional parties* when they operate within a framework of constraints imposed by the existence of other parties, the rules of electoral competition and, crucially, a distinction between the party in power (the government of the day) and state institutions (the bureaucracy, judiciary, police and so on). *Revolutionary parties*, by contrast, adopt an anti-system or anti-constitutional stance, and when such parties win power they invariably become 'ruling' or regime parties, suppressing rival parties and establishing a permanent relationship with the state machinery.

Significance

The political party is the major organizing principle of modern politics. As political machines organized to win (by elections or otherwise), and wield government power, parties are virtually ubiquitous. The only parts of the world in which they do not exist are those where they are suppressed by dictatorship or military rule. Political parties are a vital link between the state and civil society, carrying out major functions such as representation, the formation and recruitment of political elites, the articulation and aggregation of interests, and the organization of government. However, the role and significance of parties varies according to the party system. In one-party systems they effectively substitute themselves for the government, creating a fused party–state apparatus. In two-party systems the larger of the major parties typically wields government power, while the other major party constitutes the opposition and operates as a 'government in waiting'. In a multiparty system, the parties tend to act as brokers representing a narrower range of interests, and exert influence through the construction of more or less enduring electoral alliances or formal coalitions.

Criticisms of political parties have either stemmed from an early liberal fear that parties would promote conflict and destroy the underlying unity of society, and make the politics of individual conscience impossible, or that they are inherently elitist and bureaucratic bodies. The latter view was articulated most famously by Robert Michels (1911/1962) in the form of the 'iron law of oligarchy'. Some modern parties, notably green parties, style themselves as 'anti-party parties', in that they set out to subvert traditional party politics by rejecting parliamentary compromise and emphasizing popular mobilization. Among the strongest supporters of the political party has been V. I. Lenin (1902/1968), who advocated the construction of a tightly knit revolutionary party, organized on the basis of democratic centralism, to serve as the 'vanguard of the working class'. Nevertheless, the period since the late twentieth century has provided evidence of a 'crisis of party politics', reflected in a seemingly general decline in party membership and partisanship, and in the contrasting growth of single-issue protest groups and rise of new social movements. This has been explained on the basis that, as bureaucratized political machines, parties are unable to respond to the growing appetite for popular participation and activism; that their image as instruments of government means that they are inevitably associated with power, ambition and corruption; and that, given the growing complexity of modern societies and the decline of class and other traditional social identities, the social forces that once gave rise to parties have now weakened. Such factors are nevertheless more likely to lead to a transformation in the role of political parties and in the style of party politics, than to make them redundant.

POLITICAL PHILOSOPHY

Philosophy, in general terms, is the search for wisdom and understanding using the techniques of critical reasoning. However, philosophy has also been seen more specifically as a second-order discipline, in contrast to first-order disciplines which deal with empirical subjects. In other words, philosophy is not so much concerned with revealing truth in the manner of science, as with asking secondary questions about how knowledge is acquired and understanding is expressed; it has thus been dubbed the science of questions. Philosophy has traditionally addressed questions related to the ultimate nature of reality (metaphysics), the grounds of knowledge (epistemology) and the basis of moral conduct (ethics).

Political philosophy is often viewed as a subfield of ethics or moral philosophy, in that it is preoccupied with essentially prescriptive or normative questions, reflecting a concern with what *should*, *ought* or *must* be brought about, rather than what *is*. Its central questions have included 'Why should I obey the state?', 'Who should rule?', 'How should rewards be distributed?' and 'What should the limits be of individual freedom?' Academic political philosophy addresses itself to two main tasks. First, it is concerned with the critical evaluation of political beliefs, paying attention to both inductive and deductive forms of reasoning. Second, it attempts to clarify and refine the concepts employed in political discourse. What this means is that, while political philosophy may be carried out critically and scrupulously, it cannot be objective in that it is inevitably concerned with justifying certain political viewpoints at the expense of others, and with upholding a particular understanding of a concept rather than alternative ones. Political philosophy is therefore clearly distinct from political science. Despite political philosophy often being used interchangeably with political theory, the former deals strictly with matters of evaluation and advocacy, while the latter is broader, in that it also includes explanation and analysis and thus cuts across the normative/empirical divide.

Significance

Political philosophy constitutes what is called the 'traditional' approach to politics. It dates back to Ancient Greece and the work of the founding fathers of political analysis, Plato (427–347 BCE) and Aristotle (384–322 BCE). Their ideas resurfaced in the writings of medieval thinkers such as Augustine (354–430 CE) and Aquinas (1224–74). In the early modern period, political philosophy was closely associated with the social contract theories of Thomas Hobbes (1588–1679), John Locke (1632–1704) and Jean-Jacques Rousseau (1712–78), while in the nineteenth century it was advanced through J. S. Mill's (1806–73) work on freedom and Karl Marx's (1818–83) materialist conception of history. However, the status of political philosophy was gradually weakened from the late nineteenth century onwards by the rise of the empirical and scientific traditions, which led by the 1950s and 1960s to a frontal assault on the very basis of normative theorizing. Political philosophy was declared to be dead, on the grounds that its central principles, such as justice, rights, liberty and equality, are meaningless because they are not empirically verifiable entities. However, there has been a significant revival in political philosophy since the 1970s, and the tendency now is for political philosophy and political science to be seen less as distinct modes of political enquiry, and still less as rivals. Instead, they have come to be accepted simply as contrasting ways of disclosing political knowledge. This has occurred through disillusionment with behaviouralism and the recognition that values, hidden or otherwise, underpin all forms of political enquiry, and as a result of the emergence of new areas of philosophical debate, linked, for example, to feminism and to rivalry between liberalism and communitarianism.

POLITICAL SCIENCE

Science (from the Latin *scientia*, meaning knowledge) is a field of study that aims to develop reliable explanations of phenomena through repeatable experiments, observations and deductions. The 'scientific method', by which hypotheses are verified (proved true) by testing them against the available evidence, is therefore seen as a means of disclosing value-free and objective truth. Karl Popper (1902–94), however, suggested that science can only falsify hypotheses, since 'facts' can always be disproved by later experiments. Scientism is the belief that the scientific method is the only source of reliable knowledge, and so should be applied to fields such as philosophy, history and politics, as well as the natural sciences. Doctrines such as Marxism, utilitarianism and racialism are scientistic in this sense.

Political science can either be understood generally or more specifically. In general terms, it is an academic discipline which undertakes to describe, analyse and explain systematically the workings of government and the relationships between political and non-political institutions and processes. The traditional subject matter of political science, so defined, is the state, though this broadened during the twentieth century to include social, economic and other processes that influence the allocation of values and general resources. In this view, political science encompasses both descriptive and normative theory: the task of describing and analysing the operations of government institutions has often been linked to evaluative judgements about which ones work best. Defined more narrowly, political science sets out to study the traditional subject matter of politics using only the methods of the natural sciences. From this perspective, political science refers to a strictly empirical and value-free approach to political understanding that was the product of positivism, and reached its highest stage of development in the form of behaviouralism. This implies a sharp distinction between political science and political philosophy, reflecting the distinction between empirical and normative analysis. It may also, in its scientistic form, imply that the philosophical or normative approach to political understanding is, in the final analysis, worthless.

Significance

While it is widely accepted that the study of politics should be scientific in the broad sense of being rigorous and critical, the claim that it should be scientific in the stricter sense, that it can and should use the methodology of the natural sciences, is much more controversial. The attraction of a science of politics is clear. Most important, it promises an impartial and reliable means of distinguishing truth from falsehood, thereby giving us access to objective knowledge about the political world. The key to achieving this is to distinguish between 'facts' (empirical evidence) and 'values' (normative or ethical beliefs). Facts are objective in the sense that they can be demonstrated reliably and consistently; they can be proved. Values, in contrast, are inherently subjective; they are a matter of opinion.

However, any attempt to construct a science of politics meets with three difficulties. First, there is the problem of data. Human beings are not tadpoles that can be taken into a laboratory, or cells that can be observed under a microscope. We cannot get 'inside' a human being, or carry out repeatable experiments on human behaviour. What we can learn about individual behaviour is therefore limited and superficial. In the absence of exact data we have no reliable means of testing our hypotheses. Second, there are difficulties that stem from the existence of human values. The idea that models and theories of politics are entirely value-free is difficult to sustain when they are examined closely. Facts and values are so closely intertwined that it is often impossible to prise them apart. This is because theories are inevitably constructed on the basis of assumptions about human nature, society and the role of the state that have hidden political and ideological implications. Third, there is the myth of neutrality in the social sciences. Whereas natural scientists may be able to approach their studies in an objective and impartial manner, holding no presuppositions about what they are going to discover, this is difficult and perhaps impossible to achieve in politics. However politics is defined, it addresses questions relating to the structure and functioning of the society in which we live and have grown up. Family background, social experience, economic position, personal sympathies and so on thus build into each and every one of us a set of pre-conditions regarding politics and the world around us. Scientific objectivity, in the sense of absolute impartiality or neutrality, must therefore always remain an unachievable goal in political analysis.

POLITICAL THEORY

A theory is anything from a plan to a piece of abstract knowledge. In academic discourse, however, a theory is an explanatory proposition, an idea or set of ideas that in some way seeks to impose order or meaning on phenomena. As such, all enquiry proceeds through the construction of theories, sometimes thought of as hypotheses, explanatory propositions waiting to be tested. Political science, no less than the natural sciences and other social sciences, therefore has an important theoretical component. For example, theories such as that social class is the principal determinant of voting behaviour, and that revolutions occur at times of rising expectations, are essential if sense is to be made of empirical evidence. This is what is called empirical political theory.

Political theory is, however, usually regarded as a distinctive approach to the subject, even though, particularly in the USA, it is seen as a subfield of political science. Political theory involves the analytical study of ideas and doctrines that have been central to political thought. Traditionally, this has taken the form of a history of political thought, focusing on a collection of 'major' thinkers – for example, from Plato to Marx – and a canon of 'classic' texts. As it studies the ends and means of political action, political theory is concerned with ethical or normative questions, related to issues such as justice, freedom, equality and so on. This traditional approach is similar in character to literary analysis: it is interested primarily in examining what major thinkers said, how they developed or justified their views, and the intellectual context in which they worked. An alternative approach has been called formal political theory. This draws on the example of economic theory in building up models based on procedural rules, as in the case of rational choice theory. Despite political theory and political philosophy clearly overlapping (and the two terms are sometimes used interchangeably), a distinction can be drawn on the grounds that political theory may content itself with explanation and analysis, while political philosophy is inevitably involved at some level with evaluation and advocacy.

Significance

Political theory, as an approach to politics that embraces normative and philosophical analysis, can be seen as the longest and most clearly established tradition of political analysis. However, the status of political theory was seriously damaged in the twentieth century by the rise of positivism and its attack on the very normative concepts that had been its chief subject matter. While the notion that political theory was abandoned in the 1950s and 1960s is an exaggeration, the onset of the 'behavioural revolution' and the passion for all things scientific persuaded many political analysts to turn their backs on the entire tradition of normative thought. Since the 1960s, however, political theory has re-emerged with new vitality, and the previously sharp distinction between political science and political theory has faded. This occurred through the emergence of a new generation of political theorists, notably John Rawls (1971) and Robert Nozick (1974), but also through growing criticism of behaviouralism and the re-emergence of ideological divisions, brought about, for example, through anti-Vietnam war protest, the rise of feminism and the emergence of the New Right and New Left.

However, revived political theory differs in a number of respects from its earlier manifestations. One feature of modern political theory is that it places greater emphasis on the role of history and culture in shaping political understanding. While this does not imply that the study of 'major' thinkers and 'classic' texts is worthless, it does emphasize that any interpretation of such thinkers and texts must take into account context, and recognize that, to some extent, all interpretations are entangled with our own values and understanding. The second development is that political theory has become increasingly diffuse and diverse. This has occurred both through the fragmentation of liberalism and growing debate within a broad liberal tradition, but also through the emergence of new alternatives to liberal theory to add to its established Marxist and conservative rivals, the most obvious examples being feminism, communitarianism and ecologism. Finally, modern political theory has lost the bold self-confidence of earlier periods, in that it has effectively abandoned the 'traditional' search for universal values acceptable to everyone. This has occurred through a growing appreciation of the role of community and local identity in shaping values, brought about, in part, by the impact of postmodernism.

POLITICS

Politics, in its broadest sense, is the activity through which people make, preserve and amend the general rules under which they live. While politics is also an academic subject (sometimes indicated by the use of 'Politics' with a capital P), it is then clearly the study of this activity. Politics is thus inextricably linked to the phenomena of conflict and co-operation. On the one hand, the existence of rival opinions, different wants, competing needs and opposing interests guarantees disagreement about the rules under which people live. On the other hand, people recognize that, to influence these rules or ensure that they are upheld, they must work together with others – hence Hannah Arendt's (1906–75) definition of political power as 'acting in concert'. This is why the heart of politics is often portrayed as a process of conflict resolution, in which rival views or competing interests are reconciled with one another. However, politics in this broad sense is better thought of as a search for conflict resolution rather than its achievement, as not all conflicts are, or can be, resolved. From this perspective, politics arises from the facts of diversity (we are not all alike) and scarcity (there is never enough to go round).

However, four quite different notions of politics can be identified. First, it is associated specifically with the art of government and the activities of the state. This is perhaps the classical definition of politics, developed from the original meaning of the term in Ancient Greece (politics is derived from *polis*, literally meaning city-state). In this view, politics is an essentially state-bound activity, meaning that most people, most institutions and most social activities can be regarded as being 'outside' politics. Second, politics is viewed as a specifically 'public' activity in that it is associated with the conduct and management of the community's affairs rather than with the 'private' concerns of the individual. Such a view can be traced back to Aristotle's (384–322 BCE) belief that it is only within a political community that human beings can live 'the good life'. Third, politics is seen as a particular means of resolving conflict; that is, by compromise, conciliation and negotiation, rather than through force and naked power. This is what is implied when politics is portrayed as 'the art of the possible', and it suggests a distinction between 'political' solutions to problems involving peaceful debate and arbitration, and 'military' solutions. Fourth, politics is associated with the production, distribution and use of resources in the course of social existence. In this view politics is about power: the ability to achieve a desired outcome, through whatever means. Advocates of this view include feminists and Marxists.

Significance

The 'what is politics?' debate highlights quite different approaches to political analysis and exposes some of the deepest and most intractable conflicts in political thought. In the first place it determines the very subject matter and parameters of the discipline itself. The traditional view that politics boils down to 'what concerns the state' has been reflected in the tendency for academic study to focus on the personnel and machinery of government. To study politics is in essence to study government or, more broadly, to study what David Easton (1981) called the 'authoritative allocation of values'. However, if the stuff of politics is power and the distribution of resources, politics is seen to take place in, for example, the family, the workplace, and schools and universities, and the focus of political analysis shifts from the state to society.

Moreover, different views of politics embody different conceptions of social order. Definitions of politics that relate it to the art of government, public affairs or peaceful compromise are based on an essentially consensus model of society, which portrays government as being basically benign and emphasizes the common interests of the community. However, views of politics that emphasize the distribution of power and resources tend to based on conflict models of society that stress structural inequalities and injustices. Karl Marx (1818–83) thus referred to political power as 'merely the organized power of one class for oppressing another', while the feminist author Kate Millett (1970) defined politics as 'power-structured relationships, arrangements whereby one group of persons is controlled by another'. Finally, there is disagreement about the moral character of political activity and whether it can, or should, be brought to an end. On the one hand, to link politics to government is to regard it as, at worst, a necessary evil, and to associate politics with community activity and non-violent forms of conflict resolution is to portray it as positively worthwhile, even ennobling. On the other hand, those who link politics to oppression and subjugation often do so to expose structures of inequality and injustice in society, which, once overthrown, will result in the end of politics itself.

POPULISM

Populism (from the Latin *populus*, meaning 'the people') has been used to describe both a particular tradition of political thought, and distinctive political movements and forms of rule. As a political tradition, populism reflects the belief that the instincts and wishes of the people provide the principal legitimate guide to political action. Movements or parties described as populist have therefore been characterized by their claim to support the common people in the face of 'corrupt' economic or political elites. Populist politicians thus make a direct appeal to the people and claim to give expression to their deepest hopes and fears, all intermediary institutions being distrusted. Populism is therefore often viewed as a manifestation of anti-politics.

Significance

The populist political tradition can be traced back to Jean-Jacques Rousseau's (1712–78) notion of a 'general will' as the indivisible collective interest of society. Populism thus aims to establish an unmediated link between a leader and his or her people, through which the leader gives expression to the innermost hopes and dreams of the people. Populist leadership can be seen in its most developed form in totalitarian dictatorships that operate through the appeal of charismatic leaders, but it can also be found in democratic systems in which leaders cultivate a personal image and ideological vision separate from and 'above' parties, parliaments and other government institutions. Indeed, the wider use of focus groups and the increasing sophistication of political presentation and communication, particularly linked to the activities of so-called 'spin doctors', have provided greater impetus for populism in modern politics generally.

If populism is defended, it is on the basis that it constitutes a genuine form of democracy, intermediate institutions tending to pervert or misrepresent the people's will. More commonly, however, populism is subject to criticism. Two main criticisms are made of it. First, populism is seen as implicitly authoritarian, on the grounds that it provides little basis for challenging the leader's claim to articulate the genuine interests of the people. Second, it debases politics, both by giving expression to the crudest hopes and fears of the masses and by leaving no scope for deliberation and rational analysis. 'Populist democracy' is thus the enemy of both pluralist and parliamentary democracy.

POSITIVISM

Positivism is the doctrine that the social sciences, and, for that matter, all forms of philosophical enquiry, should adhere strictly to the methods of the natural sciences. The term was introduced by Claud-Henri Saint-Simon (1760–1825) and popularized by his follower, Auguste Comte (1789–1857). Positivism thus assumes that science holds a monopoly of knowledge. In the form of logical positivism, which was advanced in the 1920s and 1930s by a group of philosophers collectively known as the Vienna Circle, it rejected all propositions that are not empirically verifiable as being simply meaningless.

Significance

Positivism did much in the twentieth century to weaken the status of political philosophy and to underpin the emergence of political science. Normative concepts and theories were discarded as nonsense, on the grounds that they were 'metaphysical' and did not deal with what is externally measurable. Not only did this undermine the credentials of the philosophical approach to political analysis but it also encouraged philosophers to lose interest in moral and political issues. On the other hand, one of the chief legacies of positivism was the emergence of behaviouralism and the attempt to develop a value-free science of politics. However, the influence of positivism on philosophy and political analysis declined significantly in the second half of the twentieth century. This occurred partly because positivism was associated with a simplistic faith in science's capacity to uncover truth that has come to be regarded as naive, and partly because, in rejecting completely the beliefs, attitudes and values of political actors, it drew politics towards dull and exclusively empirical analysis.

POSTCOLONIALISM

Postcolonialism is a theoretical stance that seeks to address the cultural conditions characteristic of newly independent societies. Postcolonial thinking originated as a trend in literary and cultural studies, but from the 1970s onwards it acquired an increasingly political orientation, focusing on exposing and overturning the cultural and psychological dimensions of colonial rule. Crucial to this has been the recognition that 'inner' subjugation can persist long after the political structures of colonialism have been removed. However, as it draws inspiration from indigenous religions, cultures and traditions, postcolonial theory tends to be highly disparate. For example, it has been reflected in Gandhi's attempt to fuse Indian nationalism with an ethic of non-violence ultimately rooted in Hinduism, as well as in forms of religious fundamentalism, especially Islamic fundamentalism.

Significance

Postcolonialism has had an impact on political theory in two main areas. First, it helped to give the developing world a distinctive political voice separate from the universalist pretensions of Western thought, particularly as represented by liberalism and socialism. In this respect, it has encouraged a broader reassessment within political thought, in that, for example, Islamic and liberal ideas are increasingly considered to be equally legitimate in articulating the traditions and values of their own communities. Second, postcolonialism has served as a means of uncovering the cultural and other biases that operate within Western liberal thought. Edward Said (2003) thus developed the notion of 'Orientalism' to highlight the extent to which Western cultural and political hegemony over the rest of the world, but over the Orient in particular, has been maintained by elaborate stereotypical fictions that belittle and demean non-Western people and culture. Examples of such stereotypes include images of the 'mysterious East', 'inscrutable Chinese' and 'lustful Turks'. Critics of postcolonialism nevertheless argue that, in turning its back on the Western intellectual tradition, it has abandoned progressive politics and been used, too often, as a justification for traditional values and authority structures. This has been evident, for example, in tension between the demands of cultural authenticity and calls for women's rights.

POSTMODERNISM

Postmodernism is a controversial and confusing term that was first used to describe experimental movements in Western architecture and cultural development in general. Postmodern thought originated principally in continental Europe, especially France, and constitutes a challenge to the type of academic political theory that has come to be the norm in the Anglo-American world. Its basis lies in a perceived social shift – from modernity to postmodernity; and a related cultural and intellectual shift – from modernism to postmodernism. Modern societies are seen to have been structured by industrialization and class solidarity, social identity being largely determined by one's position within the productive system. Postmodern societies, on the other hand, are increasingly fragmented and pluralistic 'information societies' in which individuals are transformed from being producers to being consumers, and individualism replaces class, religious and ethnic loyalties. Postmodernity is thus linked to post-industrialism, the development of a society no longer dependent on manufacturing industry, but more reliant on knowledge and communication.

The central theme of postmodernism is that there is no such thing as certainty: the idea of absolute and universal truth must be discarded as an arrogant pretence. While by its nature postmodernism does not constitute a unified body of thought, its critical attitude to claims of truth stems from the general assumption that all knowledge is partial and local, a view it shares with certain forms of communitarianism. Poststructuralism, a term sometimes used interchangeably with postmodernism, emphasizes that all ideas and concepts are expressed in language that is itself enmeshed in complex relations of power.

Significance

Since the 1970s, postmodern and poststructural political theories have become increasingly fashionable. In particular they have attacked all forms of political analysis that stem from modernism. Modernism, the cultural form of modernity, is seen to stem largely from Enlightenment ideas and theories, and has been expressed politically in ideological traditions that offer rival conceptions of the good life, notably liberalism and Marxism. The chief flaw of modernist thought, from the most postmodern perspective, is that it is characterized by foundationalism, the belief that it is possible to establish objective truths and universal values, usually associated with a strong faith in progress. Jean-François Lyotard (1984) expressed the postmodern stance most succinctly in defining it as 'an incredulity towards metanarratives'. By this he meant scepticism regarding all creeds and ideologies that are based on universal theories of history that view society as a coherent totality.

Postmodernism has been criticized from two angles. In the first place it has been accused of relativism, in that it holds that different modes of knowing are equally valid, and thus rejects the idea that even science is able to distinguish reliably between truth and falsehood. Second, it has been charged with conservatism, on the grounds that a non-foundationalist political stance offers no perspective from which the existing order may be criticized, and no basis for the construction of an alternative social order. Nevertheless, the attraction of postmodern theory is its remorseless questioning of apparent solid realities and accepted beliefs. Its general emphasis on discourse, debate and democracy reflects the fact that to reject hierarchies of ideas is also to reject any political or social hierarchies.

POWER

Power can be defined broadly as the ability to achieve a desired outcome, sometimes referred to in terms of the 'power to' do something. This notion of power includes everything from the ability to keep oneself alive to the ability of government to promote economic growth. In political analysis, however, power is usually thought of as a relationship; that is, as the ability to influence the behaviour of others in a manner not of their choosing. It is referred to in terms of having 'power over' others. Power thus exists when A gets B to do something that B would not otherwise have done. Power is often distinguished from authority on the grounds that the former is based on the 'ability' to influence others, whereas the latter involves the 'right' to do so. Power may, more narrowly, be associated with the ability to punish and reward, bringing it close to force or manipulation, in contrast to 'influence', which also encompasses rational persuasion.

However, power can be exerted in various ways. This has resulted in the emergence of different conceptions of power, sometimes viewed as different dimensions or 'faces' of power. First, power is understood as decision-making: conscious judgements that in some way shape actions or influence decisions. This notion is analogous to the idea of physical or mechanical power, in that it implies that power involves being 'pulled' or 'pushed' against one's will. Keith Boulding (1989) distinguished between three ways of influencing decisions: the use of force or intimidation ('the stick'); productive exchanges involving mutual gain ('the deal'); and the creation of obligations, loyalty and commitment ('the kiss'). Second, power may take the form of agenda setting: the ability to prevent decisions being made; that is, in effect, non-decision-making. This involves the ability to prevent issues or proposals being aired; E. E. Schattschneider (1960) summed this up in his famous assertion that 'organization is the mobilization of bias'. Third, power can take the form of thought control: the ability to influence another by shaping what he or she thinks, wants or needs. This is sometimes portrayed by Lukes (2004) as the 'radical' face of power because it exposes processes of cultural and psychological control in society and, more generally, highlights the impact of ideology. The hard/soft power distinction has become increasingly influential in the theory and practice of international politics.

Significance

There is a sense in which all politics is about power. The practice of politics is often portrayed as little more than the exercise of power, and the academic subject as, in essence, the study of power. Without doubt, students of politics are students of power: they seek to know who has it, how it is used and on what basis it is exercised. However, disagreements about the nature of power run deep and have significant implications for political analysis. While it would be wrong to suggest that different 'faces' of power necessarily result in different models of the distribution of power in society, power as decision-making is commonly linked to pluralism (because it tends to highlight the influence of a number of political actors), while power as agenda setting is often associated with elitism (because it exposes the capacity of vested interests to organize issues out of politics), and power as thought control is commonly linked to Marxism (because it draws attention to forms of ideological indoctrination that mask the reality of class rule).

The concept of power is accorded particular significance by analysts who subscribe to what is called 'power politics'. Power politics is an approach to politics based on the assumption that the pursuit of power is the principal human goal. The term is generally used descriptively and is closely linked to realism. This is a tradition that can be traced back to Thomas Hobbes (1588–1679) and his assertion that the basic human urge is to seek 'power after power'. The theory of power politics portrays politics as nothing more than an arena of struggle or competition between differently interested actors. At the national level, ongoing struggle between individuals and groups is usually used to justify strong government, the virtue of government being that, as the supreme power, it alone is capable of establishing order. At the international level the power politics approach emphasizes the inherent instability of a world riven by competing national interests, and links the hope of peace to the establishment of a balance of power.

PRAGMATISM

Pragmatism, broadly defined, refers to behaviour that is shaped in accordance with practical circumstances and goals, rather than principles or ideological objectives. As a philosophical tradition, associated with 'classical pragmatists' such as William James (1842–1910) and John Dewey (1859–1952) pragmatism is used to settle metaphysical disputes that seek to clarify the meaning of concepts or propositions by identifying their practical consequences.

Significance

Pragmatism in politics has either been an ideological stance, usually associated with conservatism, or a strategy for practical politics aimed at nothing more than achieving and maintaining power. In relation to the former, it is based on the belief that the world is simply too complicated for human reason to grasp fully, in which case all abstract ideas or systems of thought are, at best, unreliable (because they claim to understand what is, ultimately, incomprehensible) and, at worst, dangerous (because they suggest solutions that may be worse than the problem being addressed). Pragmatism, in this sense, implies that the best guides to action are tradition, experience and history, relying on what 'worked' in the past. This has led to the belief, shared by many neo-revisionist socialists as well as traditional conservatives, that 'what matters is what works'.

In relation to the latter, pragmatism reflects a tendency, in particular, to follow public opinion rather then lead it. Though this might always have applied, at some level, to practical politics, this tendency has become particularly prominent in the modern age of 'de-ideologized' party politics, in which parties of both the left and the right have become increasingly detached from their ideological roots. While pragmatism in this sense may be the epitome of economic democracy (as parties end up selling 'products' – leaders or policies – to the voters), it may also mean that party politics is robbed of any sense of purpose and direction, with members and supporters losing the basis for emotional attachment to their party. When politicians believe in nothing more than winning or retaining power, they appear to believe in nothing, a perception that, as it spreads, may help to explain the rise of anti-politics.

PRESIDENT

A president is a formal head of state, a title held in other states by a monarch or emperor. However, constitutional presidents differ from executive presidents. Constitutional presidents, or non-executive presidents (found in India, Israel and Germany, for example), are a feature of parliamentary government and have responsibilities that are largely confined to ceremonial duties. In these circumstances the president is a mere figurehead, and executive power is wielded by a prime minister and/or a cabinet. Executive presidents wear 'two hats', in that they combine the formal responsibilities of a head of state with the political power of a chief executive. Presidencies of this kind constitute the basis of presidential government and conform to the principles of the separation of powers.

Significance

US-style presidential government has spawned imitations throughout the world, mainly in Latin America and, more recently, in post-communist states such as Poland, the Czech Republic and Russia. In investing executive power in a presidency, the architects of the US Constitution were aware that they were, in effect, creating an 'elective kingship'. The president was invested with an impressive range of powers, including those of head of state, chief executive, commander-in-chief of the armed forces, and chief diplomat, and was granted wide-ranging powers of patronage and the right to veto legislation. However, the modern presidency, in the USA and elsewhere, has been shaped by wider political developments as well as by formal constitutional rules. The most important of these developments have been growing government intervention in economic and social life, an increasingly interdependent or globalized international order, and the rise of the mass media, particularly television, as political institutions. Within the constraints of their political system, presidents have therefore become deliverers of national prosperity, world statesmen and national celebrities. By the 1970s this led to alarm, in the USA in particular, about the emergence of an 'imperial presidency', a presidency capable of emancipating itself from its traditional constitutional constraints. However, subsequent setbacks for presidents such as Nixon and Carter in the USA re-emphasized the enduring truth of Neustadt's (1980) classic formulation of presidential power as the 'power to persuade'; that is, the ability to bargain, encourage and even cajole, but not to dictate. While presidents appear to be more powerful than prime ministers, this is often an illusion. Combining state and governmental leadership in a single office perhaps so raises political expectations that it may make failure inevitable, and it should not disguise the fact that, unlike prime ministers, presidents do not wield direct legislative power.

Presidentialism has a number of clear advantages. Chief among these is that it makes personal leadership possible. Politics becomes more intelligible and engaging precisely because it takes a personal form: the public associates more readily with a person than it does with a political institution, such as a cabinet or political party. Linked to this is the capacity of a president to become a national figurehead, a symbol of the nation embodying both ceremonial and political authority. Presidents may thus have particularly pronounced mobilizing capacities, especially important in times of economic crisis and war. Finally, concentrating executive power in a single office ensures clarity and coherence, as opposed to the unsatisfactory and perhaps unprincipled compromises that are the stuff of collective cabinet government. On the other hand, presidentialism has its dangers. One of the most obvious of these is that personalizing politics risks devaluing it. Elections, for example, may turn into mere beauty contests and place greater emphasis on image and personal trivia than on ideas and policies. The other drawback of presidentialism is that it is based on a perhaps outdated notion of leadership, in that it implies that complex and pluralistic modern societies can be represented and mobilized through a single individual. If politics is ultimately about conciliation and bargaining, this may be better facilitated through a system of collective leadership rather than personal leadership.

PRESIDENTIAL GOVERNMENT

A presidential system of government (see Figure 11) is characterized by a constitutional and political separation of powers between the legislative and executive branches of government. Executive power is thus vested in an independently elected president who is not directly accountable to, or removable by, the assembly or parliament.

The principal features of presidential government are:

- The executive and the legislature are separately elected, and each is invested with a range of independent constitutional powers.
- There is a formal separation of personnel between the legislative and executive branches.
- The executive is not constitutionally responsible to the legislature and cannot be removed by it (except through the exceptional process of impeachment).
- The president or executive cannot 'dissolve' the legislature, meaning that the electoral terms of both branches are fixed.
- Executive authority is concentrated in the hands of the president – the cabinet and ministers merely being advisers responsible to the president.
- The roles of head of state and head of government are combined in the office of the presidency – the president 'wears two hats'.

Presidential government can be distinguished clearly from parliamentary government. However, there are a number of hybrid systems that combine elements of the two, notably semi-presidential systems. Semi-presidential government operates on the basis of a 'dual executive', in which a separately elected president works in conjunction with a prime minister and cabinet drawn from and accountable to the parliament. In some cases, policy-making responsibilities are divided between the president and the cabinet, ensuring that the former is largely concerned with foreign affairs, while the latter deals primarily with domestic issues.

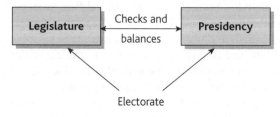

Figure 11 Presidential government

Significance

Presidential government is the principal alternative to parliamentary government in the liberal-democratic world. However, presidentialism is rarer than parliamentarianism. The USA is the classic example of a presidential system, and it is a model that has been adopted in many parts of Latin America. Semi-presidential systems can be found in states such as France and Finland. The principal strength of presidential government is that, by separating legislative from executive power, it creates internal tensions that help to protect individual rights and liberties. This, indeed, was the intention of the so-called 'founding fathers' of the US Constitution, who wished to prevent the presidency from assuming the mantle of the British monarchy. In the USA, the danger of executive domination is protected against by the range of powers vested in the Congress. For example, Congress has the right to declare war and raise taxes, the Senate may ratify treaties and confirm presidential appointments, and the two houses can combine to charge and impeach the president. Further advantages are that the president, as both head of state and head of government, and as the single politician who is nationally elected, serves as a strong focus for patriotic loyalty and national unity. The dispersal of power between the executive and the legislature also allows government to be more democratic in the sense that it is responsive to competing minorities.

However, presidential systems may also be ineffective and cumbersome, because they offer an 'invitation to struggle' to the executive and legislative branches. Critics of the US system, for example, argue that, since 'the president proposes and Congress disposes', it is nothing more than a recipe for institutional deadlock, or 'government gridlock'. This may be more likely when the White House (the presidency) and Capitol Hill (Congress) are controlled by rival parties, but it can also occur, as the Carter administration (1977–81) demonstrated, when both branches are controlled by the same party. To some extent, semi-presidential systems were constructed to overcome this problem. However, similar institutional tensions have been generated in France when presidents have been forced to work with prime ministers and cabinets drawn from a rival party or parties, giving rise to the phenomenon of 'cohabitation'.

PRESSURE GROUP

A pressure group or interest group (the terms are often, but not always, used interchangeably) is an organized association that aims to influence the policies or actions of government. Pressure groups differ from political parties in that they seek to exert influence from outside, rather than to win or exercise government power. Further, pressure groups typically focus on a narrow issue, in that they are usually concerned with a specific cause or the interests of a particular group, and seldom have the broader programmic or ideological features generally associated with political parties. Pressure groups are distinguished from social movements both by their greater degree of formal organization and by their methods of operation. Pressure groups that operate at the international level (particularly in relation to development and environmental issues) have increasingly been accorded formal recognition as non-governmental organizations (NGOs). Nevertheless, not all pressure groups have members in the formal sense; hence the preference of some commentators for the looser term 'organized interests'.

Pressure groups appear in a variety of shapes and sizes. The two most common classifications of pressure groups are between sectional and promotional groups, and between 'insider' and 'outsider' groups. Sectional groups (sometimes called protective, functional or interest groups) exist to advance or protect the (usually material) interests of their members. The 'sectional' character of such groups derives from the fact that they represent a section of society: workers, employers, consumers, an ethnic or religious group, and so on. In the USA, sectional groups are often classified as 'private interest groups', to stress that their principal concern is the betterment and well-being of their members, and not of society in general. Promotional groups (sometimes termed 'cause' or 'attitude' groups) are set up to advance shared values, ideals and principles. In the USA, promotional groups are dubbed 'public interest groups', to emphasize that they promote collective, rather than selective benefits; they aim to help groups other than their own members. Nevertheless, many pressure groups straddle the sectional/promotional divide, in that they both represent their members' interests and are concerned with ideals and broader causes. Trade unions, for example, often address the issue of social justice as well as matters such as wages, conditions and job security.

Alternatively, pressure groups can be classified on the basis of their relationship to government. Insider groups enjoy privileged and usually institutionalized access to government through routine consultation and representation on government bodies. Such groups either tend to represent key economic interests or to possess specialist knowledge and information necessary to government in the process of policy formulation. Outsider groups, on the other hand, are either not consulted by government or consulted only irregularly, and not usually at a senior level. Lacking formal access to government, these groups are forced to 'go public' in the hope of exercising indirect influence on the policy process via media and public campaigns.

Significance

Pressure groups are found only in liberal-democratic political systems, in which the rights of political association and freedom of expression are respected. However, the role pressure groups play and the importance they exert varies considerably. Among the factors that enhance group influence are a political culture that recognizes them as legitimate actors and encourages membership and participation; a fragmented and decentralized institutional structure that gives groups various points of access to the policy process; a party system that facilitates links between major parties and organized interests; and an interventionist style of public policy that requires that the government consults and co-operates with key interests, often through the emergence of corporatism.

The most positive perspective on group politics is offered by pluralist theories. These not only see organized groups as the fundamental building blocks of the political process, but also portray them as a vital guarantee of liberty and democracy. Arguments in favour of pressure groups include the idea that they strengthen representation by articulating interests and advancing views ignored by political parties; that they promote debate and discussion and thus create a more informed electorate; that they broaden the scope of political participation; that they check government power and maintain a vigorous and healthy civil society; and that they promote political stability by providing a channel of communication between government and people. A more critical view of pressure groups is advanced by corporatist, New Right and Marxist theorists. Corporatism highlights the privileged position that certain groups enjoy in relation to government, and portrays pressure groups as being hierarchically ordered and dominated by leaders who are not directly accountable to members. The New Right draws attention to the threat that groups pose in terms of over-government and economic inefficiency. Marxists argue that group politics systematically advantages business and financial interests that control the crucial employment and investment decisions in a capitalist society, and that the state is biased in favour of such interests through its role in upholding the capitalist system they dominate.

PRIME MINISTER

A prime minister (sometimes referred to as a chancellor, as in Germany; a minister-president, as in the Netherlands; or called by a local title such as the Irish Taoiseach) is a head of government whose power derives from his or her leadership of the majority party, or a coalition of parties, in the parliament or assembly. Prime ministers are formal chief executives or heads of government, but their position differs from that of a president in a number of respects. First, prime ministers work within parliamentary systems of government, or semi-presidential ones, and therefore govern in and through the parliament and are not encumbered by a constitutional separation of powers. Second, prime ministers usually operate within a formal system of cabinet government, meaning that, in theory at least, executive authority is shared collectively within the cabinet. Third, prime ministers are invested with more modest constitutional powers than presidents, and are therefore typically more reliant on the exercise of informal powers, especially those linked to their role as party leaders. Fourth, because prime ministers are parliamentary officers they are not heads of state, the latter post generally being held by a non-executive president or a constitutional monarch.

Significance

As the job of prime minister can only have a loose constitutional description, there is some truth in the old adage that the post is what its holder chooses to make of it, or, more accurately, is able to make of it. In practice, prime-ministerial power is based on the use made of two sets of relationships. The first set includes the cabinet, individual ministers and government departments; the second set is his or her party and, through it, the parliament and the public. The support of the cabinet is particularly crucial to prime ministers who operate within a system of collective cabinet government. In these cases, their power is a reflection of the degree to which, by patronage, cabinet management and the control of the machinery of government, they can ensure that ministers serve 'under' them. Nevertheless, there is no doubt that the cornerstone of prime-ministerial power lies in his or her position as party leader. Indeed, the modern premiership is largely a product of the emergence of disciplined political parties. Not only is the post of prime minister allocated on the basis of party leadership, but it also provides its holder with a means of controlling the parliament and a base from which the image of national leader can be constructed. The degree of party unity, the parliamentary strength of the prime minister's party (in particular, whether it rules alone or is a member of a **coalition**), and the **authority** vested in the parliament, or at least its first chamber, are therefore the key determinants of prime-ministerial power.

Most commentators agree that prime ministers have steadily become more significant political actors. This results in part from the tendency of the broadcast media in particular to focus on personalities, meaning that prime ministers become kinds of 'brand images' of their parties. The growth of international summitry and foreign visits has also provided prime ministers with opportunities to cultivate their statesmanship, and given them scope to portray themselves as national leaders. In some cases this has led to the allegation that prime ministers have effectively emancipated themselves from cabinet constraints and established a form of prime-ministerial government. Prime-ministerial government has two key features. First, by controlling the parliament as well as the bureaucratic machine, the prime minister is the central link between the legislative and executive branches of government. Second, executive power is concentrated in the prime minister's hands through the effective subordination of the cabinet and departmental ministers.

Such developments have led to the phenomenon of 'creeping presidentialism', in that prime ministers, under media and other pressures, have distanced themselves increasingly from their parties, cabinets and governments by cultivating a personal appeal based on their ability to articulate their own political and ideological vision. Nevertheless, though prime ministers who command cohesive parliamentary majorities and are supported by unified cabinets wield greater power than many a president, their power is always fragile because it can be exercised only in favourable political circumstances. Ultimately, prime ministers are vehicles through which parties win and retain power; prime ministers who fail in these tasks, or become unmindful of the role, rarely survive long.

PROPERTY

Property, in everyday usage, refers to inanimate objects or 'things'. However, property is better thought of as a social institution, defined by custom, convention and, in most cases, by **law**. As a political principle, property draws attention to a relationship of ownership that exists between the object in question and the person or group to whom it belongs. In that sense there is a clear distinction between property and simply making use of an object as a possession. For example, to pick up a pebble from the beach, to borrow a pen, or to drive someone else's car, does not establish ownership. Property is thus an established and enforceable claim to an object or possession; it is a **right**, not a 'thing'. The ownership of property is therefore reflected in the existence of rights and powers over an object, and the acceptance of duties and liabilities in relation to it.

However, property can be conceived of as private, common or state property. Private property is the right of an individual or institution to exclude others from the use or benefit of something. The right to 'exclude' does not necessarily deny access, however. Someone else can use 'my' car – but only with my permission. Common property is based on a shared right of access to property among members of a collective body, none of whom can exercise a 'right to exclude', except in relation to non-members. State property is private property that belongs to the **state**. Ordinary citizens, for example, have no more right of access to state property such as police cars than they do to any other private vehicle. However, the notions of state property and common property are often confused. Terms such as 'public ownership' or 'social ownership' appear to refer to property owned collectively by all citizens, but in practice usually describe property that is owned and controlled by the state. 'Nationalization' similarly implies ownership by the **nation**, but it invariably operates through a system of state control.

Significance

The question of property has been one of the deepest and most divisive issues in political and ideological debate. Indeed, ideological divisions have traditionally amounted to where one stands on property, both left-wing and right-wing political creeds practising different forms of the politics of ownership. The clash between **capitalism** and **socialism** has thus been portrayed as a choice between two rival economic philosophies, the former based on private property and the latter on common ownership.

Liberals and conservatives have generally been strong supporters of private property; among their arguments are:

- Property is a right based on 'self-ownership' – because each person has exclusive rights over him/herself, it follows that such people have an exclusive right to the product of their labour; inanimate objects have been 'mixed' with human labour to create property rights (John Locke).
- It is an incentive to labour and thus serves as a guarantee of economic prosperity and efficiency.
- It enlarges individual **freedom** in the sense that it promotes independence and self-reliance – people can 'stand on their own two feet'.
- It promotes important social values, because property owners have a 'stake' in society and are more likely to maintain **order**, to be law-abiding and to respect the property of others.
- It is a means of self-realization, an exteriorization of one's personal identity – people 'see' themselves in what they own: their cars, houses, books and so on.

Socialists and communists, on the other hand, have advanced the following arguments in favour of common property:

- It reflects the fact that labour is generally a social and collective activity depending on co-operation rather than independent effort – what is produced in common should be owned in common.
- It strengthens community and social cohesion by ensuring that all members of society have a shared interest and a collective identity.
- It guarantees equality by preventing some from accumulating wealth while others are denied it.
- It allows people to escape from greed and materialism by defining happiness not in terms of its acquisition but on the basis of personal self-development.

Nevertheless, there are clear indications that the politics of ownership has declined in significance. Though its cause was revived in the 1980s by the New Right's enthusiasm for privatization, the collapse of communism in the revolutions of 1989–91 and the de-radicalization of socialism have resulted in a widespread acceptance of at least the economic virtues of private property and therefore of the disadvantages of both common and state property.

PROPORTIONAL REPRESENTATION

Proportional representation (PR) is the principle that parties should be represented in the assembly or parliament in direct proportion to their electoral strength, their proportion of seats equalling their proportion of votes. The term is generally used not to refer to a single method of election but rather to a variety of electoral mechanisms – those able to secure proportional outcomes, or at least a high and reliable degree of proportionality. The most commonly used PR electoral system is the party list system (in which electors vote for parties, not candidates); other PR systems include the single transferable vote (STV) (which uses multi-member constituencies and a system of preferential voting) and the mixed member proportional (MMP) system (which combines the party list with the single-member plurality (SMP) system, or 'first-past-the-post').

Significance

Although the principle of PR has its origins in the late seventeenth century, PR electoral systems did not emerge until the advent of disciplined political parties in the late nineteenth century. Most modern democracies base at least lower-chamber parliamentary elections on PR, but because India and the USA in particular continue to use SMP, this does not translate into the majority of voters. The significance of PR nevertheless goes a long way beyond the issue of electoral fairness as, especially in parliamentary systems, it has an impact on the party system, the make-up of government and the relationship between the parliament and the executive. In particular, where PR is used, multiparty systems and coalition governments are more common, and the executive is less likely to be able to dominate the parliament. For supporters of PR, these tendencies bring wide-ranging benefits, not least in strengthening legitimacy, responsiveness and accountability, and helping to build a **political culture** based on **consensus** and partnership. Critics, on the other hand, associate PR with weak and unstable government, and warn that it can make small, and possibly extremist, parties disproportionately powerful.

PUNISHMENT

Punishment refers to a penalty inflicted on a person for a crime or offence. Unlike revenge, which can be random and arbitrary, punishment is formal in the sense that specific punishments are linked to particular kinds of offence. Moreover, punishment has a moral character that distinguishes it, for example, from simple vindictiveness. Punishment is not motivated by spite or the desire to inflict pain, discomfort or inconvenience for its own sake, but rather because a 'wrong' has been done. This is why what are thought of as cruel or inhuman punishments, such as torture and perhaps the death penalty, are often prohibited.

Significance

Apart from anarchists (and even they may be prepared to sanction social ostracism in some form), there is a general agreement that wrongdoing should be punished. However, there is considerable debate about the justification for punishment and the form it should take. Three key justifications for punishment have been advanced, based on the ideas of retribution, **deterrence** and rehabilitation, respectively. Retribution means to take vengeance against a wrongdoer. The idea is rooted in the religious notion of sin, the belief that there is a discernible quality of 'evil' about particular actions and, possibly, certain thoughts. Wrongdoers thus deserve to be punished; punishment is their 'just deserts'. Such thinking suggests that, because punishment is vengeance, it should be proportional to the wrong done. In short, the punishment should 'fit' the crime, in the Old Testament sense of 'an eye for an eye, a tooth for a tooth'. Retribution theory provides a clear justification, for example, for the death penalty in the case of murder.

The idea of deterrence is concerned to use punishment to shape the future conduct of others. It sees punishment primarily as a device to deter people from crime or anti-social behaviour by making them aware of the consequences of their actions. In this view, punishment should be selected on the basis of its capacity to deter other potential wrongdoers. For this reason, deterrence theory may at times justify far stricter and even more cruel punishments than retribution ever can. To punish a wrongdoer is to 'set an example' to others; the more dramatic that example, the more effective its deterrence value. As such, the idea of deterrence may come close to divorcing the wrong that has been done from the punishment meted out, and so runs the risk of victimizing the initial wrongdoer. The final justification for punishment, rehabilitation, shifts responsibility for wrongdoing away from the individual and towards society. From this perspective, crime and disorder arise not from moral deficiencies or from calculations of self-interest; rather, they are 'bred' by social problems such as unemployment, poverty, poor housing and inequality. The purpose of punishment is therefore to educate rather than penalize, seeking, above all, to integrate wrongdoers back into society on their release. However, rehabilitation theory comes dangerously close to absolving the individual from any moral responsibility for the situation.

RACE/ETHNICITY

Race refers to physical or genetic differences among humankind that supposedly distinguish one group of people from another on biological grounds, such as skin and hair colour, physique and facial features. A race is thus a group of people who share a common ancestry and 'one blood'. The term is, however, controversial, both scientifically and politically. Scientific evidence suggests that there is no such thing as 'race' in the sense of a species-type difference between peoples. Politically, racial categorization is commonly based on cultural stereotypes, and is simplistic at best and pernicious at worst. The term ethnicity is therefore sometimes preferred.

Ethnicity is the sentiment of loyalty towards a distinctive population, cultural group or territorial area. The term is complex because it has both cultural and racial overtones. The members of ethnic groups are often seen, correctly or incorrectly, to have descended from common ancestors, and the groups are thus thought of as extended kinship groups. More commonly, ethnicity is understood as a form of cultural identity, albeit one that operates at a deep and emotional level. An 'ethnic' culture encompasses values, traditions and practices but, crucially, also gives a people a common identity and sense of distinctiveness, usually by focusing on their origins and descent.

Significance

The link between race and politics was first established by the European racialism of the nineteenth century. This preached doctrines of racial superiority/inferiority and racial segregation, in the twentieth century mixing with fascism to produce Nazism, and helping to fuel right-wing nationalist or anti-immigration movements. The central idea behind such movements is that only a racially or ethnically unified society can be cohesive and successful, with multiculturalism and multiracialism always being sources of conflict and instability. Very different forms of racial or ethnic politics have developed out of the struggle against colonialism in particular, and as a result of racial discrimination and disadvantage in general. However, the conjunction of racial and social disadvantage has generated various styles of political activism.

These range from civil rights movements, such as that led in the USA in the 1960s by Martin Luther King, to militant and revolutionary movements, such as the Black Power movement and the Black Moslems (now the Nation of Islam) in the USA, and the struggle of the African National Congress (ANC) against apartheid in South Africa up to 1994. Ethnic politics, however, has become a more generalized phenomenon in the post-1945 period, associated with forms of nationalism based on ethnic consciousness and regional identity. This has been evident in the strengthening of centrifugal tendencies in states such as the UK, Belgium and Italy, and has been manifest in the rise of particularist nationalism. In the former USSR, Czechoslovakia and Yugoslavia, it led to state collapse and the creation of a series of new nation-states. The two main forces fuelling such developments are uneven patterns of social development in so-called 'core' and 'peripheral' parts of the world, and the weakening of forms of 'civic' nationalism resulting from the impact of globalization.

RACIALISM/RACISM

Racialism is, broadly, the belief that political or social conclusions can be drawn from the idea that humankind is divided into biologically distinct races. Racialist theories are thus based on two assumptions. The first is that there are fundamental genetic, or species-type, differences among the peoples of the world – racial differences are meaningful. The second is that these genetic divisions are reflected in cultural, intellectual and/or moral differences, making them politically or socially significant. Political racialism is manifest in calls for racial segregation (for example, apartheid) and in doctrines of 'blood' superiority or inferiority (for example, Aryanism or anti-Semitism).

'Racialism' and 'racism' are commonly used interchangeably, but the latter is better used to refer to prejudice or hostility towards a people because of their racial origin, whether or not this is linked to a developed racial theory. 'Institutionalized' racism is racial prejudice that is entrenched in the norms and values of an organization or social system, and so is not dependent on conscious acts of discrimination or hostility. Nevertheless, the term is highly contentious and has been used, among other things, to refer to unwitting prejudice, insensitivity to the values and culture of minority groups, racist stereotyping, racism as a deliberate act of policy, and racial oppression as an ideological system (as in Nazism).

Significance

Racial theories of politics first emerged in the nineteenth century in the work of theorists such as Count Gobineau (1816–82) and H. S. Chamberlain (1855–1929). They developed through the combined impact of European imperialism and a growing interest in biological theories associated with Darwinism. By the late nineteenth century, the idea that there were racial differences between the 'white', 'black' and 'yellow' peoples of the world was widely accepted in European society, extending beyond the political right and including many liberals and even socialists. Overt political racialism has been most clearly associated with fascism in general and Nazism in particular. However, covert or implicit forms of racialism have operated more widely in campaigns against immigration by far-right groups and parties such as the French National Front and the British National Party (BNP). Anti-immigration racialism is based ideologically on conservative nationalism, in that it highlights the danger to social cohesion and national unity that is posed by multiculturalism. The attraction of racialism is that it offers a simple, firm and apparently scientific explanation for social divisions and national differences. However, racialism has little or no empirical basis, and it invariably serves as a thinly veiled justification for bigotry and oppression. Its political success is associated largely with its capacity to generate simple explanations and solutions, and to harness personal and social insecurities to political ends.

RATIONAL CHOICE

Rational choice is a broad theoretical approach to the study of politics whose principal subdivisions include public choice theory, social choice theory and game theory. Sometimes called formal **political theory**, it draws heavily on the example of economic theory in building up models based on procedural rules, usually about the rationally self-interested behaviour of individuals. Rational choice theorists use a method that dates back to Thomas Hobbes (1588–1679) and is employed in **utilitarianism**, in assuming that political actors consistently choose the most efficient means to achieve their various ends. In the form of public choice theory it is concerned with the provision of so-called public goods, goods that are delivered by **government** rather than the **market**, because, as with clean air, their benefit cannot be withheld from individuals who choose not to contribute to their provision. In the form of social choice theory it examines the relationship between individuals' preferences and social choices such as voting. In the form of **game theory** it has developed more from the field of mathematics than from the assumptions of neo-classical economics, and entails the use of first principles to analyse puzzles regarding individual behaviour. The best-known example of game theory is the 'prisoners' dilemma', (see Figure 2), which demonstrates that rationally self-interested behaviour is generally less beneficial than co-operation.

Significance

Rational choice theory emerged as a tool of political analysis in the 1950s and gained greater prominence from the 1970s onwards. Most firmly established in the USA, and associated in particular with the so-called Virginia School, it has been used to provide insights into the actions of voters, lobbyists, bureaucrats and politicians. It has had its broadest impact on political analysis in the form of what is called institutional public choice theory. Supporters of rational choice theory argue that it has introduced greater rigour into the discussion of political phenomena, by allowing political analysts to develop explanatory models in the manner of economic theory. The rational choice approach to political analysis, however, has by no means been universally accepted.

It has been criticized for overestimating human rationality, in that it ignores the fact that people seldom possess clear sets of preferred goals and rarely make decisions in the light of full and accurate knowledge. Furthermore, in proceeding from an abstract model of the individual, rational choice theory pays insufficient attention to social and historical factors, failing to recognize, among other things, that human self-interestedness may be socially conditioned rather than innate. Finally, rational choice theory is sometimes seen to have a conservative value bias, stemming from its initial assumptions about human behaviour, and reflected in its use by theorists such as Buchanan and Tulloch (1962) to defend the free market and support a minimal state.

RATIONALISM

Rationalism is the belief that the world has a rational structure, and that this can be disclosed through the exercise of human reason and critical enquiry. As a philosophical theory, rationalism is the belief that knowledge flows from reason rather than experience, and thus it contrasts with empiricism. As a general principle, however, rationalism places a heavy emphasis on the capacity of human beings to understand and explain their world, and to find solutions to problems. While rationalism does not dictate the ends of human conduct, it certainly dictates how these ends should be pursued. It is associated with an emphasis on principle and reason-governed behaviour, as opposed to a reliance on custom or tradition, or non-rational drives and impulses.

Significance

Rationalism was one of the core features of the Enlightenment, the intellectual movement that reached its height in the eighteenth century and challenged traditional beliefs in religion, politics and learning generally in the name of reason. Enlightenment rationalism provided the basis for both liberalism and socialism, and established the intellectual framework within which conventional political and social analysis developed. Rationalist approaches to understanding have a number of characteristics. First, they tend to place a heavy emphasis on progress and reform. Reason not only enables people to understand and explain their world, but it also helps them to re-shape the world for the better. Rationalism thus promises to emancipate humankind from the grip of the past and the weight of custom and tradition. Each generation is able to advance beyond the previous one as the stock of human knowledge and understanding progressively increases. Second, rationalism is associated with the attempt to uncover values and structures that are universally applicable to humankind. Reason, in this sense, constitutes a higher reference point for human conduct than do the inherited values and norms of a particular society. Third, rationalism highlights the importance of debate and discussion over the use of force or aggression, and implies a broad faith in democracy. If people are reason-guided creatures they have both the ability to settle disputes through debate and negotiation, and a capacity to identify and express their own best interests.

However, rationalistic approaches to political understanding have never been universally accepted. A form of anti-rationalism took root in the late nineteenth century as thinkers started to reflect on the limits of human reason and draw attention to other, perhaps more powerful, drives and impulses. For example, Friedrich Nietzsche (1844–1900) proposed that human beings are motivated by deep-seated emotions, their 'will' rather than the rational mind, and in particular by what he called the 'will to power'. In their most extreme form, associated with fascism, such ideas were manifested in a reverence for strength and military power, and the rejection of intellectual enquiry as cold, dry and lifeless. In the form of traditional conservatism, they gave rise to the much more modest belief that tradition and history are surer guides for human conduct than reason and principle, because the world is simply too complicated for people to grasp fully. Faith in rationalism also waned, particularly in the final decades of the twentieth century. This occurred, among other things, because of a growing acceptance that particular individuals, groups and societies possess their own intrinsic values and that these are not susceptible to rational ordering, and through a recognition that rationalism is linked to Western values and that the Enlightenment project of which it is a part is merely a form of cultural imperialism. Such reservations about rationalism have been expressed by both communitarian and postmodern theorists.

REALISM

Realism, in its broadest sense, is a tradition of political theorizing that is 'realistic' in the sense that it is hard-headed and (as realists see it) devoid of wishful thinking and deluded moralizing. Key early thinkers in this tradition included Niccolò Machiavelli (1469–1527) and Thomas Hobbes (1588–1679). Realism has nevertheless had its greatest impact as a theory of international relations. Realist international theory is, primarily, about power and self-interest. The realist power-politics model of international politics is based on two core assumptions. First, human nature is characterized by selfishness and greed, meaning that states, the dominant actors on the international stage, exhibit essentially the same characteristics. Second, as states operate in a context of anarchy, they are forced to rely on self-help and so prioritize security and survival. Realist theory can therefore be summed up in the equation: egoism plus anarchy equals power politics.

Some have suggested that the formulation betrays a basic theoretical fault line within realism, dividing it into two distinct schools of thought. One of these – *classical realism* – explains power politics in terms of egoism, while the other – *neorealism*, or *structural realism* – explains it in terms of anarchy. However, these alternative approaches reflect more a difference of emphasis within realism rather than a division into rival 'schools', as the central assumptions of realism are common to most realist theorists, even though they may disagree about which factors are ultimately the most important. By no means, however, do realists assume that the combination of egoism and anarchy must result in restless conflict and unending war. Instead, realists insist that the pattern of conflict and co-operation within the international system conforms largely to the requirements of the balance of power.

Significance

Realism can claim to be the oldest theory of international politics. It can be traced back to Thucydides' account of the Peloponnesian War (431–404 BCE), and to Sun Tzu's classic work on strategy, *The Art of War*, written at roughly the same time in

China. However, as a theory of international relations, realism took shape from the 1930s onwards as a critique of the then-dominant liberal internationalism, dismissed by some realists as 'utopianism'. With the end of World War II and the onset of the Cold War, realism became the pre-eminent theory of international relations during the Cold War period. Among the reasons for realism's dominance was that the Cold War, characterized as it was by superpower rivalry and a nuclear arms race, made the politics of power and security appear to be undeniably relevant and insightful.

However, in a process that began during the 1970s, but was significantly accelerated by the end of the Cold War, more and more aspects of world politics came to be shaped by developments that either ran counter to realist expectations or highlighted the limitations of realist analysis. These included the end of the Cold War itself, the growing impact of non-state actors, the advance of globalization and the increased significance of human rights. Critics of realism have also objected to its tendency to divorce politics from morality, arguing that this has tended to legitimize military escalation and the hegemonic ambitions of great powers. Nevertheless, realism continues to form a part of the analytical toolkit of most serious students of international politics. This applies, in part, because the acceptance that anarchy (albeit modified by other developments) remains the basic feature of world politics extends well beyond realism. Neorealist thinking about the structural dynamics of the international system is therefore seldom dismissed out of hand.

REFERENDUM

A referendum is a vote in which the electorate can express a view on a particular issue of public policy. It differs from an election in that the latter is essentially a means of filling a public office and does not provide a direct or reliable method of influencing the content of policy. The referendum is therefore a device of direct democracy. However, it is typically used not to replace representative institutions, but to supplement them. Referendums may either be advisory or binding; they may also raise issues for discussion, or be used to decide or confirm policy questions (propositions or plebiscites). Whereas most referendums are called by the government, initiatives (used especially in Switzerland and California) are placed on the ballot through some form of popular petition.

Significance

The use of the referendum can be traced back to sixteenth-century Switzerland. However, referendums have always had a dual character. On the one hand, they are a form of popular government in that they give expression to 'bottom-up' pressures within the political system. On the other hand, they have also been used as 'top-down' instruments of political control. This was seen most clearly in the case of Hitler and other 1930s dictators, who used plebiscites as a means of legitimizing dictatorship, but it has also applied to democratic politicians who wish to neutralize opposition within representative institutions.

The wider use of referendums is supported for a number of reasons, including:

- They strengthen democracy by allowing the public to speak for themselves rather than through the inevitably distorted views of their representatives.
- They check the power of elected governments, keeping them in line with public opinion between elections.
- They promote political participation, thus helping to create a more engaged, better-educated and better-informed electorate.
- Unlike elections, they provide the public with a way of expressing their views on specific issues.
- They provide a means of settling major constitutional questions.

On the other hand, referendums have been associated with the following disadvantages and dangers:

- They place political decisions in the hands of those who have the least education and experience, and are most susceptible to media and other influences.
- They provide, at best, only a snapshot of public opinion at a single point in time.
- They allow politicians to absolve themselves of responsibility for making difficult decisions.
- They enable leaders to manipulate the political agenda (especially when governments call referendums and can use public resources and their publicity machine to back their preferred outcome).
- They tend to simplify and distort political issues, reducing them to questions that have a simple yes/no answer.

REFORM

Reform means, most basically, to create a new form of something, to make it anew. The term 'reform' nevertheless always carries positive overtones, implying betterment or improvement. Strictly speaking, therefore, it is contradictory to condemn or criticize what is acknowledged to be a reform. However, reform denotes improvement of a particular kind, in at least two senses. First, reform indicates changes within a person, institution or system that may remove their undesirable qualities, but do not alter their fundamental character: in essence, they remain the same person, institution and system. Reform thus endorses change while maintaining continuity. Second, the change that reform stands for tends to have piecemeal character: it advances bit by bit, rather than through a sudden or dramatic upheaval. As a longer-term and gradual process of change, reform differs markedly from revolution.

Significance

As a style of political change, reform is linked, most commonly, to liberalism and parliamentary socialism. Liberal reformism is often associated with utilitarianism. Founded on the assumption that all individuals seek to maximize their own happiness, and applying the principle of general utility – 'the greatest happiness for the greatest number'– utilitarian thinkers advocated a wide range of legal, economic and political reforms, following the lead of Jeremy Bentham (1748–1832). These reforms included the codification of the legal system, the removal of barriers to trade and economic competition, and the extension of democracy. Socialist reformism, which emerged towards the end of the nineteenth century, consciously built on these liberal foundations. In the UK, this was reflected in the Fabian Society's faith in 'the inevitability of gradualism'. Openly rejecting the ideas of revolutionary socialism, as represented by Marxism, Fabian socialists proposed instead that a socialist society would gradually emerge out of liberal capitalism through a process of incremental and deliberate reform. Similar thinking was advanced in Eduard Bernstein's *Evolutionary Socialism* (1898/1962), which championed the idea of a gradual and peaceful transition from capitalism to socialism.

Reform has two key advantages. In the first place, by trying to balance change against continuity, reform can usually be brought about peacefully and without disrupting social cohesion. Even when the cumulative effect of reform amounts to fundamental change, because it is brought about in a piecemeal fashion, and over an extended period, it is more likely to be acceptable, even to those who are at first unsympathetic. Second, reform is founded on the best empirical traditions of scientific enquiry. As an incremental process, reform advances through 'trial and error': the impact of earlier reforms can be assessed and adjustments can be made through a further set of reforms, as necessary. Critics of reform have nevertheless condemned it as little more than a sham. This is because it serves to perpetuate what it appears to oppose. Revolutionary socialists, for example, have alleged that that reform may actually have strengthened capitalism; indeed that capitalism's susceptibility to reform may be the secret of its survival.

REGIONALISM

Regionalism, broadly, is a process through which geographical regions become significant political and/or economic units, serving as the basis for co-operation and, possibly, identity. At the institutional level, regionalism involves the growth of norms, rules and formal structures through which this co-operation is brought about. Regionalism has two faces, however. In the first place it is a sub-national phenomenon, a process that takes place *within* countries. As such, regionalism implies decentralization, but without calling the integrity of the state and the final authority of national government into question. Regionalism, in this sense, may take the form of devolution, in either its administrative or its legislative guise, or it may involve federalism, in which case regional or provincial bodies are constitutionally entrenched and exercise a share of sovereignty. The second face of regionalism is international rather than sub-national. Regionalism, in this sense, refers to a process of co-operation or integration between countries in the same region of the world. Regionalism at an international level may take the form of intergovernmentalism or supranationalism.

Significance

Sub-national regionalism has generally become more respectable and has, in states ranging from the UK, France and Spain to Canada and India, become a more powerful political movement since the 1960s. The forces supporting regionalism include the growth of ethnic and cultural nationalism, and the declining capacity of the nation-state to maintain a high level of political allegiance in an increasingly globalized world. In that sense, regionalism may be a counterpart to globalization. However, it is sometimes argued that regionalism is only appropriate to certain states, notably to relatively large and culturally diverse states in which there are strong and meaningful traditions of regional political loyalty. Criticisms of this form of regionalism usually focus on one of two issues. Regionalism is seen either as a threat to the nation's territorial integrity, in that it strengthens regional loyalties and identities at the expense of national ones, or, from a separatist perspective, as a device employed by central government to contain and control centrifugal pressures within the state. This latter view implies that regionalism may take the form of 'regionalization', the process by which central authorities respond to regional demand without redistributing policy-making power.

International regional organizations have sprung up in all parts of the world since 1945. The first phase of this process peaked in the 1960s, but the advance of regionalism has been particularly notable since the late 1980s. This has given rise to the phenomenon of 'new' regionalism. Whereas earlier forms of regionalism had promoted regional co-operation over a range of issues – security, political and economic issues and so on – 'new' regionalism has been reflected in the creation of new regional trading blocs, or the strengthening of existing ones, largely, once again, in response to challenges linked to globalization. Some, as a result, have drawn attention to an emerging 'world of regions', arguing that regionalism may be both the successor to the nation-state and an alternative to globalization. Others, however, point out both that there is no evidence that regionalism can rival nationalism's capacity to generate identity and belonging, and that, far from being an alternative to globalization, regionalism has generally been used by states as a means of engaging more effectively with the global economy.

RELIGIOUS FUNDAMENTALISM

Fundamentalism (from the Latin *fundamentum*, meaning 'base') is a style of ideological thought in which certain principles are recognized as essential 'truths' that have unchallengeable and overriding authority, regardless of their content. Substantive fundamentalisms therefore have little or nothing in common except that their supporters tend to evince an earnestness or fervour born out of doctrinal certainty. Fundamentalism in this sense can be found in a variety of political creeds. For example, Marxism and communism are sometimes viewed as forms of fundamentalist socialism (as opposed to the revisionist socialism endorsed by social democracy), on the grounds of their absolute and unequivocal rejection of capitalism. Even liberal scepticism can be said to incorporate the fundamental belief that all theories should be doubted (apart from this one). Though the term is often used pejoratively to imply inflexibility, dogmatism and authoritarianism (and may therefore be avoided by fundamentalists themselves), fundamentalism may suggest selflessness and a devotion to principle.

Religious fundamentalism is characterized by a rejection of the distinction between religion and politics – 'politics is religion'. This implies that religious principles are not restricted to personal or 'private' life, but are also seen as the organizing principles of 'public' existence, including law, social conduct and the economy as well as politics. The fundamentalist impulse therefore contrasts sharply with secularism, the belief that religion should not intrude into secular (worldly) affairs, reflected in the separation of church from state. While some forms of religious fundamentalism coexist with pluralism (for example, Christian fundamentalism in the USA and Jewish fundamentalism in Israel) because their goals are limited and specific, other forms are revolutionary (for example, Islamic fundamentalism, or Islamism, in Iran, Pakistan and Sudan) in that they aim to construct a theocracy in which the state is reconstructed on the basis of religious principles, and political position is linked to one's place within a religious hierarchy. In some cases, but not necessarily, religious fundamentalism is defined by a belief in the literal truth of sacred texts.

Significance

Religious fundamentalism has been a growing political force since the 1970s. Its most important form has been Islamic fundamentalism, associated most closely with the 'Islamic revolution' in Iran since 1979 but also evident throughout the Middle East and in parts of north Africa and Asia. However, forms of Christian fundamentalism (USA), Jewish fundamentalism (Israel), Hindu fundamentalism and Sikh fundamentalism (India), and even Buddhist fundamentalism (Sri Lanka) have also emerged. It is difficult to generalize about the causes of this fundamentalist upsurge, because in different parts of the world it has taken different doctrinal forms and displayed different ideological features. What is clear, however, is that fundamentalism arises in deeply troubled societies, particularly societies afflicted by an actual or perceived crisis of identity. Among the factors that have contributed to such crises since the final decades of the twentieth century have been secularization and the apparent weakening of society's 'moral fabric'; the search in post-colonial states for a non-Western and perhaps anti-Western political identity; the declining status of revolutionary socialism; and the tendency of globalization to weaken 'civic' nationalism and stimulate the emergence of forms of 'ethnic' nationalism. There is nevertheless considerable debate about the long-term significance of religious fundamentalism. One view is that fundamentalist religion is merely a symptom of the difficult adjustments that modernization brings about, but it is ultimately doomed because it is out of step with the secularism and liberal values that are implicit in the modernization process. The rival view holds that secularism and liberal culture are in crisis, and that fundamentalism exposes their failure to address deeper human needs and their inability to establish authoritative values that give social order a moral foundation.

The great strength of fundamentalism is its capacity to generate political activism and mobilize the faithful. Fundamentalism operates on both psychological and social levels. Psychologically, its appeal is based on its capacity to offer certainty in an uncertain world. Being religious, it addresses some of the deepest and most perplexing problems confronting humankind; and being fundamentalist, it provides solutions that are straightforward, practical and, above all, absolute. Socially, while its appeal has extended to the educated and professional classes, religious fundamentalism has been particularly successful in addressing the aspirations of the economically and politically marginalized.

The main criticisms of religious fundamentalism are that it breeds, or legitimizes, political extremism, and that it is implicitly oppressive, even totalitarian. While the popular image of fundamentalists as bombers and terrorists is unbalanced and misleading, it is impossible to deny that some forms of religious fundamentalism have expressed themselves through militancy and violence. The most common fundamentalist justification for such acts is that, as they are intended to eradicate evil, they fulfil the will of God. The association between fundamentalism and oppression derives from its insistence on a single, unquestionable truth and a single, unchallengeable source of political authority. This creates profound tension between religious fundamentalism and core features of the Western political tradition such as pluralism and liberal democracy.

REPRESENTATION

To represent means, in everyday language, to 'portray' or 'make present', as when a picture is said to represent a scene or a person. As a political principle, representation is a relationship through which an individual or group stands for, or acts on behalf of, a larger body of people. Representation differs from democracy in that, while the former acknowledges a distinction between government and the governed, the latter, at least in its classical sense, aspires to abolish this distinction and establish popular self-government. Representative democracy may nevertheless constitute a limited and indirect form of democratic rule, provided that representation links government and the governed in such a way that the people's views are effectively articulated or their interests secured.

However, there is no single, agreed theory of representation. The term may have one of four sets of implications. First, a representative may be a trustee, a person who is vested with formal responsibility for another's property or affairs. This was classically expressed by Edmund Burke (1729–97), who argued that representatives serve their constituents by thinking for themselves and using their own mature judgement. Second, a representative may be a delegate, a person who is chosen to act for another on the basis of clear guidance or instructions. Delegation implies acting as a conduit conveying the views of others, without expressing one's own views or opinions; examples include sales representatives and ambassadors. Third, a representative may be a person who carries out a mandate, in the sense that such people are obliged to carry out the promises on which they fought an election. This theory implies that political parties rather than individual politicians are the principal agents of representation. Fourth, a representative may typify or resemble the group he or she claims to represent, usually coming from the group itself. This notion is embodied in the idea of a 'representative cross-section', and implies that a representative government or **parliament** would constitute a microcosm of the larger society, containing members drawn from all groups and sections in society, and in numbers that are proportional to the size of the groups in society at large.

Significance

Representation is widely viewed as the only practicable form of democracy in modern circumstances. Interest in it developed alongside the wider use of popular election as the principal means of political recruitment, though pre-democratic forms of representation supposedly operated through, for example, the obligation of monarchs to consult major landed, clerical and other interests. The general benefits of representation are that it provides the people with a mechanism through which they can replace unpopular politicians or unsuccessful governments, while relieving ordinary citizens of the everyday burdens of decision-making, thus making possible a division of labour in **politics**. Representation therefore allows government to be placed in the hands of those with better education, expert knowledge and greater experience.

Nevertheless, there are very different views about what representation does, or should, imply in practice. Burke's model of trusteeship, for example, views representation as a moral duty that can be invested in an educated and social elite. Its virtue is that it does not bind representatives to the ill-considered and ignorant views of their constituents, but its disadvantage is that it may allow representatives to advance their own interests or defend the general interests of the social elite. Representation as delegations emerged specifically to counter such tendencies by realizing the ideal of popular **sovereignty**; however, it appears to rob governments and parliaments of their vital deliberative function as forums of debate and discussion. The doctrine of the mandate has the advantage that it helps to imbue elections with meaning by authorizing governments only to carry out policies that have been properly endorsed, but it is questionable whether voters are influenced by issues or policies, and, as with delegation, it allows governments little freedom of debate or manoeuvre. The resemblance model supposedly ensures that representatives can fully identify with the group they represent because they have a common background and shared experiences, but the idea that only a woman can represent women, or only a black person can represent other black people, is perhaps unnecessarily narrow as well as simplistic. Others, however, question the very idea of representation. This is done most commonly by those who argue that representation is simply a substitute for democracy, in that the former always has elitist implications because government is carried out by a small group of professional politicians and the people are kept at arm's length from political **power**.

REPUBLICANISM

Republicanism refers, most simply, to a preference for a republic over a **monarchy**. However, the term republic suggests not merely the absence of a monarch but, in the light of its Latin root, *res publica* (meaning common or collective affairs), it implies a distinctively public arena and popular rule. Republicanism has thus developed into a broader school of political theory that advocates certain moral precepts and institutional structures. The moral concern of republicanism is expressed in a belief in civic virtue, understood to include public-spiritedness, honour and patriotism. Above all, it is linked to a stress on public over private activity. The institutional focus of republicanism has, however, shifted its emphasis over time. Whereas classical republicanism was usually associated with mixed government that combined monarchical, aristocratic and democratic elements, the American and French revolutions reshaped republicanism by applying it to whole nations rather than small communities, and by endorsing the implications of modern democratic government. In the US version this means an acceptance of divided government achieved through federalism and the separation of powers; but in the French version it is associated more closely with radical democracy and the idea of the 'general will'.

Significance

Republican political ideas can be traced back to the ancient Roman Republic, its earliest version being Cicero's (106–43 BCE) defence of mixed government developed in *The Republic* (2008). It was revived in Renaissance Italy as a model for the organization of Italian city-states that supposedly balanced civic freedom against political stability. Further forms of republicanism were born out of the English, American and French revolutions. The major defence of republican forms of government, particularly in their anti-monarchical form, is their emphasis on civic freedom. Republican freedom combines liberty, in the sense of protection against arbitrary and tyrannical government, with the full and active participation of citizens in public and political life. In the form of 'civic republicanism', advocated since the 1960s by communitarian thinkers in particular, it amounts to the attempt to re-establish the public domain as the principal source of personal fulfilment, and thus rejects the tendency towards privatization and the 'rolling back' of the political sphere, as advocated by the New Right. Republicanism is therefore associated with the notion of active citizenship. The main criticisms of republicanism are that it is politically incoherent, in that it has been associated with such a wide variety of political forms; and that it is illiberal, in that it rejects the idea of freedom as privacy and non-interference, and has been used to justify the expansion of government responsibilities.

RESPONSIBILITY

Responsibility can be understood in three contrasting ways. First, it means to have control or authority, in the sense of being responsible for something or someone. Personal responsibility thus implies being responsible for oneself and one's own economic and social circumstances, while social responsibility implies being responsible for others. Second, responsibility means accountability or answerability, in the sense of being responsible to someone. This suggests the existence of a higher authority to which an individual or body is subject, and by which it can be controlled. Government is responsible in this sense if its actions are open to scrutiny and criticism by a parliament or assembly that has the ability to remove it from power. This also has an important moral dimension: it implies that the government is willing to accept blame and bear an appropriate penalty. Third, responsibility means to act in a sensible, reasonable or morally correct fashion, often in the face of pressure to behave otherwise. A government may thus claim to be responsible when it resists electoral pressures, and risks unpopularity by pursuing policies designed to meet long-term public interests.

Significance

Responsibility, as it applies to individuals, has different implications depending on what citizens are deemed to be responsible for, and to whom. However, the idea of responsible government has clearer applications, linked to the wider use of electoral and democratic procedures. Responsible government, in the sense of accountable government, is usually associated with two important benefits. The first is that it facilitates representation by binding government to the electorate viewed as a higher authority. Responsible government thus means that the government is responsible to, and removable by, the public, presumably through the mechanism of competitive elections. The second advantage is that it exposes government to scrutiny and oversight, checking the exercise of its power and exposing its policies to analysis and debate. This is a function that is usually vested in the parliament; it is carried out through procedures for debate and questioning and, in a more specific manner, by the use of committee.

In the UK system, responsible government has been elaborated into the conventions of collective and individual ministerial responsibility. Collective responsibility obliges all ministers to 'sing the same song', on the grounds that they are collectively responsible to and removable by Parliament. Individual responsibility holds that ministers are personally responsible to Parliament for departmental blunders or policy failures. Nevertheless, the adequacy of responsible government has been widely doubted. This occurs when doctrines of responsibility lose their political edge and become mere constitutional principles. For example, UK governments have little fear of collective responsibility so long as they have majority control of the House of Commons; and individual responsibility no longer, at least in its traditional form, results in ministerial resignations. Responsibility in the sense of governments acting in a morally correct fashion has always been deeply controversial. Its danger is that, by contrast with the idea of accountability, it divorces government from the people by suggesting that only the former has the ability to judge the best interests of the latter. Doubtless, all governments would view themselves as being responsible in this sense, supported by the knowledge that no other body could challenge this designation.

REVOLUTION

The term revolution, in its earliest usage, meant cyclical change (from the verb 'to revolve'), as in the restoration of 'proper' political order in the so-called Glorious

Revolution of 1688 in England. The French Revolution (1789), however, established the modern concept of revolution as a process of dramatic and far-reaching change, involving the destruction and replacement of the old order. Revolutions nevertheless may have a political, social or cultural character.

Political revolutions are popular uprisings involving extra-legal mass actions; they are often, though not necessarily, violent in character. This distinguishes a revolution from a coup d'état, which is a seizure of power by a small group. Revolutions differ from rebellions and revolts in that they bring about fundamental change, a change in the political system itself, as opposed to merely the displacement of a governing elite or a change of policy. *Social revolutions* are changes in the system of ownership or the economic system; in Marxist theory they are changes in the 'mode of production', as when capitalism replaced feudalism and when communism would replace capitalism. For Marxists, social revolutions are more fundamental than political ones, the latter being the political manifestation of a deeper and more long-term transformation of the class system. *Cultural revolutions* involve the rooting out of values, doctrines and beliefs that supported the old order, and the establishment in their place of a set of new ones. All revolutions have a crucial cultural dimension, reflecting the fact that any stable system of rule must, to some extent, be culturally and ideologically embedded. Many political revolutions are consolidated through a conscious process of re-education to establish a new set of system-sustaining values and aspirations.

Significance

The modern world has been formed through a series of crucial revolutions. These began with the English Revolution of the 1640s and 1650s, which overthrew monarchical absolutism and established early principles of constitutionalism and parliamentary government. The American Revolution (1776) led to the creation of a constitutional republic independent of Britain, and gave practical expression to the principle of representation. The French Revolution set out to destroy the old order under the banner of 'liberty, equality and fraternity', advanced democratic ideals and sparked an 'age of revolution' in early-nineteenth-century Europe. The Russian Revolution (1917), the first 'communist' revolution, provided a model for many of the subsequent twentieth-century revolutions, including the Chinese Revolution (1949), the Cuban Revolution (1959), the Vietnamese Revolution (1975) and the Nicaraguan Revolution (1979).

Debate about revolutions centres on their causes and their consequences. Among the general theories of revolutions are the following. The Marxist theory of revolution holds that they are essentially social phenomena arising out of contradictions that exist in all class societies. Systems theorists argue that revolution results from 'disequilibrium' in the political system, brought about by economic, social, cultural or international changes to which the system itself is incapable of responding – the 'outputs' of government become structurally out of line with the 'inputs'. The idea of a 'revolution of rising expectations' suggests that revolutions occur when a period of economic and social development is abruptly reversed, creating a widening gap between popular expectations and the capabilities of government.

The social-structural explanation implies that regimes usually succumb to revolution when, through international weakness and/or domestic ineffectiveness, they lose the ability, or the political will, to maintain control through the exercise of coercive power.

The consequences of revolution also cause deep disagreement. Revolutionaries themselves argue that revolution is by its nature a popular phenomenon, the unleashing of naked democratic pressure. They also tend to portray revolution as a purifying and ennobling struggle, a rooting-out of corruption, injustice and oppression; for this reason, revolutionary movements usually subscribed to some form of utopianism. Critics of revolution, however, point out that revolutions in practice invariably fail to live up to the high ideals of their perpetrators. This occurs for a variety of reasons, including that, despite the image of popular revolt, revolutions are invariably brought about by small cliques that are typically unwilling to relinquish their newly won power; that any regime that is established through the use of force and violence is compelled to continue using them and is thus forced down the road of authoritarianism; and that revolutions dismantle or crucially weaken institutions and governmental structures, leaving revolutionary leaders with potentially unchecked power.

RIGHTS

A right is an entitlement to act or be treated in a particular way (though in its original meaning it stood for a power or privilege, as in the rights of the nobility or divine right). Rights, however, can be either legal or moral in character. *Legal rights* are laid down in law or in a system of formal rules and so are enforceable. *Moral rights*, in contrast, exist only as moral claims or philosophical assertions. Human rights, and their predecessors, natural rights, are essentially moral rights, despite their having been translated increasingly into international law and sometimes domestic law. A further distinction can be made between negative and positive rights. *Negative rights* are rights that mark out a realm of unconstrained action, and thus impose restrictions on the behaviour of others, particularly the government. Traditional civil liberties, such as freedom of speech and freedom of movement, are therefore negative rights; our exercise of them requires that government and fellow citizens leave us alone. *Positive rights* are rights that impose demands on others, and particularly government, in terms of the provision of resources or supports, and thus extend their responsibilities. Social or welfare rights, such as the right to education or the right to benefits, are positive rights. Our exercise of them requires that the government provides services and guarantees social support.

Significance

The doctrine of rights emerged in the seventeenth and eighteenth centuries through the idea of natural or God-given rights, particularly as used by social contract theorists. Rights thus developed as, and in an important sense, remain, an expression of liberal individualism. However, the language of rights has come to be adopted by almost all political traditions and thinkers, meaning that political debate is littered with assertions of rights – the right to education, the right to free speech, the right to abortion, the rights of animals and so on. This reflects the fact that rights are the most convenient means of translating political commitments into principled claims. The most significant divisions over rights therefore focus not on whether or not they exist, but on which rights should be given priority and with what implications. Negative rights, for example, have traditionally been supported by liberals, who see them as a means of defending the individual from arbitrary government, but have been attacked by socialists on the grounds that they may merely uphold private property and thus class inequality. Positive rights, on the other hand, are favoured by socialists who wish to defend welfare provision and economic intervention, but are condemned by some liberals and supporters of the New Right because they breed dependency and weaken self-reliance.

Moreover, whereas liberals treat rights as being strictly individual entitlements, others have developed the idea of group rights, as in the case of socialist support for trade union rights and the nationalist emphasis on the rights of national self-determination. The idea of minority rights, in reference to the rights of groups such as women (a minority, of course, only in terms of elite representation), homosexuals, disabled people, children and ethnic minorities, has provoked particular debate. In many cases these are rights of equality; demands, in other words, for equal treatment on behalf of people who suffer from some form of discrimination or social disadvantage. In other cases, minority rights articulate demands that arise from the special needs of particular groups, examples including contraception and abortion rights for women, and mobility rights for people who use wheelchairs. Further controversy has arisen as a result of attempts to apply rights to non-humans, most obviously in the form of animal rights, but also more generally in the idea of the rights of the planet.

Nevertheless, some thinkers object to the very idea of rights. Marxists have traditionally portrayed rights as an example of bourgeois ideology, in that they establish a bogus equality that disguises the workings of the capitalist class system; utilitarians reject rights as nonsense, on the grounds that they constitute untestable philosophical assertions; and conservatives and some communitarians have warned that a 'culture of rights' breeds egoism and weakens social norms, an obsession with individual rights being a threat to the idea of what is morally right.

RULE OF LAW

The rule of law is the principle that the law should 'rule', in the sense that it establishes a framework within which all citizens should act and beyond which no one, neither private citizen nor government official, should go. This principle is enshrined in the German concept of the *Rechtsstaat*, a state based on law, which encouraged the development of codified constitutional systems across much of continental Europe. In the USA, the rule of law is linked to the doctrine of 'due process', which both restricts the discretionary power of public officials and establishes key individual rights, including the right to a fair trial and to equal treatment under the law. The

UK has traditionally been taken to represent an alternative conception of the rule of law. As outlined in A. V. Dicey (1835–1922), it embraces four features:

- No one should be punished except for breaches of the law
- Equality before the law
- When the law is broken there must be a certainty of punishment
- The rights and liberties of the individual are embodied in the 'ordinary law' of the land (though this may have been superseded in the UK by the passage of the Human Rights Act 1998, which enjoys a semi-entrenched status).

Significance

In its broad sense, the rule of law is a core liberal-democratic principle, embodying ideas such as **constitutionalism** and limited government to which most modern states aspire. In particular, the rule of law imposes significant constraints on how law is made and how it is adjudicated. For example, it suggests that all laws should be 'general', in the sense that they do not select particular individuals or groups for special treatment, for good or ill. Further, it is vital that citizens know 'where they stand'; laws should therefore be framed precisely and accessible to the public. Retrospective legislation, for example, is clearly unacceptable on such grounds, as it allows citizens to be punished for actions that were legal at the time they occurred. Above all, the principle implies that the courts should be impartial and accessible to all. This can only be achieved if the **judiciary** enjoys independence from government.

Nevertheless, the rule of law also has its critics. Some have, for example, suggested that it is possible to claim that the rule of law was observed in the Third Reich and in the USSR, simply on the grounds that in these cases oppression wore the cloak of legality. Marxist critics go further, however, arguing that, as law reflects the economic structure of society, the rule of law effectively protects private property, social inequality and class domination. Feminists have also drawn attention to biases that operate through the system of law, in this case biases that favour the interests of men at the expense of women, as a result, for example, of a predominantly male judiciary and legal profession. Multicultural theorists, for their part, have argued that law reflects the values and attitudes of the dominant cultural group and so is insensitive to the values and concerns of minority groups.

SECURITY

Security is the condition of being safe from (usually physical) harm; it therefore consists in being free from threat, intimidation and violence. However, a distinction is commonly drawn between the maintenance of security in the domestic sphere and its maintenance in the international sphere. In a domestic context, security refers to the **state**'s capacity to uphold **order** within its own borders, using the instruments of the coercive state, the police and, at times, the military. In an international context, security refers to the capacity of the state to provide protection against threats from beyond its borders, especially the ability of its armed forces to fight **wars** and resist military attack.

Significance

Security is widely viewed as being the deepest and most abiding issue in **politics**. This is because insecurity and fear make a decent and worthwhile existence impossible. High-sounding values such as **freedom**, **justice** and **toleration** thus only merit consideration once security is upheld. However, the issue of security is often thought of as being especially pressing in international politics because, while the domestic sphere is ordered and stable, by virtue of the existence of a sovereign state, the international sphere is anarchical and therefore threatening and unstable by its nature. There is nevertheless considerable debate about how security in international affairs can and should be upheld. Realists understand security primarily in terms of 'national' security. In a world of self-help, all states are under at least potential threat from all other states, so each state must have the capacity for self-defence. National security therefore places a premium on military power, reflecting the assumption that the more militarily powerful a state is, the more secure it is likely to be. However, this focus on military security draws states into dynamic, competitive relationships with one another, based on what is called the **security** dilemma.

The state-centric idea of national security has nevertheless been challenged. Liberals, for example, have long supported the notion of 'collective' security, reflecting the belief that aggression can best be resisted by united action taken by a number of states, often acting under the auspices of international bodies such as the United Nations or NATO. Furthermore, the advent of new security threats, and particularly the emergence of transnational **terrorism**, has encouraged some to argue that security should be recast in terms of 'global' security. This has happened as a result of trends and development, not least those associated with **globalization**, that has seen a substantial growth of cross-border movements of people, goods, money and ideas, perhaps rendering the distinction between security in the domestic and international spheres irrelevant. A final development has been the tendency to rethink the concept of security at a still deeper level, usually linked to the notion of 'human security', which brings a wide variety of other threats into focus, elated to poverty, environmental degradation, lack of food, lack of healthcare and so on.

SECURITY DILEMMA

The security dilemma describes a condition in which a military build-up for defensive purposes by one state is always liable to be interpreted by other states as potentially or actually aggressive, leading to retaliatory military build-ups and so on. This formulation reflects two component dilemmas (Booth and Wheeler, 2008). First, there is a dilemma of *interpretation* – what are the motives, intentions and capabilities of others in building up military power? As weapons are inherently ambiguous symbols (they can be either defensive or aggressive), there is irresolvable uncertainty about these matters. Second, there is a dilemma of *response* – should they react in kind, in a militarily confrontational manner, or should they seek to signal reassurance and attempt to defuse tension? Misperception here may lead either to an unintended **arms race** or to national disaster.

Significance

The security dilemma has been viewed as the quintessential dilemma of international politics. For realist theorists in particular, it is one of the key reasons why relations between states are characterized by permanent insecurity and an inescapable tendency towards war. This is because uncertainty about motives forces states to treat all other states as enemies. However, while liberal theorists may accept that co-operation and trust are always fragile in the international sphere, they are more optimistic than realists about the extent to which the impact of the security dilemma can be mitigated by, for example, synchronized diplomacy, institutions of collective security and international organizations such as the United Nations. Constructivists, for their part, emphasize the way that states interpret and respond to the actions of other states depends not just on the remorseless logic of the security dilemma, but also on how these other states are perceived in terms of their identities and interests, and, crucially, whether they are viewed as friends or enemies.

SEPARATION OF POWERS

The separation of powers (see Figure 12) is a doctrine proposing that the three chief functions of government (legislation, execution and adjudication) should be entrusted to separate branches of government (the legislature, the executive and the judiciary, respectively). In its formal sense the separation of powers demands independence, in that there should be no overlap of personnel between the branches. However, it also implies interdependence, in the form of shared powers to ensure that there are checks and balances. The separation of powers is applied most strictly in presidential systems of government, as in the USA, where it is the basis of the constitution, but the principle is respected in some form in all liberal democracies, notably in the principle of judicial independence. A full separation of powers

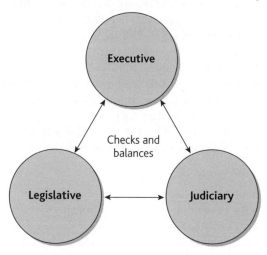

Figure 12 Separation of powers

requires the existence of a written constitution to define the formal powers and responsibilities of each of the branches of government.

Significance

The principle of the separation of power can be found in the writings of John Locke (1632–1704) but was more fully elaborated by C.-L. Montesquieu (1689–1775). The separation of powers is one of the classic means of fragmenting government power in order to defend liberty and keep tyranny at bay. An important feature of liberal constitutionalism, its advantages are that it both cuts the power of any branch of government down to size and establishes a network of internal tensions that ensure the exercise of power is never unchecked. This is evident in Richard Neustadt's (1980) description of the US system as 'separated institutions sharing powers'. However, few liberal democracies operate on the basis of a strict separation of powers. Its major drawback is that it offers an 'invitation to struggle' to the executive and legislative branches of government. It may therefore be nothing more than a recipe for institutional conflict, or 'government gridlock'. From this point of view it is a device that may suit only large and highly differentiated societies such as the USA, in which political stability requires that competing groups and interests have a wide variety of access points to government. Elsewhere, institutionalized links have been forged between the legislature and executive through parliamentary systems or hybrid semi-presidential systems.

SOCIAL CLASS

A social class is, broadly, a group of people who share a similar social and economic position. For Marxists, class is linked to economic power, which is defined by the individual's relationship to the means of production. From this perspective, class divisions are divisions between capital and labour, that is, between the owners of productive wealth (the bourgeoisie) and those who live off the sale of their labour power (the proletariat). Non-Marxist definitions of class are usually based on income and status differences between occupational groups. The most common notion of occupational class distinguishes between 'middle' class, white-collar (or non-manual) workers, and 'working' class, blue-collar (or manual) workers. A more sophisticated marketing-based distinction, used, with variations, by sociologists and political scientists, is made between higher professionals (class A), professionals (B), clerical workers (C1), skilled manual workers (C2), semi-skilled and unskilled workers (D), and those who are unemployed, unavailable for work or unable to work (E).

Significance

The leading proponents of the theory of class politics have been Marxists. Marxists regard social class as the most fundamental, and politically the most significant, social division. In Karl Marx's (1818–83) view, classes are the key actors on the political stage, and they have the ability to make history. The proletariat was destined to be the 'grave digger' of capitalism. It would fulfil this destiny once it had achieved 'class consciousness' and became aware of its genuine class interests, thus recognizing the fact of its own exploitation. The proletariat would therefore be transformed from a 'class *in*-itself' (an economically defined category) to a 'class *for*-itself' (a revolutionary force). This, Marx believed, would be a consequence of the deepening crisis of capitalism and the declining material conditions, or immiseration, of the working class. The Marxist two-class model has, however, been discredited by the failure of Marx's predictions to materialize, and by declining evidence of class struggle, at least in advanced capitalist societies. Modern Marxists have attempted to refine the crude two-class model, while still emphasizing the importance of wealth ownership, accepting, for example, that an 'intermediate' class of managers and technicians has emerged, and that there are internal divisions within both the bourgeoisie and the proletariat.

The decline in class politics is usually linked to the emergence of a post-industrial society, a society no longer dependent on manufacturing industry, but more reliant on knowledge and communication. The solidaristic class culture that was rooted in clear political loyalties and, usually, strong union organization, has thus been displaced by more individualistic and instrumentalist attitudes. For some, this is reflected in a transition from a 'Fordist' to a 'post-Fordist' era, from a system of mass production and mass consumption to one characterized by social and political fragmentation. One aspect of this has been the phenomenon of class de-alignment, the weakening of the relationship between social class and party support, evident in the UK, the USA and elsewhere since the 1970s. Another aspect is growing political interest in the so-called 'underclass' – those who suffer from multiple deprivation (unemployment or low pay, poor housing, inadequate education and so on) and are socially marginalized – 'the excluded'. However, whereas left-wing commentators define the underclass in terms of structural disadvantage and the changing balance of the global economy, right-wing commentators tend to explain the emergence of the underclass largely in terms of welfare dependency and personal inadequacy.

SOCIAL DEMOCRACY

Social democracy is an ideological position, usually, but not necessarily, associated with democratic socialism, which endorses a reformed or 'humanized' capitalist system though the term was originally used by Marxists to distinguish between the narrow goal of political democracy and the more radical task of collectivizing, or democratizing, productive wealth). Social democracy therefore advocates a balance between the market and the state, and between the individual and the community. At the heart of the social democratic position is an attempt to establish a compromise between, on the one hand, an acceptance of capitalism as the only reliable mechanism for generating wealth, and, on the other, a desire to distribute social rewards in accordance with moral, rather than market, principles. The chief characteristic of social democracy is thus a belief in reform within capitalism, underpinned by a general concern for the underdogs in society, the weak and vulnerable.

However, social democracy can take a variety of forms. In its classical form, associated with ethical socialism, it embodies an underlying commitment to equality and the politics of social justice. Nevertheless, social democracy may also be informed by modern liberal ideas, such as positive freedom and even by a paternalistic conservative emphasis on social duty, as in the case of the One Nation tradition. In terms of public policy, the three traditional pillars of social democracy have been the mixed economy (and therefore selective nationalization), economic management (usually in the form of Keynesianism – the use of fiscal policies to achieve the goal of full employment, as recommended by J. M. Keynes (1883–1946), and the welfare state (serving as a redistributive mechanism). Modernized or 'new' social democracy is usually associated with a fuller acceptance of market economics, and with sympathy for communitarian ideas such as mutual obligations and responsibility, breaking, or at least weakening, the traditional link between social democracy and egalitarianism.

Significance

Social democratic ideas and policies had their greatest impact in the early post-1945 period. Advanced by socialist and sometimes liberal and conservative parties, they resulted in the extension of economic and social intervention in most Western states. Social democracy has therefore often been credited with having contained the vagaries of capitalism and delivering wider prosperity and general social stability. However, the 'forward march' of social democracy went hand-in-hand with the 'long boom' of the post-war period, and, when this came to an end with the recessions of the 1970s and 1980s, the underlying contradiction of social democracy (between maintaining capitalism and promoting equality) came to the surface. This has resulted in a widespread abandonment of traditional social democratic positions and the adoption of more market-orientated values and policies. However, just as the flaws of the social democratic pro-state position created opportunities for the New Right in the 1980s, growing doubts about the New Right's pro-market position may open up fresh opportunities for modernized or 'new' social democracy.

The attraction of social democracy is that it has kept alive the humanist tradition, within socialist thought in particular. Its attempt to achieve a balance between efficiency and equality has been, the centre ground to which politics in most developed societies has tended to gravitate, regardless of whether socialist, liberal or conservative governments are in power. From the Marxist perspective, however, social democracy amounts to a betrayal of socialist principles, and attempts to prop up a defective capitalist system in the name of socialist ideals. Nevertheless, social democracy's central weakness is its lack of firm theoretical roots. While social democrats have an enduring commitment to equality and social justice, the kind and extent of equality they support, and the specific meanings they have given to social justice, have constantly been revised. For example, to the extent that social democracy has been recast in terms of the politics of community, it can be said to have assumed an essentially conservative character. Instead of being a vehicle for social transformation, it has developed into a defence of duty and responsibility, and so serves to uphold established institutions and ways of life.

SOCIAL JUSTICE

Social justice refers to a morally defensible distribution of benefits or rewards in society, evaluated in terms of wages, profits, housing, medical care, welfare benefits and so on. Social justice is therefore about 'who *should* get what'. In the view of some commentators, however, the very notion of social justice is mistaken. They argue that the distribution of material benefits has nothing to do with moral principles such as justice, but can only be evaluated in the light of economic criteria, such as efficiency and growth.

Significance

A distinctive concept of social justice, as opposed to the more ancient ideal of justice, first emerged in the early nineteenth century. This reflected both the fact that the onset of industrialization made it possible, perhaps for the first time, to envisage the eradication of poverty, and that the issue of social justice has always been linked to debates about the impact, for good or ill, of capitalism on material distribution. The issue, however, has been concerned less with whether social questions can be evaluated in moral terms – since most people are unwilling to reduce material distribution to mere economics – and more with how social justice should be conceived. Competing conceptions of social justice have thus developed, and these have been based, respectively, on the ideas of needs, rights and deserts.

The idea that material benefits should be distributed on the basis of needs has been proposed most commonly by socialist thinkers, for whom needs, unlike wants or preferences, reflect the fundamental requirements of the human condition. Any needs-based theory of social justice clearly has egalitarian implications, as the needs of one person (for food, water, clothing, health care, personal security and so on) are broadly the same as those of any other person. That said, for modern social democrats, social justice is associated with the goal of relative equality, particularly linked to equality of opportunity, rather than absolute equality, a stance associated not with the abolition of the capitalist system, but with its reform. The idea of rights, which has been favoured by many liberal and libertarian thinkers, serves, by contrast, to justify higher levels of social inequality and lower levels of social intervention. It does this by endorsing meritocracy, thereby implying that those who are talented and hard-working should be rewarded at the expense of the lazy and feckless. Finally, the idea of deserts, which has attracted support among traditional conservatives in particular, has also been used to uphold social equality, but it has done this by suggesting that justice reflects the 'natural order of things', rather than principles dreamed up by philosophers or social theorists.

SOCIAL MOVEMENT

A social movement is a particular form of collective behaviour in which the motive to act springs largely from the attitudes and aspirations of members, typically acting within a loose organizational framework. Being part of a social movement requires a level of commitment and political activism, rather than formal or card-carrying membership; above all, movements move. A movement is different from spontaneous mass action (such as an uprising or rebellion) in that it implies a measure of intended or planned action in pursuit of a recognized social goal. Not uncommonly, social movements embrace **pressure groups** and may even spawn **political parties**; trade unions and socialist parties, for example, can be seen as part of a broader labour movement. So-called *new social movements* – the women's movement, the ecological or green movement, the peace movement, and so on – differ from more traditional social movements in three respects. First, they typically attract support from the young, the better-educated and the relatively affluent, rather than the oppressed or disadvantaged. Second, they usually have a post-material orientation, being more concerned with 'quality of life' issues than with material advancement. Third, while traditional movements had little in common and seldom worked in tandem, new social movements subscribe to a common, if not always clearly defined, set of New Left values and beliefs.

Significance

Social movements can be traced back to the early nineteenth century. The earliest were the labour movement, which campaigned for improved conditions for the growing working class; various nationalist movements, usually struggling for independence from multinational European empires; and, in central Europe in particular, a Catholic movement that fought for emancipation through the granting of legal and political rights to Catholics. In the twentieth century it was also common for fascist and right-wing authoritarian groups to be seen as movements rather than as conventional political parties. However, the experience of **totalitarianism** in the inter-war period encouraged mass society theorists such as Erich Fromm (1900–80) and Hannah Arendt (1906–75) to see movements in distinctly negative terms. From the mass society perspective, social movements reflect a 'flight from freedom', an attempt by alienated individuals to achieve security and identity through fanatical commitment to a cause, and obedience to a (usually fascist) leader.

In contrast, new social movements are generally interpreted as rational and instrumental actors, whose use of informal and unconventional means merely reflects the resources available to them. The emergence of new social movements is widely seen as evidence of the fact that **power** in postindustrial societies is increasingly dispersed and fragmented. The class politics of old has thus been replaced by a 'new politics', which turns away from 'established' parties, pressure groups and representative processes towards a more innovative and theatrical form of protest politics. Not only do new movements offer new and rival centres of power, but they also diffuse power more effectively by resisting bureaucratization and developing more spontaneous, effective and decentralized forms of organization. Nevertheless, while the impact of movements such as the women's movement and the gay and lesbian movement cannot be doubted, it is difficult to assess in practical terms because of the broad nature of their goals and the less tangible character of the cultural strategies they tend to adopt.

SOCIALISM

Socialism is an ideology defined by its opposition to capitalism and its attempts to provide a more humane and socially worthwhile alternative. The core of socialism is a vision of human beings as social creatures united by their common humanity; as the poet John Donne put it, 'No man is an island entire of itself; every man is a piece of the continent, a part of the main.' This highlights the degree to which individual identity is fashioned by social interaction and the membership of social groups and collective bodies. Socialists therefore prefer co-operation to competition, and favour collectivism over individualism. The central, and some would say defining, value of socialism is equality, socialism sometimes being portrayed as a form of egalitarianism. Socialists believe that a measure of social equality is the essential guarantee of social stability and cohesion, and that it promotes freedom in the sense that it satisfies material needs and provides the basis for personal development. The socialist movement has traditionally articulated the interests of the industrial working class, seen as being systematically oppressed or structurally disadvantaged within the capitalist system. The goal of socialism is thus to reduce or abolish class divisions.

Socialism, however, contains a bewildering variety of divisions and rival traditions. *Ethical socialism*, or utopian socialism, advances an essentially moral critique of capitalism. In short, socialism is portrayed as being morally superior to capitalism because human beings are ethical creatures, bound to one another by the ties of love, sympathy and compassion. *Scientific socialism* undertakes a scientific analysis of historical and social development which, in the form of Marxism, does not suggest that socialism should replace capitalism, but predicts that, inevitably, it *would* replace capitalism.

A second distinction is regarding the 'means' of achieving socialism, namely the difference between revolution and reform. *Revolutionary socialism*, reflected most clearly in the communist tradition, holds that socialism can only be introduced by the revolutionary overthrow of the existing political and social system, usually based on the belief that existing state structures are irredeemably linked to capitalism and the interests of the ruling class. *Reformist socialism* (sometimes termed evolutionary, parliamentary or democratic socialism), on the other hand, believes in 'socialism through the ballot box', and thus accepts basic liberal democratic principles such as consent, constitutionalism and party competition. Finally, there are profound divisions over the 'end' of socialism; that is, the nature of the socialist project. *Fundamentalist socialism* aims to abolish and replace the capitalist system, viewing socialism as qualitatively different from capitalism. Fundamentalist socialists, such as Marxists and communists, generally equate socialism with common ownership in some form. *Revisionist socialism* aims not to abolish capitalism but to reform it, looking to reach an accommodation between the efficiency of the market and the enduring moral vision of socialism. This is expressed most clearly in social democracy.

Significance

Socialism arose as a reaction to the social and economic conditions generated in Europe by the growth of industrial capitalism. The birth of socialist ideas was closely linked to the development of a new but growing class of industrial workers, who suffered the poverty and degradation that are so often a feature of early industrialization. For over 200 years socialism has constituted the principal oppositional force within capitalist societies, and has articulated the interests of oppressed and disadvantaged peoples in many parts of the world. The principal impact of socialism has been in the form of the twentieth-century communist and social-democratic movements. However, since the late twentieth century socialism has suffered a number of major reverses, leading some to proclaim the 'death of socialism'. The most spectacular of these was the collapse of communism in the Eastern European Revolutions of 1989–91. Partly in response to this, and partly as a result of globalization and changing social structures, parliamentary socialist parties in many parts of the world have re-examined, and sometimes rejected, traditional socialist principles.

The moral strength of socialism derives not from its concern with what people are like, but with what they have the capacity to become. This has led socialists to develop utopian visions of a better society in which human beings can achieve genuine emancipation and fulfilment as members of a community. In that sense, despite its late-twentieth-century setbacks, socialism is destined to survive if only because it serves as a reminder that human development can extend beyond market individualism. Critics of socialism nevertheless advance one of two lines of argument. The first is that socialism is irrevocably tainted by its association with statism. The emphasis on collectivism leads to an endorsement of the state as the embodiment of the public interest. Both communism and social democracy are in that sense 'top-down' versions of socialism, meaning that socialism amounts to an extension of state control and a restriction of freedom. The second line of argument highlights the incoherence and confusion inherent in modern socialist theory. In this view socialism was only ever meaningful as a critique of, or alternative to, capitalism. The acceptance by socialists of market principles therefore demonstrates either that socialism itself is flawed or that their analysis is no longer rooted in genuinely socialist ideas and theories.

SOVEREIGNTY

Sovereignty, in its simplest sense, is the principle of absolute and unlimited power. However, a distinction is commonly made between legal and political sovereignty. *Legal sovereignty* refers to supreme legal authority; that is, an unchallengeable right to demand compliance, as defined by law. *Political sovereignty*, in contrast, refers to unlimited political power; that is, the ability to command obedience, which is typically ensured by a monopoly of coercive force. The term sovereignty is used in two distinct though related senses, usually understood as external and internal sovereignty. *External sovereignty* relates to a state's place in the international order and its capacity to act as an independent and autonomous entity. This is what is meant by terms such as 'national sovereignty' and 'sovereign state'. *Internal sovereignty* is the notion of a supreme power/authority within the state, located in the body that makes decisions that are binding on all citizens, groups and institutions within the state's territorial boundaries. This is how the term is used in cases such as 'parliamentary sovereignty' and 'popular sovereignty'.

Significance

The concept of sovereignty emerged in the sixteenth and seventeenth centuries, as a result of the development in Europe of the modern state. As the authority of transnational institutions, such as the Catholic Church and the Holy Roman Empire faded, centralizing monarchs in England, France, Spain and elsewhere were able to claim to exercise supreme power, and they did this in a new language of sovereignty. In the writings of Jean Bodin (1530–96) and Thomas Hobbes (1588–1679), sovereignty was used as a justification for monarchical absolutism. For Bodin, law amounted to little more than the command of the sovereign, and subjects were required simply to obey. However, whereas Bodin accepted that the sovereign monarch was constrained by the will of God or natural law, Hobbes defined sovereignty as a monopoly of coercive power and advocated that it be vested in the hands of a single, unchallengeable rule. The basic justification for internal sovereignty as developed by Bodin and Hobbes is that the existence of a single focus of allegiance and a supreme source of law within a state is the only sure guarantee of order and stability. Hobbes in particular offered citizens a stark choice between absolutism and anarchy.

Other versions of internal sovereignty, such as Jean-Jacques Rousseau's (1712–78) notion of popular sovereignty, expressed in the idea of the 'general will', and John Austin's (1790–1859) doctrine of parliamentary sovereignty, viewed as the 'monarch in Parliament', linked sovereignty to democracy and constitutionalism, respectively. What all such thinkers, however, had in common is that they believed that sovereignty could be, and should be, located in a determinate body. In an age of pluralistic and democratic government this 'traditional' doctrine of sovereignty has attracted growing criticism. Its opponents argue either that it is intrinsically linked to its absolutist past, and if so is frankly undesirable, or that it is no longer applicable to modern systems of government, which operate according to networks of checks and balances. It has been suggested, for example, that liberal democratic principles are the very antithesis of sovereignty in that they argue for a distribution of power among a number of institutions, none of which can meaningfully claim to be sovereign. This is particularly evident in the case of federalism, which is based on the paradoxical notion of shared sovereignty.

While questions about internal sovereignty have appeared increasingly outdated in a democratic age, the issue of external sovereignty has become absolutely vital. Indeed, some of the deepest divisions in modern politics, from the Arab–Israeli conflict to tensions in former Yugoslavia, involve disputed claims to such sovereignty. Historically, the notion of external sovereignty has been closely linked to the struggle for popular government, the two ideas fusing to create the modern notion of 'national sovereignty'. External sovereignty has thus come to embody the principles of national independence and self-government. Only if a nation is sovereign are its people capable of fashioning their own destiny according to their particular needs and interests. To ask a nation to surrender its sovereignty is tantamount to asking its people to give up their freedom. This is why external or national sovereignty is so keenly felt and, when it is threatened, so fiercely defended. The potent appeal of political nationalism is the best evidence of this. However, external sovereignty has been criticized on both moral and theoretical grounds. Moral concerns about external sovereignty arise from its capacity to block interference in the affairs of other states, even when they are violating the natural rights of their citizens. Theoretical problems stem from the fact that the notion of an independent or sovereign state may no longer be meaningful in an increasingly interdependent world. Globalization, for example, may mean that political sovereignty is impossible, while legal sovereignty has been reduced to merely a diplomatic nicety.

STATE

The state can, most simply, be defined as a political association that establishes sovereign jurisdiction within defined territorial borders and exercises authority via a set of permanent institutions. It is possible to identify five key features of the state. First, the state exercises sovereignty – it exercises absolute and unrestricted power in that it stands above all other associations and groups in society; Thomas Hobbes (1588–1679), for this reason, portrayed the state as a 'leviathan', a gigantic monster. Second, state institutions are recognizably 'public', in contrast to the 'private' institutions of civil society – state bodies are responsible for making and enforcing collective decisions in society and are funded at the public's expense. Third, the state is an exercise in legitimation – its decisions are usually (though not necessarily) accepted as being binding on its citizens, because, it is claimed, it reflects the permanent interests of society. Fourth, the state is an instrument in domination – it possesses the coercive power to ensure that its laws are obeyed and that transgressors are punished; as Max Weber (1864–1920) put it, the state has a monopoly of the means of 'legitimate violence'. Fifth, the state is a territorial association – it exercises jurisdiction within geographically defined borders. In international politics, however, the state is usually defined from an external perspective, and so embraces civil society. In this view, the state is characterized by four features: a defined territory; a permanent population; an effective government; and sovereignty.

States nevertheless come in different shapes and sizes. *Minimal states* or 'nightwatchman' states, advocated by classical liberals and the New Right, are merely protective bodies whose sole function is to provide a framework of peace and social order within which citizens can conduct their lives as they think best. *Developmental states*, found, for example, in the 'tiger' economies of East and Southeast Asia, operate through a close relationship between the state and major economic interests, notably big business, and aim to develop strategies for national prosperity in a context of transnational competition. *Social-democratic states*, the ideal of both modern liberals and democratic socialists, intervene widely in economic and social life to promote growth and maintain full employment, reduce poverty and bring about a more equitable distribution of social rewards. *Collectivized states*, found in orthodox communist countries, abolished private enterprise completely and set up centrally planned economies administered by a network of economic ministries and planning committees. *Totalitarian states*, often associated with the state form found as constructed in Hitler's Germany and Stalin's USSR, penetrate every aspect of human existence through a combination of comprehensive surveillance and terroristic policing, and a pervasive system of ideological manipulation and control.

Significance

The state has always been central to political analysis, to such an extent that politics is often understood as the study of the state. This is evident in two key debates. The first and most fundamental of these focuses on the need for the state and the basis of political obligation. The classic justification for the state is provided by social contract theory, which constructs a picture of what life would be like in a stateless society, a so-called 'state of nature'. In the view of thinkers such as Hobbes and John Locke (1632–1704), as the state of nature would be characterized by an unending civil war of each against all, people would be prepared to enter into an agreement – a social contract – through which they would sacrifice a portion of their liberty to create a sovereign body without which orderly and stable existence would be impossible. In the final analysis, then, individuals should obey the state because it is the only safe-guard they have against disorder and chaos. The rival view, advanced by anarchism, is based on markedly more optimistic assumptions about human nature, and places a heavier emphasis on natural order and spontaneous co-operation among individuals. Anarchists have also looked to a range of social institutions, such as common owner-ship or the market mechanism, to underpin social stability in the absence of a state.

The second area of debate concerns the nature of state power. Much of political theory deals specifically with rival theories of the state. The major positions in this debate can be summarized as follows. Liberals view the state as a neutral arbiter among competing interests and groups in society, a vital guarantee of social order; the state is at worst a 'necessary evil'. Marxists have portrayed the state as an instru-ment of class oppression, a 'bourgeois' state, or, allowing for its 'relative autonomy' from the ruling class, have emphasized that its role is to maintain stability within a system of unequal class power. Democratic socialists often regard the state as an embodiment of the common good, highlighting its capacity to rectify the injus-tices of the class system. Conservatives have generally linked the state to the need for authority and discipline to protect society from incipient disorder, hence their traditional preference for a strong state. The New Right has highlighted the non-legitimate character of the state by drawing attention to the extent to which it articulates its own interests separately from those of the larger society and often to the detriment of the economic performance. Feminists have viewed the state as an instrument of male power, the 'patriarchal' state serving to exclude women from, or subordinate them within, the 'public' or political sphere of life. Finally, anarchists argue that the state is nothing less than legalized oppression operating in the inter-ests of the powerful, propertied and privileged.

Since the late 1980s, however, debate about the state has been overshadowed by assertions about its 'retreat' or 'decline'. The once-mighty leviathan – widely seen to have been co-extensive with politics itself – had seemingly been humbled, state authority having been undermined by the growing importance of, among other things, the global economy, the market, transnational corporations, non-state actors of various kinds, and international organizations. The clamour for 'state-centric' approaches to domestic and international politics to be rethought, or abandoned completely, therefore grew. Nevertheless, a simple choice between 'state-centrism' and 'retreat-ism' is, at best, misleading. For example, while states and markets are commonly portrayed as being rival forces, they also interlock and complement each other. Apart from anything else, markets cannot function without a system of property rights that only the state can establish and preserve. Moreover, though states may have lost authority in recent decades in certain respects, in relation to matters such as war-making and homeland security (in the aftermath of 9/11) and financial and banking regulation (in the aftermath of the 2007–09 global financial crisis), they may have become stronger.

SUBSIDIARITY

Subsidiarity (from the Latin *subsidiarii*, meaning a contingent of supplementary troops) is, broadly, the devolution of decision-making from the centre to lower levels. However, it is understood in two crucially different ways. In federal states such as Germany, subsidiarity is understood as a political principle that implies decentralization and popular participation, benefiting local and provincial institutions often at the expense of national ones. This is expressed in the idea that decisions should be 'taken as closely as possible to the citizen'. However, subsidiarity is also interpreted as a constitutional principle that defends national sovereignty against the encroachment of supranational bodies. This is expressed in the commitment that the competence of supranational bodies should be restricted to those actions that cannot be sufficiently achieved sufficiently well by nation-states.

Significance

The principle of subsidiarity is important because it addresses the question of the most appropriate level within a political system at which decisions should be made. In advocating that political decisions should always be made at the lowest possible level of government, it clearly endorses decentralization. However, it is better thought of as providing a test of appropriateness: if a governmental function can be carried out as efficiently or effectively by smaller or lower bodies, then it should be devolved, otherwise larger or higher bodies should take responsibility. The notion of subsidiarity is established most firmly established in federal systems such as those in Germany and Switzerland, where it has been used in its political sense in allocating powers appropriately between federal government and provincial bodies, and sometimes between provincial bodies and local government. The term has gained a wider currency, however, since its use in the Treaty of the European Union (Maastricht Treaty) of 1993. Opponents of Euro-federalism have used subsidiarity in a narrow constitutional sense as an embodiment of the rights of member states, and as a defence against the growth of a European 'super-state'.

SUPERPOWER

A superpower, in simply terms, is a power that is greater than a traditional great power. According to Fox (1944), superpowers possess great power 'plus great mobility of power'. As the term tended to be used to refer specifically to the USA and the USSR during the Cold War period, it is of more historical than conceptual significance. To describe the USA and the USSR as superpowers implied that they possessed:

- A global reach
- A predominant economic and strategic role within their respective ideological bloc or sphere of influence
- Preponderant military capacity, especially in terms of nuclear weaponry.

Significance

The term 'superpower' was born in the final phase of World War II, and reflected the reconfiguration of global power that the war had brought about. The USA and the USSR emerged as the preponderant actors on the world stage through the decisive role each had played in defeating the Axis powers, their status later being enhanced by the onset of the Cold War and the emergence of tensions between an increasingly US-dominated West and a Soviet-dominated East. By comparison with the USA and the USSR, the great powers of the pre-war period – France, the UK, Germany, Japan and so on – had thus been relegated to second-order status. However, the notion that the Cold War amounted to a 'superpower era' may conceal as much as it reveals. For example, to consider the USA and the USSR as super-powers is to suggest a broad equivalence of power between them that may never have existed. In particular, the USSR was never a superpower in economic terms (despite perceptions to the contrary that lingered long in the West). The gulf in productive capacity between the USA and the USSR widened consistently from the 1960s onwards, to such an extent that Soviet attempts to match increased US military spending under President Reagan in the 1980s threatened to bring about economic collapse and contributed to the USSR's eventual demise. In addition, the concept of a superpower has shifted over time, first through the tendency to refer to Japan and Germany from the 1980s onwards, and to China from the 2000s onwards, as 'economic' superpowers, and second through the emergence of the USA in the post-Cold War period as the world's sole superpower, often seen as a 'hyperpower' or a 'global hegemon'.

SUPRANATIONALISM

Supranationalism is the existence of an authority that is 'higher' than that of the nation-state and capable of imposing its will on it. Supranationalism thus differs from intergovernmentalism in that the latter allows for international co-operation only on the basis of the sovereign independence of individual states. While, strictly speaking, empires are supranational bodies, being structures of political domination that comprise a diverse collection of cultures, ethnic groups and nationalities, supranationalism usually refers to international bodies that have been established by voluntary agreement among states, and which serve limited and specific functions. The best examples of supranational bodies are therefore international federations, such as the European Union (EU), in which sovereignty is shared between central and peripheral bodies. However, the EU is a difficult body to categorize, as it encompasses a mixture of intergovernmental and supranational elements and is thus more accurately described as a federalizing than a federal body.

Significance

The advance of supranationalism has been one of the most prominent features of post-1945 world politics. It reflects the growing interdependence of states, particularly in relation to economic and security decision-making, but also in matters such as environmental protection, and the recognition that globalization has perhaps made the notion of state sovereignty irrelevant. From this point of view, the shift from intergovernmentalism to supranationalism is likely to be a continuing trend, as intergovernmental action requires unanimous agreement and does not allow for action to be taken against recalcitrant states. For example, the United Nations (UN), strictly speaking an intergovernmental body, acted in a supranational capacity during the Gulf War of 1991 by sanctioning military action against one of its member states, Iraq. This drift towards supranationalism is supported by those who warn that respect for state sovereignty is simply misguided, or that it is dangerous in that it allows states to treat their citizens however in whatever way they wish, and produces an anarchical international order that is prone to conflict and war. Supranationalism is therefore one of the faces of internationalism. Opponents of supranationalism continue, on the other hand, to stand by the principle of the nation-state, and argue that supranational bodies have not, and can never can, rival the nation-state's capacity to generate political allegiance and ensure democratic accountability.

SUSTAINABLE DEVELOPMENT

Sustainable development is development that respects the requirements of ecological sustainability, and so has the capacity to continue in existence for an extended period of time. The Brundtland Report's (1987) highly influential definition of the term is:

> Sustainable development is development that meets the needs of the present without compromising the ability of future generations to meet their own needs. It contains two key concepts:

> - The concept of *need*, in particular the essential needs of the world's poor, to which overriding priority should be given
> - The concept of *limitations*, imposed by the state of technology and social organization on the environment's ability to meet present and future needs.

Significance

Since the 1980s, sustainable development is the watchword of reformist ecologism. It reflects the recognition that there are 'limits to growth', in that environmental degradation (in the form of, for example, pollution or the use of non-renewable resources) ultimately threatens prosperity and economic performance. From this perspective, 'growthism', placing priority on economic growth over all other considerations, is ultimately self-defeating. 'Getting rich slower' therefore makes economic as well as ecological sense. However, despite near universal rhetorical support for the principle of sustainable development, the extent to which development goals and strategies have in practice been modified in the light of ecological concerns has been limited. This is because electoral and other pressures on societies, rich and poor, to deliver economic growth have often proved to be irresistible. Nevertheless, it would be a mistake to assume that all ecologists endorse the idea of sustainable development. Radical ecologists, and in particular deep ecologists, have challenged the notion of a compromise between economic and ecological goals, and see these, instead, as being incompatible. In this anti-growth view, sustainable development is a contradiction in terms.

SYSTEMS THEORY

Systems theory sets out to explain the entire political process, as well as the function of major political actors, through the application of systems analysis. A 'system' is an organized or complex whole, a set of interrelated and interdependent parts that form a collective entity. To analyse politics from this perspective is to construct the model of a political system. A political system consists of linkages between what are viewed as 'inputs' and 'outputs' (see Figure 13). Inputs into the political system consist of demands and supports from the general public. Demands can range from pressure for higher living standards, improved employment prospects and more

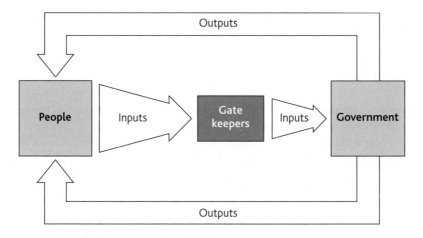

Figure 13 The political system

generous welfare payments, to greater protection for minority and individual rights. Supports, on the other hand, are ways in which the public contributes to the political system by paying taxes, offering compliance and being willing to participate in public life. Outputs consist of the decisions and actions of government, including the making of policy, the passing of laws, the imposition of taxes, and the allocation of public funds. These outputs generate 'feedback', which in turn shapes further demands and supports. The key insight offered by the systems model is that the political system tends towards long-term equilibrium or political stability, as its survival depends on outputs being brought into line with inputs.

Significance

Systems analysis was first employed in political science in the 1950s, the pioneering work having been done by Easton (1953/1981). Linked to behaviouralism, the systems approach was part of the attempt to introduce more scientific rigour into the study of politics, in this case through the application of models of ecological systems from biology. Systems theory has provided a rich source of insights into, for example, the role of 'gatekeepers' such as political parties and pressure groups, which regulate the flow of inputs into the political system, and into the general policy process and the nature of its outputs. Its strengths include the breadth of its scope, which extends well beyond state institutions, and even the class system, to include all politically significant actors, and its tendency to foster holistic thinking. However, the systems model is at best a device for drawing out understanding; it does not in itself constitute reliable knowledge. For example, institutions such as parties and pressure groups are more interesting and complex than their designation as 'gatekeepers' suggests; for example, they play an important role in managing public perceptions and thus help to shape the nature of public demands. Moreover, the systems model is more effective in explaining how and why political systems respond to popular pressures than in explaining why they employ repression and coercion, as, to some degree, all do. Finally, the systems model is implicitly conservative, in that it highlights the responsiveness and inherent stability of liberal democracy, thereby arguably concealing its structural weaknesses and inherent contradictions.

TERRORISM

Terrorism is a form of political violence that aims to achieve its objectives by creating a climate of fear and apprehension. As such, it uses violence in a very particular way: not primarily to bring about death and destruction, but rather to create unease and anxiety about possible future attacks. Terrorist violence is therefore clandestine and involves an element of surprise, if not arbitrariness, designed to create uncertainty and widening apprehension. Terrorism therefore often takes the form of seemingly indiscriminate attacks on civilian targets, though attacks on symbols of power and prestige, and the kidnapping or murder of prominent businessmen, senior government officials and political leaders, are usually also viewed as acts of terrorism. Different forms of terrorism have nevertheless been identified:

- *Insurrectionary terrorism* – aimed at the revolutionary overthrow of a state (examples include anarchist and revolutionary communist terrorism)
- *Loner or issue terrorism* – aimed at the promotion of a single cause (examples include the 1995 sarin nerve gas attack on the Tokyo subway by the religious cult Aum Shinryko)
- *Nationalist terrorism* – this aims to overthrow colonial rule or occupation, often with the goal of gaining independence for an ethnic, religious or national group (examples include the FLN in Algeria, and the Tamil Tigers of Tamil Eelam in Sri Lanka)
- *Transnational or global terrorism* – this aims to inflict damage and humiliation on a global power or at transforming global civilizational relations (examples include al-Qaeda and other forms of Islamist terrorism).

However, the term 'terrorism' is ideologically contested and emotionally charged; some even refuse to use it on the grounds that it is either hopelessly vague or carries unhelpful pejorative implications. Its negative associations mean that the word is almost always applied to the acts of one's opponents, and almost never to similar acts carried out by one's own group or a group one supports. Terrorism thus tends to be used as a political tool, a means of determining the legitimacy, or illegitimacy, of a group or political movement under consideration. This also raises questions as to whether terrorism is evil in itself and beyond moral justification. Whereas mainstream approaches to terrorism usually view it as an attack on civilized or humanitarian values, even as an example of nihilism (literally a belief in nothing), radical scholars sometimes argue that terrorism and other forms of political violence may advance the cause of political justice and counter other, more widespread, forms of violence or abuse, suggesting that they are justifiable (Honderich, 1989).

Significance

The attacks on New York and Washington on 11 September 2001 (9/11) are widely believed to have brought about a profound shift in the significance of terrorism, even having established terrorism as the pre-eminent security threat in the twenty-first century. This has occurred for at least three reasons. First, thanks largely to globalization, terrorism has acquired a genuinely transnational if not global character. Together with other non-state groups, terrorist organizations have proved to be particularly adept at exploiting the potential of the modern, hyper-mobile world with its 'porous' borders, creating the impression that they can strike anywhere, at any time. Second, the potential scope and scale of terrorism has greatly increased as a result of modern technology, and in particular the prospect of weapons of mass destruction (WMD) falling into the hands of terrorists. Specifically, concern has been expressed about the possibility of nuclear terrorism. Third, some argue that modern terrorists, increasingly inspired by a radical politico-religious ideology, such as Islamism, are more willing to countenance widespread death and destruction than the largely secular terrorist of old. Terrorism has thus become a religious imperative, even a sacred duty, rather than a pragmatically selected political strategy.

However, the threat of terrorism, even of global terrorism, may have been greatly overstated. For example, there are doubts about its military effectiveness. While particular terrorist attacks may have a devastating impact, by its nature terrorism consists of a series of sporadic attacks on a variety of targets, which is very different from the concerted, sustained and systematic destruction that is wreaked by mass warfare conducted between states. Moreover, where terrorist campaigns have been successful, they have usually been linked to attempts to advance or defend the interests of a national or ethnic group, in which case its goals have enjoyed a significant measure of popular support. Where this is not the case, terrorism may well be counter-productive, provoking popular hostility and outrage (rather than fear and apprehension) among the civilian population, as well as military retaliation from the government. Finally, fears about terrorism may be exaggerated because they are based on the idea of a conflict of civilization between Islam and the West that do not stand up to examination.

THIRD WAY

The 'third way' is a slogan that encapsulates the idea of an alternative to both capitalism and socialism. It draws attention to an ideological position that has attracted political thinkers from various traditions. The term originated within Italian fascism and was first used publicly by Mussolini (who claimed to have coined it). The fascist 'Third Way' took the form of corporatism, a politico-economic system in which major economic interests are bound together under the auspices of the state. The organic unity of fascist corporatism was supposedly superior to the rampant individualism of profit-orientated capitalism and the stultifying state control of communism. In the post-1945 period a very different 'third way' was developed in relation to Keynesian social democracy, found in its most developed form in Sweden. The Swedish economic model attempted to combine elements of both socialism and capitalism. Productive wealth was concentrated largely in private hands, but social justice was maintained through a comprehensive welfare system funded by a steeply progressive tax regime. More recently, the idea of the 'third way' has resurfaced in association with 'new' social democratic or post-socialist thought. Widely associated with the government of Tony Blair and 'new' Labour in the UK, but also influenced by the Bill Clinton administration in the USA, this 'third way' is defined as an alternative to 'top-down' state intervention (and therefore traditional social democracy) and free-market capitalism (and therefore Thatcherism or Reaganism). The ideological character of this post-social democratic 'third way' is, however, unclear. In most forms it involves a general acceptance of the market and of globalized capitalism, qualified by a communitarian emphasis on social duty and the reciprocal nature of rights and responsibilities.

Significance

The recurrence of the idea of a 'third way' highlights deep, but perhaps incoherent, dissatisfaction with the two dominant twentieth-century models of economic organization: market capitalism and state socialism. Proponents of 'third way' politics in effect attempt to develop a non-socialist critique of an unregulated market economy. While the philosophical and ideological basis of this critique changes, the major reservations about capitalism remain remarkably similar: a concern about the random and often immoral implications of market competition. The flaw of capitalism, from this point of view, is that it is a constant threat to social cohesion and stability. At the same time, however, 'third way' thinkers reject socialism because of its association with state control and because they believe that collectivization and planning fail to provide a viable alternative to the capitalist market. Two key criticisms are advanced of 'Third Way' politics. The first is that the idea of the 'third way' is merely a populist slogan devoid of political or economic content. The second is that 'third way' theories are inherently contradictory because, while criticizing competition and market individualism, they are not capable of looking beyond a capitalist model of economic organization.

TOLERATION

Toleration means forbearance, a willingness to accept views or actions with which one disagrees or of which one disapproves. Toleration should therefore be distinguished from both permissiveness and indifference. Permissiveness is a social attitude that allows people to act as they wish or as they choose; it reflects either moral indifference (the belief that the actions in question cannot be judged in moral terms) or moral relativism (the belief that moral judgements can be made only from the perspective of the individuals concerned). Toleration, on the other hand, is based on two separate moral judgements. The first is disapproval of a form of behaviour or set of beliefs; the second is a deliberate refusal to impose one's own views on others. Toleration thus does not simply mean 'putting up with' what cannot be changed – for example, a battered wife who stays with her abusive husband out of fear can hardly be said to 'tolerate' his behaviour. Moreover, toleration does not imply non-interference. While toleration does not allow for interference with, or constraint on, others, it allows influence to be exerted through moral example and rational persuasion. A distinction is sometimes made between 'negative' toleration, a passive acceptance of diversity or willingness to 'live and let live', and 'positive' toleration, a celebration of diversity and pluralism viewed as enriching for all.

Significance

Toleration is a core principle of liberalism and one of the central values of liberal democracy. Liberals have usually viewed toleration as a guarantee of individual freedom and a means of social enrichment. John Locke (1632–1704) defended toleration, particularly religious toleration, on the grounds that the state has no right to meddle in 'the care of men's souls'. However, his central argument was based on a belief in human rationality. 'Truth' will only emerge out of free competition among ideas and beliefs and therefore must be left to 'shift for herself'. J. S. Mill (1806–73) treated toleration as one of the faces of individual liberty, suggesting that it represents the goal of personal autonomy, and that, in promoting debate and argument, it stimulates the intellectual development and moral health of society at large. Such views are consistent with support for pluralism in its moral, cultural and political forms.

Nevertheless, even liberals recognize the limits of toleration, particularly in the need to protect toleration from the intolerant. This may, for example, provide a justification for banning anti-democratic and anti-constitutional political parties, on the grounds that, if they came to power, they would establish dictatorial rule and abolish toleration. Other concerns about toleration include that it places a heavy, perhaps over-heavy, faith on rationalism and the ability of people to resist 'bad' ideas; that it may allow groups with offensive views, such as racists and fascists, to operate legally and gain respectability; and that it weakens society in the sense that it makes it impossible to develop shared values and a common culture.

TORYISM

'Tory' was used in eighteenth-century Britain to refer to a parliamentary faction that (as opposed to the Whigs) supported monarchical power and the Church of England, and represented the landed gentry; in the USA it implied loyalty to the British crown. In the mid-nineteenth century the British Conservative Party emerged out of the Tories, and in the UK 'Tory' is still widely (but unhelpfully) used as a synonym for Conservative, but Toryism is best understood as a distinctive ideological stance within broader conservatism. Its characteristic features are a belief in hierarchy, tradition, duty and an organic society. While 'high' Toryism articulates a neo-feudal belief in a ruling class and a pre-democratic faith in established institutions, the Tory tradition is also hospitable to welfarist and reformist ideas, provided these serve the cause of social and institutional continuity. One Nation conservatism can thus be seen as a form of 'welfare Toryism' or 'Tory democracy'. Tory democracy is an idea developed in the late nineteenth century by Randolph Churchill, who proclaimed that the way to generate wider popular support for traditional institutions was through advancing the cause of social reform.

Significance

Toryism amounts to the vestiges of the feudal political tradition, the remnants of the ideological stance of the landed aristocracy. Tory ideas survived because they were absorbed into conservative ideology, their attraction being both that they served the interests of new capitalist elites and, because they are not expressed in terms of abstract principles, they proved to be ideologically flexible and adaptable. However, the match between Toryism and conservatism has always been imperfect, as the latter has accommodated, to a greater or lesser extent, capitalist values such as individualism, self-striving and competition. The rise of the New Right in the 1970s pushed Toryism, and its associated One Nation ideals, to the margins of conservative politics. The attraction of Toryism is that it advances a vision of a stable, if hierarchical, social order, in which the strong take some responsibility for the weak and vulnerable. The disadvantages of Toryism are that it legitimizes the class system and articulates values that are entirely out of step with a modern, meritocratic society.

TOTALITARIANISM

Totalitarianism is an all-encompassing system of political rule that is typically established by pervasive ideological manipulation and open terror and brutality. Totalitarianism differs from both autocracy and authoritarianism, in that it seeks 'total power' through the politicization of every aspect of social and personal existence. Totalitarianism thus implies the outright abolition of civil society: the abolition of 'the private'. Friedrich and Brzezinski (1966) defined totalitarianism in terms of a six-point 'syndrome of interrelated traits and characteristics':

- The existence of an 'official' ideology
- A one-party state, usually led by an all-powerful leader
- A system of terroristic policing
- A monopoly of the means of mass communication
- A monopoly of the means of armed combat
- State control of all aspects of economic life.

Significance

The phenomenon of totalitarianism is usually believed to have arisen in the twentieth century, pervasive ideological manipulation and systematic terror requiring the resources of a modern industrialized state. The idea of totalitarianism originated in fascist Italy as a belief in the state as an all-consuming 'ethical community' that reflects the altruism and mutual sympathy of its members. This was developed into the doctrine: 'everything for the state, nothing outside the state, nothing against the state'. The term was subsequently adopted to describe the perhaps uniquely oppressive character of twentieth-century dictatorships, in particular Adolf Hitler's Germany and Joseph Stalin's USSR. Totalitarian analysis achieved its greatest prominence in the 1950s and 1960s, when it was widely used to highlight totalitarian parallels between fascism and communism, and to divide the world into rival democratic (liberal democratic) and totalitarian states.

However, the totalitarian classification has a number of drawbacks. First, it became part of Cold War ideology and was used as a sometimes crude form of anti-communist propaganda. Second, it tended to obscure important differences between fascism and communism, particularly in relation to their ideological orientation and the degree to which they tolerated capitalism. Third, the idea of 'total' state power is misleading, because some form of resistance or opposition always persists, even in the most technologically advanced and brutal of states. Nevertheless, even though the apparent precision of the six-point syndrome is misleading, the concept of totalitarianism is useful in highlighting distinctions

224 Key Concepts in Politics and International Relations

between modern and traditional dictatorships, and in drawing attention to the importance of charismatic leadership. The latter consideration has given rise to the idea of 'totalitarian democracy', the phenomenon whereby a leader justifies his or her unchecked power through a claim to possess a monopoly of ideological wisdom and to articulate the 'true' interests of his/her people. A very different theory of totalitarianism was advanced by Herbert Marcuse (1964), who identified totalitarian tendencies in advanced industrial societies, viewing them as 'one-dimensional societies' in which rising affluence helps to subdue argument and debate and absorb all forms of opposition.

TRADITION

Tradition refers to ideas, practices or institutions that have endured through time and have therefore been inherited from an earlier period. However, it is difficult to determine precisely how long something has to survive before it can be regarded as a tradition. Tradition is usually thought to denote continuity between generations; traditions are things that have been transmitted from one generation to the next. However, the line between the traditional and the merely fashionable is often indistinct. Tradition should nevertheless be distinguished from both progress and reaction. Whereas progress implies a movement forward, building on the past, and reaction suggests 'turning the clock back', reclaiming the past, tradition stands for continuity or conservation: the absence of change.

Significance

Tradition is one of the key principles, some would say the defining principle, of conservatism. The original conservative justification for tradition rested on the idea of natural order and the belief that tradition reflected God-given institutions and practices has now effectively been abandoned except by religious fundamentalists. The remaining conservative case for tradition is twofold. First, tradition reflects the accumulated wisdom of the past, institutions and practices that have been 'tested by time' and should be preserved for the benefit of the living and for generations to come. This is embodied in Edmund Burke's (1729–97) assertion that society is a partnership between 'those who are living, those who are dead and those who are to be born'. Second, tradition engenders a sense of belonging and identity in the individual that is rooted in history, as well as fostering social cohesion by establishing in society a moral and cultural bedrock. Tradition thus gives people, individually and collectively, a sense of who they are.

However, developments in modern society have generally eroded respect for tradition, with lingering forms of traditionalism, such as the neo-conservative defence of traditional values, often being seen as part of the difficult adjustment to a post-traditional society. The most important of these developments has been the accelerating pace of change in technologically advanced societies, and the spread of rationalism, suggesting that reason and critical understanding are a better test of 'value' than mere survival. The two most common criticisms of tradition are that it amounts to the 'despotism of custom' (J. S. Mill), in that it enslaves the present generation to the past and denies the possibility of progress, and that tradition serves the interests not of the many but of the few, the elite groups that dominated past societies.

TRANSNATIONAL CORPORATION

A transnational corporation (TNC) is a company that controls economic activity in two or more countries. The 'parent' company is usually incorporated in one state (the 'home'), with 'subsidiaries' in others (the 'hosts'), though subsidiaries may be separately incorporated affiliates. Such companies are now generally referred to as transnational corporations rather than multinational corporations –TNCs as opposed to MNCs – to reflect the extent to which their corporate strategies and processes transcend national borders rather than merely crossing them. As such, TNCs are the principal economic face of transnationalism. Integration across economic sectors and the growing importance of intra-firm trade has allowed TNCs to operate, in effect, as economies in their own right.

Significance

Some early transnational corporations developed in association with the spread of European colonialism, the classic example being the Dutch East India Company, established in 1602. However, the period since 1945 has witnessed a dramatic growth in the number, size and global reach of TNCs. The number of powerful companies with subsidiaries in several countries has risen from 7,000 in 1970 to 38,000 in 2009. TNCs currently account for about 50 per cent of world manufacturing production and over 70 per cent of world trade, often dwarfing states in terms of their economic size. Based on a comparison between corporate sales and countries' GDP, 51 of the world's 100 largest economies are corporations; only 49 of them are countries. However, economic size does not necessarily translate into political power or influence; states, after all, can do things that TNCs can only dream about, such as make laws and raise armies. What gives TNCs their strategic advantage over national governments is their ability to transcends territory through the growth of 'trans-border', even 'trans-global', communications and interactions, reflected, in particular, in the flexibility they enjoy over the location of production and investment. TNCs can, in effect, 'shop around', looking for circumstances that are conducive to profitability. This creates a relationship of structural dependency between governments and TNCs whereby governments rely on TNCs to provide jobs and capital inflows, but can only attract them by providing circumstances favourable to their interests.

Defenders of TNCs argue that they bring massive economic benefits and that they have been 'demonized' by the anti-globalization movement, which has greatly exaggerated their political influence From this perspective, TNCs have been successful because they have worked. Their two huge economic benefits are their efficiency and their high level of consumer responsiveness. Greater efficiency has resulted from their historically unprecedented ability to reap the benefits from economies of scale, and from the development of new productive methods and the application of new technologies. The consumer responsiveness of TNCs is demonstrated by their huge investment in research and development (R&D) and product innovation. Critics nevertheless portray a much more sinister image of TNCs, arguing that they distort markets through their disproportionate economic power, exert undue political influence by the impact their policies have on employment and investment levels, and uphold a 'brand culture' that pollutes the public sphere through the proliferation of commercial images, and manipulates personal preferences. The influence of TNCs on the developing world has attracted particular criticism, with allegations ranging from the exploitation of workers through low wages and bans on union organization to the disruption of production patterns that had previously been geared to meeting local needs.

TRANSNATIONALISM

Transnationalism refers to sustained relationships, patterns of exchange, affiliations and social formations that cross national borders. As such, transnationalism implies that the domestic/international divide in politics has been fatally undermined, casting doubt on the continuing importance of both sovereignty and the state. Transnationalism differs from internationalism, in that the latter implies co-operation or solidarity between established nations (and so is compatible with nationalism), rather than the removal or abandonment of national identities completely.

Significance

Transnationalism comes in a variety of shapes and forms, and is more relevant to some areas of human existence than to others. Most debate about transnationalism centres on its relationship to globalization, which is commonly viewed either as the chief cause of transnationalism or as its primary manifestation. Indeed, in absorbing national economies, to a greater or lesser extent, into an interlocking global economy, globalization can be thought of as a comprehensive system of economic transnationalism. Among the implications of this is the changing balance between the power of territorial states and 'deterritorialized' transnational corporations, which can switch investment and production to other parts of the world if state policy is not conducive to profit maximization and the pursuit of corporate interests. Economic sovereignty, then, may no longer be meaningful in what Ohmae (1990) called a 'borderless world'. However, the rhetoric of a 'borderless' global economy can be taken too far. For example, there is evidence that, while globalization may have changed the strategies that states adopt to ensure economic success, it has by no means rendered the state redundant as an economic actor. Indeed, rather than globalization having been foisted on unwilling states by forces beyond their control, economic globalization has largely been created by states and for states.

An alternative form of transnationalism has emerged from the upsurge in recent decades, partly fuelled by globalization, of international migration. This has led to speculation about the growth of 'transnational communities' or diasporas. A transnational community is a community whose cultural identity, political allegiances and psychological orientations cut across national borders; they are often thought of as 'deterritorialized nations' or 'global tribes'. For a transnational community to be established, an immigrant group must forge and, crucially, sustain relations that link its society of origin and its society of settlement, something that has been made substantially easier through the advent of cheap transport and improved communications, not least the internet and the mobile phone. Nevertheless. it is by no means clear that transnational loyalties are as stable and enduring as those built around the nation. This is because social ties that are not territorially rooted and geographically defined may not prove to be viable in the long term. Moreover, the social and cultural cohesion of transnational communities should not be over-stated, as, albeit to differing degrees, they encompass divisions based on factors such as gender, social class, ethnicity, religion, age and generation.

UTILITARIANISM

Utilitarianism is a moral philosophy that suggests that the 'rightness' of an action, policy or institution can be established by its tendency to promote happiness. This is based on the assumption that individuals are motivated by self-interest and that these interests can be defined as the desire for pleasure, or happiness, and the wish to avoid pain or unhappiness. Individuals thus calculate the quantities of pleasure and pain each possible action would generate and choose whichever course promises the greatest pleasure over pain. Utilitarian thinkers believe that it is possible to quantify pleasure and pain in terms of 'utility', taking into account their intensity, duration and so on. Human beings are therefore utility maximizers, who seek the greatest possible pleasure and the least possible pain. The principle of utility can be applied to society at large using Jeremy Bentham's (1748–1832) classic formula: 'the greatest happiness of the greatest number'.

Utilitarianism, however, has developed into a cluster of theories. Classical utilitarianism is *act-utilitarianism*, in that it judges an act to be right if its consequences produce at least as much pleasure-over-pain as those of any alternative act. *Rule-utilitarianism*, in contrast, judges an act to be right if it conforms to a rule which, if generally followed, would produce good consequences. What is called *utilitarian generalization* assesses an act's rightfulness, not in terms of its own consequences but on the basis of its consequences if the act were to be performed generally. *Motive-utilitarianism* places emphasis on the intentions of the actor rather than on the consequences of each action.

Significance

Utilitarian theory emerged in the late eighteenth century as a supposedly scientific alternative to natural rights theories. In the UK, during the nineteenth century, utilitarianism provided the basis for a wide range of social, political and legal reforms, advanced by the so-called philosophic radicals. It provided one of the major foundations for classical liberalism and remains perhaps the most important branch of moral philosophy, certainly in terms of its impact on political issues.

The attraction of utilitarianism is its capacity to establish supposedly objective grounds on which moral judgements can be made. Rather than imposing values on society, it allows each individual to make his or her own moral judgement as each alone is able to define what is pleasurable and what is painful. Utilitarian theory thus upholds diversity and freedom, and demands that we respect others as pleasure-seeking creatures. Its drawbacks are philosophical and moral. Philosophically, utilitarianism is based on a highly individualistic view of human nature that is both asocial and ahistorical. It is by no means certain, for example, that consistently self-interested behaviour is a universal feature of human society. Morally, utilitarianism may be nothing more than crass hedonism, a view expressed by J. S. Mill (1806–73) in his declaration that he would rather be 'Socrates dissatisfied than a fool satisfied' (though Mill himself subscribed to a modified form of utilitarianism). Utilitarianism has also been criticized for endorsing acts that are widely considered to be wrong, such as the violation of basic human rights, if they serve to maximize the general utility of society.

UTOPIANISM

A utopia (from the Greek *utopia*, meaning 'no place', or the Greek *eutopia*, meaning 'good place') is literally an ideal or perfect society. The term was coined by Thomas More (1478–1535), and was first used in his *Utopia* (1516/1965). Utopianism is a style of social theorizing that develops a critique of the existing order by constructing a model of an ideal or perfect alternative. As such, it usually exhibits three features. First, it embodies a radical and comprehensive rejection of the status quo; present social and political arrangements are deemed to be fundamentally defective and in need of root-and-branch change. Second, utopian thought highlights the potential for human self-development, based either on highly optimistic assumptions about human nature or optimistic assumptions regarding the capacity of economic, social and political institutions to ameliorate baser human drives and instincts. Third, utopianism usually transcends the 'public/private' divide in that it suggests the possibility of complete or near-complete personal fulfilment. For an alternative society to be ideal, it must offer the prospect of emancipation in the personal realm as well as in the political or public realms.

However, utopianism is not a political philosophy or an ideology. Substantive utopias differ from one another, and utopian thinkers have not advanced a common conception of the good life. Nevertheless, most utopias are characterized by the abolition of want, the absence of conflict and the avoidance of violence and oppression. Socialism in general, and anarchism and Marxism in particular, have a marked disposition towards utopianism, reflecting their belief in the human potential for sociable, co-operative and gregarious behaviour. Socialist utopias, as a result, are strongly egalitarian and typically characterized by collective property ownership and a reduction in, or eradication of, political authority. Feminism and ecologism have also spawned utopian theories. Liberalism's capacity to generate utopian thought is restricted by its stress on human self-interestedness and competition;

however, an extreme belief in free-market capitalism can be viewed as a form of market utopianism. Other utopias have been based on faith in the benign influence of government and political authority. More's society, for example, was hierarchical, authoritarian and patriarchal, albeit within a context of economic equality.

Significance

The utopian approach to political understanding was most popular in the nineteenth century, generally stimulated by the immense political and social upheavals generated by industrialization. Since the early twentieth century, however, utopianism has become distinctly unfashionable. Criticisms of utopian thought fall into two categories. The first (in line with the pejorative, everyday use of the term 'utopian') suggests that utopianism is deluded or fanciful thinking, a belief in an unrealistic and unachievable goal. Karl Marx (1818–83), for example, denounced 'utopian socialism' on the grounds that it advances a moral vision that is in no way grounded in historical and social realities. By contrast, 'scientific socialism' sought to explain how and why a socialist society would come into being (Marxism's utopian character is nevertheless evident in the nature of its ultimate goal: the construction of a classless, communist society). The second category of criticisms holds that utopianism is implicitly totalitarian, in that it promotes a single set of indisputable values and so is intolerant of free debate and diversity.

However, a revival of utopianism has occurred since the 1960s, associated with the rise of New Left and the writings of thinkers such as Herbert Marcuse (1898–1979), Ernst Bloch (1885–1977) and Paul Goodman (1911–72). The strength of utopianism is that it enables political theory to think beyond the present and to challenge the 'boundaries of the possible'. The establishment of 'concrete' utopias is a way of uncovering the potential for growth and development within existing circumstances. Without a vision of what could be, political theory may simply be overwhelmed by what is, and thereby lose its critical edge.

WAR

War is a condition of armed conflict between two or more political groups. It has been distinguished from other forms of violence by at least four factors. First, wars have traditionally been fought by states, with inter-state war, often over territory or resources – 'wars of plunder' – being thought of as the archetypal form of war. However, inter-state war has become significantly less common in recent years, most modern wars (sometimes called 'new' wars), being civil wars, featuring the involvement of non-state actors such as guerrilla groups, resistance movements and terrorist organizations. Second, conventional warfare is a highly organized affair. It is carried out by armed forces or trained fighters who are subject to uniforms, drills, saluting and ranks, and who operate according a strategy of some sort, as opposed to carrying out random and sporadic attacks. Modern warfare has nevertheless become a less organized affair, often involving irregular fighters who may be difficult to distinguish from the civilian population, and employing improvised tactics.

Third, war is usually distinguished by its scale or magnitude. A series of small-scale attacks involve only a handful of deaths is seldom referred to as a war. The United Nations thus defines a 'major conflict' as one in which at least 1,000 deaths occur annually. However, this figure is arbitrary, and would, for example, exclude the Falklands War of 1982, which is widely regarded as a war. Finally, as they involve a series of battles or attacks, wars usually take place over a significant period of time. That said, some wars are very short, such as the Six-Day War of 1967 between Israel and the neighbouring states of Egypt, Syria and Jordan. Other wars are nevertheless so protracted, sometimes involving lengthy periods of peace, that there may be confusion about exactly when a war starts and ends. For example, though World War I and World War II are usually portrayed as separate conflicts, some historians prefer to view them as part of a single conflict interrupted by a 20-year truce. Confusion about the beginning and end of a war has, indeed, become more common in recent years, as the declining use of formal 'declarations of war' has meant that it is often difficult to determine when an armed conflict has become a war.

Significance

War has traditionally been the principal way in which states establish their place within the hierarchy of states. Warfare both enables a state to protect its territory and people from external aggression, and to pursue its interests abroad through conquest and expansion. Recent decades have nevertheless witnessed a marked decline in warfare in many parts of the world, a trend that certainly applies to large-scale, high-intensity military conflict. This has encouraged liberals in particular to declare that war is becoming obsolete as a means of determining international and global outcomes. At least four factors have been associated with this development. These are: the spread of democratic governance, in line with the democratic peace thesis; the expansion of free trade and the emergence of an alternative, non-military route to national prosperity; the growth of a system of international law and changed moral attitudes to the use of force; and the development of nuclear weapons, which have dramatically intensified fears about the escalation of war.

However, the decline of traditional inter-state war does not mean that the world has become a safer place. Rather, new, and in some ways more challenging security threats have emerged, not least related to terrorism. War and warfare have not ended, but, as demonstrated by the counter-insurgency wars in Afghanistan and Iraq, their form has clearly changed. Moreover, the decline of inter-state war may prove to be a temporary phenomenon. This is a warning associated most clearly with realist theorists, who emphasize that the underlying biases within the international system continue to favour conflict over co-operation. These biases may have been kept in check in recent years by factors such as the advance of globalization and the USA's massive military predominance, but there is no guarantee that these will persist. The revived prospect of inter-state war, and even of great-power war, is most often linked to rising multipolarity and the increased instability and fluidity it may bring in its wake

WELFARE

Welfare, in its simplest form, means happiness, prosperity or well-being in general; it implies not merely physical survival but also some measure of health and contentment. As a political principle, however, welfare stands for a particular means through which social well-being is maintained: collectively provided welfare, delivered by government, through what is termed a welfare state. The term 'welfare state' is used either to refer to a state that assumes broad responsibilities for the social well-being of its citizens, or, more narrowly, to the health, education, housing and social security systems through which these responsibilities are carried out. Welfare states nevertheless come in many different shapes and forms. Esping-Andersen (1990) distinguished between three types of welfare state: liberal or 'limited' welfare states (as in the USA and Australia) aim to provide little more than a 'safety net' for those in need; conservative or 'corporate' welfare states (as in Germany) provide a comprehensive range of services that depend heavily on the 'paying-in' principle and link benefits closely to jobs; and social democratic or 'Beveridge' welfare states (as traditionally existed in Sweden and the UK, modelled on the 1942 Beveridge Report) incorporate a system of universal benefits and are based on national insurance and full employment.

Significance

Interest in welfare emerged during the nineteenth century as industrialization created a spectre of urban poverty and social division that, in different ways, disturbed conservative, liberal and socialist politicians alike. Early support for social reform and welfare reflected elite fears about the danger of social revolution and the desire to promote national efficiency in both economic and military terms, as well as the more radical wish to abolish poverty and counter the injustices of the capitalist system. This, in turn, gave rise to quite different forms of welfare support in different states. While a welfare consensus developed in the early post-1945 period as paternalistic conservatives, modern liberals and social democrats unified in support for at least the principle of welfare, the 1980s and 1990s witnessed a general retreat from welfare, even among socialists, brought about in part by the pressures of economic globalization. Nevertheless, welfare remains one of the central fault lines in ideological debate, dividing pro-welfarist social democrats and modern liberals from anti-welfarist libertarians and supporters of the New Right. Among the arguments in favour of welfare are:

- It promotes social cohesion and national unity, in that it gives all citizens a 'stake' in society and guarantees at least basic social support.
- It enlarges freedom in the sense that it safeguards people from poverty and provides conditions in which they can develop and realize their potential.
- It ensures prosperity by countering the effects of social deprivation and helping those who cannot help themselves.
- It serves as a redistributive mechanism that promotes greater equality and strengthens a sense of social responsibility.

Arguments against welfare include:

- It creates a culture of dependency and so restricts freedom in the sense of individual responsibility and self-reliance.
- It amounts to legalized theft, and so is unjust, in that it transfers resources from the prosperous to the lazy without the formers' consent.
- It is economically damaging because welfare spending pushes up taxes and fuels inflation.
- It is inefficient because it is provided through monopolistic public bureaucracies that are not driven by a profit motive.

LIST OF FIGURES

GLOSSARY OF KEY POLITICAL THINKERS

Theodor Adorno (1903–69)   A German philosopher, sociologist and musicologist, Adorno was a leading member of the Frankfurt School of critical theory. His best-known works include *The Authoritarian Personality* (1950), and *Minima Moralia* (1951).

Thomas Aquinas (1224–74)   An Italian Dominican monk, theologian and philosopher, Aquinas argued that reason and faith are compatible and explored the relationship between human law and God's natural law. His best-known work is *Summa Theologiae*, begun in 1265.

Hannah Arendt (1906–75)   A German political theorist and philosopher, Arendt wrote widely on issues such as the nature of modern mass society and the importance of political action in human life. Her best-known works include *The Origins of Totalitarianism* (1951) and *The Human Condition* (1958).

Aristotle (384–322 BCE)   A Greek philosopher, Aristotle's work ranged over physics, metaphysics, astronomy, meteorology, biology, ethics and politics; it became the foundation of Islamic philosophy and was later incorporated into Christian theology. His best known political work is *Politics*.

Augustine of Hippo (354–430)   A theologian and political philosopher, Augustine developed a defence of Christianity that drew on neo-Platonic philosophy, Christian doctrine and biblical history. His major work is *City of God* (413–25).

Mikhail Bakunin (1814–76)   A Russian propagandist and revolutionary, Bakunin supported a collectivist form of anarchism that was based on a belief in human sociability, expressed in the desire for freedom within a community of equals.

Jeremy Bentham (1748–1832)   A British philosopher and legal reformer, Bentham was the founder of utilitarianism and a major influence on the reform of social administration, government and economics in nineteenth-century Britain. His major works include *Fragments on Government* (1776) and *Principles of Morals and Legislation* (1789).

Jean Bodin (1530–96)   A French political philosopher, Bodin was the first important theorist of sovereignty, which he defined as 'the absolute and perpetual power of a commonwealth'. His most important work is *The Six Books of the Commonwealth* (1576).

Edmund Burke (1729–97)   A Dublin-born British statesman and political theorist, Burke was the father of the Anglo-American conservative tradition that accepts the principle of 'change in order to conserve'. His most important work is *Reflections on the Revolution in France* (1790).

Robert Cox (1926–)   A Canadian international economist and leading exponent of critical theory, Cox has examined issues ranging from the role of social forces in the making of history to the implications of globalization and the nature of US global hegemony. His seminal work is *Production, Power and World Order* (1987).

Friedrich Engels (1820–95)   A German socialist theorist and life-long friend and collaborator of Marx, Engels elaborated Marx's ideas and theories for the benefit of the growing socialist movement in the late nineteenth century. His major works include *The Origins of the Family, Private Property and the State* (1884) and *Dialectics of Nature* (1925).

Michel Foucault (1926–84)   A French philosopher, Foucault was a major influence on poststructuralism and was concerned with forms of knowledge and the construction of the human subject. His most important works include *Madness and Civilisation* (1961), *The Archaeology of Knowledge* (1969) and *History of Sexuality* (1976–84).

Erich Fromm (1900–80)   A German-born psychoanalyst and social philosopher, Fromm developed a critique of modern society that blended the ideas of Freud, Marx and, in later life, Buddhism. His best-known works include *Fear of Freedom* (1941), *The Sane Society* (1955) and *To Have or To Be?* (1976).

Francis Fukuyama (1952–)   A US social analyst and political commentator, Fukuyama has advanced a strong defence of US-style market capitalism and liberal-democratic political structures. His works include *The End of History and the Last Man* (1992) and *Trust* (1996).

Antonio Gramsci (1891–1937)   An Italian Marxist and social theorist, Gramsci rejected 'scientific' determinism by stressing, through the theory of hegemony, the importance of the political and intellectual struggle. His major work is *Prison Notebooks* (1929–35).

Jürgen Habermas (1929–)   A German philosopher and social theorist, Habermas is the leading exponent of the 'second generation' of the Frankfurt School of critical theory. His main works include *Towards a Rational Society* (1970), *Legitimation Crisis* (1973) and *The Theory of Communicative Competence* (1984).

Georg Wilhelm Friedrich Hegel (1770–1831)   A German philosopher, Hegel was the founder of modern idealism and advanced an organic theory of the state that portrayed it as the highest expression of human freedom. His main works include *Phenomenology of Spirit* (1807) and *Philosophy of Right* (1821).

Thomas Hobbes (1588–1679)   An English political philosopher, Hobbes developed the first comprehensive theory of nature and human behaviour since Aristotle and advanced a rationalist defence of absolutism. His major work is *Leviathan* (1651).

Samuel P. Huntington (1927–2008) A US political commentator and academic, Huntington made influential contributions to military politics, US and comparative politics, and the politics of less developed societies, but was best known for *The Clash of Civilization and the Making of World Order* (1996). His other works include *The Third Wave* (1991) and *Who Are We?* (2004).

Immanuel Kant (1724–1804) A German philosopher, Kant advanced an ethical individualism that stressed the importance of morality in politics and has had considerable impact on liberal thought. His most important works include *Critique of Pure Reason* (1781), *Critique of Practical Reason* (1788) and *Critique of Judgement* (1790).

Robert Keohane (1941–) A US international relations theorist and exponent of neoliberal institutionalism, Keohane, with Joseph Nye, advanced a critique of realism based on the theory of 'complex interdependence', developed in *Power and Interdependence* (1977). In his later writing, Keohane attempted to synthsize structural realism and complex interdependence.

John Maynard Keynes (1883–1946) A British economist, Keynes developed a critique of neoclassical economics that underlined the need for 'demand management' by government. His major work is *The General Theory of Employment, Interest and Money* (1936).

Pyotr Kropotkin (1842–1921) A Russian geographer and anarchist theorist, Kropotkin drew attention to the human propensity for freedom and equality, based on the idea of mutual aid. His major works include *Mutual Aid* (1897), *Fields, Factories and Workshops* (1901) and *The Conquest of Bread* (1906).

Vladimir Ilyich Lenin (1870–1924) A Russian Marxist theorist and revolutionary, Lenin built on the theories of Marx by emphasising the issues of organisation and revolution. His most important works include *What is to be Done?* (1902), *Imperialism, the Highest Stage of Capitalism* (1916) and *State and Revolution* (1917).

John Locke (1632–1704) An English philosopher and politician, Locke was a key thinker of early liberalism and a powerful advocate of consent and constitutionalism. His most important political works are *A Letter Concerning Toleration* (1689) and *Two Treatises of Government* (1690).

Niccolò Machiavelli (1469–1527) An Italian politician and author, Machiavelli portrayed politics in strictly realistic terms and highlighted the use by political leaders of cunning, cruelty and manipulation. His major work is *The Prince* (1513).

James Madison (1751–1836) A US statesman and political theorist, Madison was a leading proponent of pluralism and divided government, urging the adoption of federalism, bicameralism and the separation of powers as the basis of US government. His best-known political writings are his contributions to *The Federalist* (1787–8).

Joseph de Maistre (1753–1821) A French aristocrat and political thinker, de Maistre was a fierce critic of the French Revolution and an implacable supporter of monarchical absolutism. His chief political work is *Du pape* (1817).

Herbert Marcuse (1898–1979)   A German political philosopher and social theorist, Marcuse developed a radical critique of advanced industrial society but emphasised both its repressive character and the potential for liberation. His most important works include *Reason and Revolution* (1941), *Eros and Civilisation* (1958) and *One Dimensional Man* (1964).

Karl Marx (1818–83)   A German philosopher, economist and political thinker, Marx advanced a teleological theory of history that held that social development would eventually culminate with the establishment of communism. His classic work is *Capital* (1867, 1885 and 1894); his best-known work is *Communist Manifesto* (1848).

Giuseppe Mazzini (1805–72)   An Italian nationalist and apostle of liberal republicanism, Mazzini was an early advocate of the universal right to national self-determination, viewed as the key to freedom and international harmony.

Robert Michels (1876–1936)   A German politician and social theorist, Michels drew attention to elite tendencies within all organisations, summed up in the 'iron law of oligarchy'. His major work is *Political Parties* (1911).

James Mill (1773–1836)   A Scottish philosopher, historian and economist, Mill helped to turn utilitarianism into a radical reform movement. His best-known work is *Essay on Government* (1820).

John Stuart Mill (1806–73)   A British philosopher, economist and politician, Mill was an important liberal thinker who opposed collectivist tendencies and tradition and upheld the importance of individual freedom, based on a commitment to individuality. His major writings include *On Liberty* (1859), *Considerations on Representative Government* (1861) and *The Subjection of Women* (1869).

Kate Millett (1934–   )   A US writer and sculptor, Millett developed radical feminism into a systematic theory that clearly stood apart from established liberal and socialist traditions. Her major work is *Sexual Politics* (1970).

Charles-Louis de Secondat Montesquieu (1689–1775)   A French political philosopher, Montesquieu emphasised the need to resist tyranny by fragmenting government power, particularly through the device of the separation of powers. His major work is *The Spirit of the Laws* (1748).

Hans Morgenthau (1892–1982)   A German-born US international relations theorist, Morgenthau developed a 'science of power politics' based on the belief of what he called 'political man's insatiable desire to dominate others'. His major writings include *Politics Amongst Nations* (1948), *In Defence of the National Interest* (1951) and *The Purpose of American Politics* (1960).

Gaetano Mosca (1857–1941)   An Italian elite theorist, Mosca argued that a cohesive minority will always be able to manipulate and control the masses, even in a parliamentary democracy. His major work is *The Ruling Class* (1896).

Friedrich Nietzsche (1844–1900)   A German philosopher, Nietzsche's complex and ambitious work stressed the importance of will, especially the 'will to power', and anticipated modern existentialism in emphasising that people create their own world and make their own values. His best-known writings include *Thus Spoke Zarathustra* (1883–84), *Beyond Good and Evil* (1886) and *On the Genealogy of Morals* (1887).

Robert Nozick (1938–2002)   A US academic and political philosopher, Nozick developed a form of libertarianism that was close to Locke's and has had considerable impact on the New Right. His major works include *Anarchy, State and Utopia* (1974) and *Philosophical Explanations* (1981).

Michael Oakeshott (1901–90)   A British political philosopher, Oakeshott was a leading proponent of conservative traditionalism and an advocate of a non-ideological style of politics. His best-known works include *Rationalism in Politics and Other Essays* (1962) and *On Human Conduct* (1975).

Robert Owen (1771–1858)   A British industrialist and pioneer trade unionist, Owen developed a utopian form of socialism that emphasised the capacity of the social environment to influence character. His best-known work is *A New View of Society* (1812).

Vilfredo Pareto (1848–1923)   An Italian economist and social theorist, Pareto developed a form of elitism that is based largely on the different psychological propensities of leaders and followers. His major work is *The Mind and Society* (1917–18).

Plato (427–347 BCE)   A Greek philosopher, Plato taught that the material world consists of imperfect copies of abstract and eternal 'ideas', and described the 'ideal state' in terms of a theory of justice. His major writings include *The Republic* and *The Laws*.

Karl Popper (1902–94)   An Austrian-born British philosopher, Popper's political writings upheld liberalism and the free society and condemned authoritarian and totalitarian tendencies. His main political work is *The Open Society and its Enemies* (1945).

Pierre-Joseph Proudhon (1809–65) A French anarchist, Proudhon attacked both traditional property rights and communism, arguing instead for mutualism, a cooperative productive system geared towards need rather than profit. His best-known work is *What is Property?* (1840).

John Rawls (1921–2002)   A US academic and political philosopher, Rawls used a form of social contract theory to reconcile liberal individualism with the principles of redistribution and social justice. His major works include *A Theory of Justice* (1971) and *Political Liberalism* (1993).

Jean-Jacques Rousseau (1712–78)   A Geneva-born French moral and political philosopher, Rousseau developed a philosophy that reflects a deep belief in the goodness of 'natural man' and the corruption of 'social man'. His best-known political work is *The Social Contract* (1762).

Adam Smith (1723–90)   A Scottish economist and philosopher, Smith developed the first systematic analysis of the workings of the economy in market terms, crucially influencing emergent classical liberalism. His most famous work is The *Wealth of Nations* (1776).

Richard Henry Tawney (1880–1962)   A British social philosopher and historian, Tawney advocated a form of socialism that was firmly rooted in a Christian social moralism unconnected with Marxist class analysis. His major works include *The Acquisitive Society* (1921), *Equality* (1931) and *The Radical Tradition* (1964).

Kenneth Waltz (1924–2013)   A US international relations theorist, Waltz was the key figure in the development of neorealism. In *Theory of International Politics* (1979), he used systems theory to explain how international anarchy shapes the actions of states, placing a particular focus on the distribution of capabilities between and among states.

Max Weber (1864–1920)   A German political economist and sociologist, Weber was one of the founders of modern sociology and championed a scientific and value-free approach to scholarship. His most influential works include *The Protestant Ethic and the Spirit of Capitalism* (1902), *The Sociology of Religion* (1920) and *Economy and Society* (1922).

Alexander Wendt (1958–   )   A German-born international relations theorist who has worked mainly in the USA, Wendt is a meta-theorist who has used constructivism to develop a critique of both neorealism and neoliberal institutionalism. His major works include 'Anarchy is What States Make of It' (*International Organization*, 1992) and *Social Theory of International Politics* (1999).

BIBLIOGRAPHY

Adorno, T. *et al.* (1950) *The Authoritarian Personality* (New York: Hooper).

Almond, G. A. and Verba, S. (1963) *The Civic Culture: Political Attitudes and Democracy in Five Nations* (Princeton, NJ: Princeton University Press).

Almond, G. A. and Verba, S. (1980) *The Civic Culture Revisited* (Boston, MA: Little, Brown).

Anderson, B. (1991) *Imagined Communities: Reflections on the Origins and Spread of Nationalism* (London: Verso).

Arblaster, A. (1994) *Democracy* (Milton Keynes: Open University Press).

Axford, B. (1995) *The Global System: Economics, Politics and Culture* (Cambridge: Polity Press).

Baggott, R. (1995) *Pressure Groups Today* (Manchester/New York: Manchester University Press).

Ball, A. and Millward, F. (1986) *Pressure Politics in Industrial Societies* (London: Macmillan).

Ball, T. (1997) 'Political Theory and Conceptual Change', in A. Vincent (ed.), *Political Theory: Tradition and Diversity* (Cambridge: Cambridge University Press).

Ball, T. (1988) *Transforming Political Discourse: Political Theory and Critical Conceptual History* (Oxford: Basil Blackwell).

Ball, T., Farr, J. and Hanson, R. L. (eds) (1989) *Political Innovation and Conceptual Change* (Cambridge: Cambridge University Press).

Barbalet, J. M. (1988) *Citizenship* (Milton Keynes: Open University Press).

Barber, B. (2003) *Jihad vs McWorld* (London: Corgi).

Barker, J. (1987) *Arguing for Equality* (London and New York: Verso).

Barry, B. and Hardin, R. (eds) (1982) *Rational Man and Irrational Society?* (Beverly Hills, CA: Sage).

Barry, N. (1987) *The New Right* (London: Croom Helm).

Barry, N. (1990) *Welfare* (Milton Keynes: Open University Press).

Batley, R. and Stoker, G. (eds) (1991) *Local Government in Europe: Trends and Developments* (London: Macmillan).

Baxter, B. (2000) *Ecologism: An Introduction* (Edinburgh: Edinburgh University Press).

Beetham, D. (1991) *The Legitimation of Power* (London: Macmillan).

Beetham, D. (ed.) (1994) *Defining and Measuring Democracy* (London: Sage).

Bell, D. (1960) *The End of Ideology* (Glencoe, IL: Free Press).

Bellamy, R. (ed.) (1993) *Theories and Concepts of Politics: An Introduction* (Manchester/New York: Manchester University Press).

Bentham, J. (1948) *A Fragment on Government and an Introduction to the Principles of Morals and Legislation* (Oxford: Blackwell).

Berlin, I. (1958) *Four Essays on Liberty* (Oxford: Oxford University Press).

Berman, P. (2003) *Terror and Liberalism* (New York: W. W. Norton).

Bernstein, E. (1898/1962) *Evolutionary Socialism* (New York: Schocken).

Berry, C. (1986) *Human Nature* (London: Macmillan).

Birch, A. H. (1964) *Representative and Responsible Government: An Essay on the British Constitution* (London: George Allen & Unwin).

Birch, A. H. (1972) *Representation* (London: Macmillan).

Birch, A. H. (2007) *The Concepts and Theories of Modern Democracy* (London/New York: Routledge).

Blau, P. and Meyer, M. (eds) (1987) *Bureaucracy in Modern Society* (New York: Random House).

Bobbio, N. (1996) *Left and Right* (Cambridge: Polity Press).

Bogdanor, V. (1979) *Devolution* (Oxford: Oxford University Press).

Bogdanor, V. (ed.) (1988) *Constitutions in Democratic Politics* (Aldershot: Gower).

Booth, K. and Wheeler, N. (2008) *The Security Dilemma: Fear, Cooperation and Trust in World Politics* (Basingstoke: Palgrave Macmillan).

Bottomore, T. (1985) *Theories of Modern Capitalism* (London: George Allen & Unwin).

Bottomore, T. (1993) *Elites and Society* (London: Routledge).

Boulding, K. (1989) *Three Faces of Power* (Newbury Park, CA: Sage).

Brandt Report (1980) *North-South: A Programme for Survival* (London: Pan Books).

Brundtland Report (1987) *Our Common Future* (London: Routledge).

Bryson, V. (1995) *Feminist Political Theory: An Introduction* (London: Macmillan).

Buchanan, J. and Tulloch, G. (1962) *The Calculus of Consent* (Ann Arbor, MI: Michigan University Press).

Bull, H. (1977) *The Anarchical Society* (London: Macmillan).

Bull, H. (2012) *The Anarchical Society: A Study of World Order* (Basingstoke: Palgrave Macmillan).

Burchill, S. and Linklater, A. (1996) *Theories of International Relations* (London: Macmillan).

Calvert, P. (1990) *Revolution and Counter-Revolution* (Buckingham: Open University Press).

Camilleri, J. and Falk, P. (1992) *The End of Sovereignty? The Politics of a Shrinking and Fragmented World* (Aldershot: Edward Elgar).

Chalmers, A. F. (1986) *What Is This Thing Called Science?* (Milton Keynes: Open University Press).

Cicero (2008) *The Republic and The Laws* (Oxford: Oxford University Press).

Clarke, P. (1979) *Liberals and Social Democrats* (Cambridge: Cambridge University Press).

Cohen, G. A. (1978) *Karl Marx's Theory of History: A Defence* (Oxford: Clarendon Press).

Cox, R. (1981) 'Social Forces, States and World Order: Beyond International Relations Theory', *Millennium*, 10 (June): 126–55.

Cox, R. (1987) *Production, Power and World Order: Social Forces in the Making of History* (New York: Columbia University Press).

Dahl, R. (2006) *A Preface to Democratic Theory* (Chicago, IL: University of Chicago Press).

Dallmayr, F. and McCarthy, T. (eds) (1997) *Understanding and Social Inquiry* (Notre Dame, IN: University of Notre Dame Press).

Devlin, P. (1968) *The Enforcement of Morals* (Oxford: Oxford University Press).

Doyle, M. (1986) 'Liberalism and World Politics', *American Political Science Review*, 80.

Dunleavy, P. (1991) *Democracy, Bureaucracy and Public Choice: Economic Explanations in Political Science* (Hemel Hempstead: Harvester Wheatsheaf).

Dunleavy, P. and O'Leary, B. (1987) *Theories of the State: The Politics of Liberal Democracy* (London: Macmillan).

Easton, D. (1979) *A Framework for Political Analysis* (Chicago, IL: University of Chicago Press).

Easton, D. (1953/1981) *The Political System* (Chicago, IL: University of Chicago Press).

Eatwell, R. and O'Sullivan, N. (eds) (1989) *The Nature of the Right: European and American Politics and Political Thought since 1789* (London: Pinter).

Elgie, R. (1995) *Political Leadership in Liberal Democracies* (London: Macmillan).

Esping-Andersen, G. (1990) *The Three Worlds of Welfare Capitalism* (Cambridge: Polity Press).

Etzioni, A. (1995) *The Spirit of Community: Rights, Responsibilities and the Communitarian Agenda* (London: Fontana).

Finifter, A. (ed.) (1993*) Political Science: The State of the Discipline* (Washington, DC: American Political Science Association).

Flatham, R. (1980) *The Practice of Political Authority* (Chicago, IL: Chicago University Press).

Fox, W. (1944) *The Super-Powers: The United States, Britain and the Soviet Union – Their Responsibility for Peace* (New York: Harcourt, Brace).

Freeden, M. (1991) *Rights* (Minneapolis, MN: University of Minnesota Press).

Freeden, M. (1996) *Ideologies and Political Theory: A Conceptual Approach* (Oxford: Clarendon Press).

Friedrich, C. J. and Brzezinski, Z. (eds) (1966) *Totalitarian Dictatorship and Autocracy* (Cambridge, MA: Harvard University Press).

Fromm, E. (1984) *The Fear of Freedom* (London: Ark).

Fukuyama, F. (1989) 'The End of History?', *National Interest*, Summer.

Fukuyama. F. (1992) *The End of History and the Last Man* (Harmondsworth: Penguin).

Gallie, W. B. (1955–6) 'Essentially Contested Concepts', *Proceedings of the Aristotelian Society*, 56: 157–97.

Gellner, E. (1983) *Nations and Nationalism* (Oxford: Basil Blackwell).

Gibbins, J. (ed.) (1989) *Contemporary Political Culture: Politics in a Postmodern Age* (London: Sage).

Giddens, A. (1998) *The Third Way: The Renewal of Social Democracy* (Cambridge: Polity Press).

Goodin, R. (1995) *Utilitarianism as a Public Philosophy* (Cambridge: Cambridge University Press).

Goodin, R. E. and Pettit, P. (1995) *A Companion to Contemporary Political Philosophy* (Oxford: Basil Blackwell).

Graham, B. D. (1993) *Representation and Party Politics: A Comparative Perspective* (Oxford: Basil Blackwell).

Gramsci, A. (1929–35/1971) *Selections from the Prison Notebooks* (London: Lawrence & Wishart).

Gray, J. (1995) *Liberalism* (Milton Keynes: Open University Press).

Gray, T. (1990) *Freedom* (London: Macmillan).

Green, L. (1988) *The Authority of the State* (Oxford: Clarendon Press).

Griffin, R. (ed.) (1995) *Fascism* (Oxford/New York: Oxford University Press).

Habermas, J. (1973) *Legitimation Crisis* (Boston, MA: Beacon).

Hague, R., Harrop, M. and Breslin, S. (1992) *Comparative Government and Politics: An Introduction* (London: Macmillan).

Hailsham, Lord (1976) *Elective Dictatorship* (London: BBC Publications).

Hall, S. and Jacques, M. (eds) (1983) *The Politics of Thatcherism* (London: Lawrence & Wishart).

Hart, H. L. A. (1961) *The Concept of Law* (Oxford: Oxford University Press).

Harvey, D. (1989) *The Condition of Postmodernity: An Enquiry into the Origins of Cultural Change* (London: Basil Blackwell).

Hay, C. (2002) *Political Analysis: A Critical Introduction* (Basingstoke: Palgrave Macmillan).

Held, D. (1990) *Political Theory and the Modern State* (Cambridge: Polity Press).

Held, D. (ed.) (1991) *Political Theory Today* (Cambridge: Polity Press).

Hennessy, P. (1986) *Cabinet* (Oxford: Blackwell).

Heywood, A. (1998) *Political Ideologies: An Introduction* (London: Macmillan).

Heywood, A. (2015) *Political Theory: An Introduction* (Basingstoke: Palgrave).

Hindley, F. H. (1986) *Sovereignty* (New York: Basic Books).

Hirst, P., Thompson, G. and Bromley, S. (1995) *Globalization in Question* (Cambridge: Polity Press).

Hitler, A. (1925/1969) *Mein Kampf*, trans. R. Mannheim (London: Hutchinson).

Holden, B. (1993) *Understanding Liberal Democracy* (Hemel Hempstead: Harvester Wheatsheaf).

Honderich, T. (1989) *Violence for Equality: Inquiries in Political Philosophy* (London: Routledge.

Horton, J. (1992) *Political Obligation* (London: Macmillan).

Huntington, S. (1991) *Third Wave: Democratization in the Late Twentieth Century* (Norman, OK/London: Oklahoma University Press).

Huntington, S. (1996) *The Clash of Civilizations and the Remaking of World Order* (New York: Simon & Schuster).

Hutcheon, L. (1989) *The Politics of Postmodernism* (New York: Routledge).

Johnson, N. (1989) *The Limits of Political Science* (Oxford: Clarendon Press).

Kagan, R. (2008) *The Return of History: And the End of Dreams* (New York: Alfred A. Knopf).

Kant, I. (1795/1970) *Political Writings* (Cambridge: Cambridge University Press).

Kegley, C. (ed.) (1995) *Controversies in International Relations Theory: Realism and the Neoliberal Challenge* (New York: St Martin's Press).

Kegley, C. and Wittkopf, E. (1995) *World Politics: Trend and Transformation* (New York: St Martin's Press).

Kenny, M. (1995) *The First New Left: British Intellectuals after Stalin* (London: Lawrence & Wishart).

Keohane, R. and Nye, J. (1977) *Power and Interdependence: World Politics in Transition* (Boston, MA: Little, Brown).

King, P. (1982) *Federalism and Federation* (London: Croom Helm).

Kingdom, J. (1992) *No Such Thing as Society? Individualism and Community* (Buckingham: Open University Press).

Kirchheimer, O. (1966) 'The Transformation of the Western European Party Systems', in J. la Palombara and M. Weiner (eds), *Political Parties and Political Development* (Princeton, NJ: Princeton University Press).

Kolakowski, L. (1979) *Main Currents of Marxism*, 3 vols (Oxford: Oxford University Press).

Kuhn, T. (1962) *The Structure of Scientific Revolutions* (Chicago, IL: Chicago University Press).

Kumar, K. (1991) *Utopianism* (Milton Keynes: Open University Press).

Kymlicka, W. (1990) *Contemporary Political Philosophy: An Introduction* (Oxford/New York: Oxford University Press).

Kymlicka, W. (1995) *Multicultural Citizenship* (Oxford: Oxford University Press).

Laclau, E. and Mouffe, C. (1985) *Hegemony and Socialist Strategy* (London: Verso).

LeDuc, L., Niemi, R. and Norris, P. (eds) (1996) *Comparing Democracies: Elections and Voting in Global Perspective* (London: Sage).

Leftwich, A. (ed.) (1984) *What Is Politics? The Activity and Its Study* (Oxford/New York: Basil Blackwell).

Lenin, V. I. (1902/1968) *What Is to Be Done?* (Harmondsworth/New York: Penguin).

Lewis, B. (2005) *The Crisis of Islam: Holy Wars and Unholy Terror* (New York: Random House).

Lijphart, A. (1977) *Democracy in Plural Societies: A Comparative Exploration* (New Haven, CT: Yale University Press).

Lijphart, A. (ed.) (1992) *Parliamentary Versus Presidential Government* (Oxford: Oxford University Press).

Lindblom, C. (1959) 'The Science of Muddling Through', *Public Administration Review*, **19**: 79–88.

Linklater, A. (1990) *Beyond Realism and Marxism: Critical Theory and International Relations* (London: Macmillan).

Linklater, A. (1998) *The Transformation of Political Community: Ethical Foundations of the Post-Westphalian Era* (Cambridge: Cambridge University Press).

Lukes, S. (2004) *Power: A Radical View* (Basingstoke: Palgrave).

Lyotard, J.-F. (1984) *The Postmodern Condition: The Power of Knowledge* (Minneapolis, MN: University of Minnesota Press).

MacCallum, G. (1991) 'Negative and Positive Freedom', in D. Miller (ed.), *Liberty* (Oxford: Oxford University Press).

MacIntyre, A. (1981) *After Virtue* (Notre Dame, IL: University of Notre Dame Press).

Mair, C. (1987) *In Search of Stability: Explorations in Historical Political Economy* (Cambridge: Cambridge University Press).

Marcuse, H. (1964) *One-Dimensional Man: Studies in the Ideology of Advanced Industrial Society* (Boston, MA: Beacon).

Marsh, D. and Stoker, G. (eds) (1995) *Theory and Methods in Political Science* (London: Macmillan).

Marty, M. E. and Appleby, R. S. (eds) (1993) *Fundamentalisms and the State: Re-making Polities, Economies, and Militance* (Chicago, IL/London: University of Chicago Press).

Marx, K. and Engels, F. (1848/1967) *The Communist Manifesto* (Harmondsworth: Penguin).

Matchan, T. R. (ed.) (1982) *The Libertarian Reader* (Totowa, NJ: Rowan & Littlefield).

McDowell, L. and Pringle, R. (eds) (1992) *Defining Women: Social Institutions and Gender Divisions* (Cambridge: Polity Press).

McLellan, D. (1986) *Ideology* (Milton Keynes: Open University Press).

McLennan, G. (1995) *Pluralism* (Buckingham: Open University Press).

Mendus, S. (1989) *Toleration and the Limits of Liberalism* (London: Macmillan).

Meny, Y. and Wright, V. (eds) (1995) *Centre–Periphery Relations in Western Europe* (London: Croom Helm).

Merleau-Ponty, M. (1993) *Adventures of the Dialectic* (London: Heinemann).

Michels, R. (1911/1962) *Political Parties: A Sociological Study of the Oligarchal Tendencies of Modern Democracy* (New York: Collier).

Miller, D. (1984) *Anarchism* (London: Dent).

Millett, K. (1970) *Sexual Politics* (London: Virago).

Mills, C. Wright. (1956) *The Power Elite* (New York: Oxford University Press).

More, T. (1516/1965) *Utopia*, trans. P. Turner (Harmondsworth: Penguin).

Nairn, T. (1988) *The Enchanted Glass: Britain and Its Monarchy* (London: Picador).

Negrine, R. (1996) *The Communication of Politics* (London: Sage).

Neumann, S. (1956) *Modern Political Parties* (Chicago, IL: University of Chicago Press).

Neustadt, R. (1980) *Presidential Power: The Politics of Leadership from FDR to Carter* (New York: John Wiley).

Norton, P. (ed.) (1990a) *Legislatures* (Oxford: Oxford University Press).

Norton, P. (ed.) (1990b) *Parliaments in Western Europe* (London: Frank Cass).

Nozick, R. (1974) *Anarchy, State and Utopia* (Oxford: Basil Blackwell).

Nye, J. (2004) *Soft Power: The Means to Succeed in World Politics* (New York: PublicAffairs).

Oakeshott, M. (1962) *Rationalism in Politics and Other Essays* (London: Methuen).

Ohmae, K. (1990) *The Borderless World: Power and Strategy in the Interlinked Economy* (New York: Free Press).

Oilman, B. (1993) *Dialectical Investigations* (London: Routledge).

O'Neill, J. (ed.) (1993) *Modes of Individualism and Collectivism* (London: Gregg Revivals).

Pakulski, J. (1990) *Social Movements: The Politics of Protest* (Melbourne: Longman).

Parsons, W. (1995) *Public Policy: Introduction to the Theory and Practice of Policy Analysis* (Aldershot: Edward Elgar).

Pettit, P. (1997) *Republicanism: A Theory of Freedom and Government* (Oxford: Oxford University Press).

Pinkney, R. (1990) *Right-Wing Military Government* (London: Pinter).

Przeworski, A. (1991) *Democracy and the Market: Political and Economic Reforms in Eastern Europe and Latin America* (Cambridge/New York: Cambridge University Press).

Rawls, J. (1971) *A Theory of Justice* (London: Oxford University Press).

Raz, J. (1986) *The Authority of Law* (Oxford: Clarendon Press).

Regan, T. (2004) *The Case for Animal Rights* (Oakland, CA: University of California Press).

Rex, J. and Mason, D. (eds) (1992) *Theories of Race and Ethnic Relations* (Cambridge: Cambridge University Press).

Reynolds, C. (1981) *Modes of Imperialism* (Oxford: Martin Robertson).

Ritterberger, V., Zangl, B. and Kruck, A. (2012) *International Organization: Polity, Politics and Policies* (Basingstoke: Palgrave Macmillan).

Rorty, R. (ed.) (1967) *The Linguistic Turn* (Chicago, IL: University of Chicago Press).

Rose, R. (1991) *The Postmodern Presidency: The White House Meets the World* (New York: Chartham House).

Rose, R. and Suleiman, E. N. (eds) (1980) *Presidents and Prime Ministers* (Washington, DC: American Enterprise Institute).

Rosenau, J. and Czenpiel, E.-O. (1992) *Governance without Government: Order and Change in World Politics* (Cambridge: Cambridge University Press).

Ruggie, J. (1993) *Multilateralism Matters: Theory and Praxis of an International Form* (New York: Columbia University Press).

Ryan, A. (1987) *Property* (Milton Keynes: Open University Press).

Said, E. (2003) *Orientalism* (London: Penguin).

Sandel, M. (1982) *Liberalism and the Limits of Justice* (Cambridge: Cambridge University Press).

Sartori, G. (1976) *Parties and Party Systems: A Framework for Analysis* (Cambridge: Cambridge University Press).

Saunders, P. (1990) *Social Class Stratification* (London: Routledge).

Saunders, P. (1995) *Capitalism: A Social Audit* (Buckingham: Open University Press).

Schattschneider, E. E. (1960) *The Semisovereign People* (New York: Holt, Rinehart & Winston).

Schmitter, P. C. and Lehmbruch, G. (eds) (1979) *Trends towards Corporatist Intermediation* (London: Sage).

Scruton, R. (1984) *The Meaning of Conservatism* (London: Macmillan).

Sen, A. (1999) *Development as Freedom* (Oxford: Oxford University Press).

Sil, R. and Katzenstein, J. (2010) *Beyond Paradigms: Analytic Eclecticism in the Study of World Politics* (Basingstoke: Palgrave Macmillan).

Simon, H. (1983) *Models of Bounded Rationality* (Cambridge, MA: MIT Press).

Smith, A. D. (1991) *Theories of Nationalism* (London: Duckworth).

Tam, H. (1998) *Communitarianism: A New Agenda for Politics and Citizenship* (London: Macmillan).

Taylor, P. and Groom, A. J. R. (eds) (1978) *International Organisations: A Conceptual Approach* (London: Pinter).

Thompson, G., Frances, J., Levacic, R. and Mitchell, J. (1991) *Markets, Hierarchies and Networks: The Coordination of Social Life* (London: Sage).

Tivey, L. (ed.) (1980) *The Nation-State* (Oxford: Martin Robertson).

Tormey, S. (1995) *Making Sense of Tyranny: Interpretations of Totalitarianism* (Manchester/New York: Manchester University Press).

Verney, D. V. (1959) *The Analysis of Political Systems* (London: Routledge & Kegan Paul).

Vincent, A. (1995) *Modern Political Ideologies* (Oxford: Basil Blackwell).

Vincent, A. (1997) *Political Theory: Tradition and Diversity* (Cambridge: Cambridge University Press).

Waltman, J. and Holland, K. (eds) (1988) *The Political Role of Law Courts in Modern Democracies* (New York: St Martin's Press).

Waltz, K. (1959) *Man, the State, and War* (New York: Columbia University Press).

Waltz, K. (1979) *Theory of International Politics* (Reading, MA: Addison-Wesley).

Weaver, R. K. and Rockman, B. A. (eds) (1993) *Do Institutions Matter?* (Washington, DC: Brookings Institution).

Weller, P. (1985) *First Among Equals: Prime Ministers in Westminster Systems* (Sydney: George Allen & Unwin).

Wendt, A. (1992) 'Anarchy Is What States Make of It: The Social Construction of Power Politics', *International Organization*, 46(2): 391–425.

Wendt, A. (1999) *Social Theory of International Politics* (Cambridge: Cambridge University Press).

White, J. B. (1984) *When Words Lose Their Meaning* (Chicago, IL: University of Chicago Press).

Williams, P. (1989) *Mahayana Buddhism* (London and New York: Routledge).

Wilson, D. and Game, C. (1994) *Local Government in the United Kingdom* (London: Macmillan).

Wright, A. (1987) *Socialisms: Theories and Practices* (Oxford/New York: Oxford University Press).

INDEX

bold type = extended discussion; f = figure